THE Ultimate Instant Pot® HEALTHY COOKBOOK

Instant Pot
Ultra
www.InstantPot.com
Pressure Cook
Soup/Broth
Meat/Stew
Bean/Chili
Steam
Slow Cook
Sauté
Warm
Rice
Porridge
Multigrain
Cake
Egg
Sterilize
Yogurt
Ultra
On
Pressure
High
Keep Warm
ON
Pre-heating
Cancel
Start

THE Ultimate Instant Pot® HEALTHY COOKBOOK

150 DELICIOUSLY SIMPLE RECIPES
FOR YOUR ELECTRIC PRESSURE COOKER

Coco Morante

Photography by Jennifer Davick

TEN SPEED PRESS
California | New York

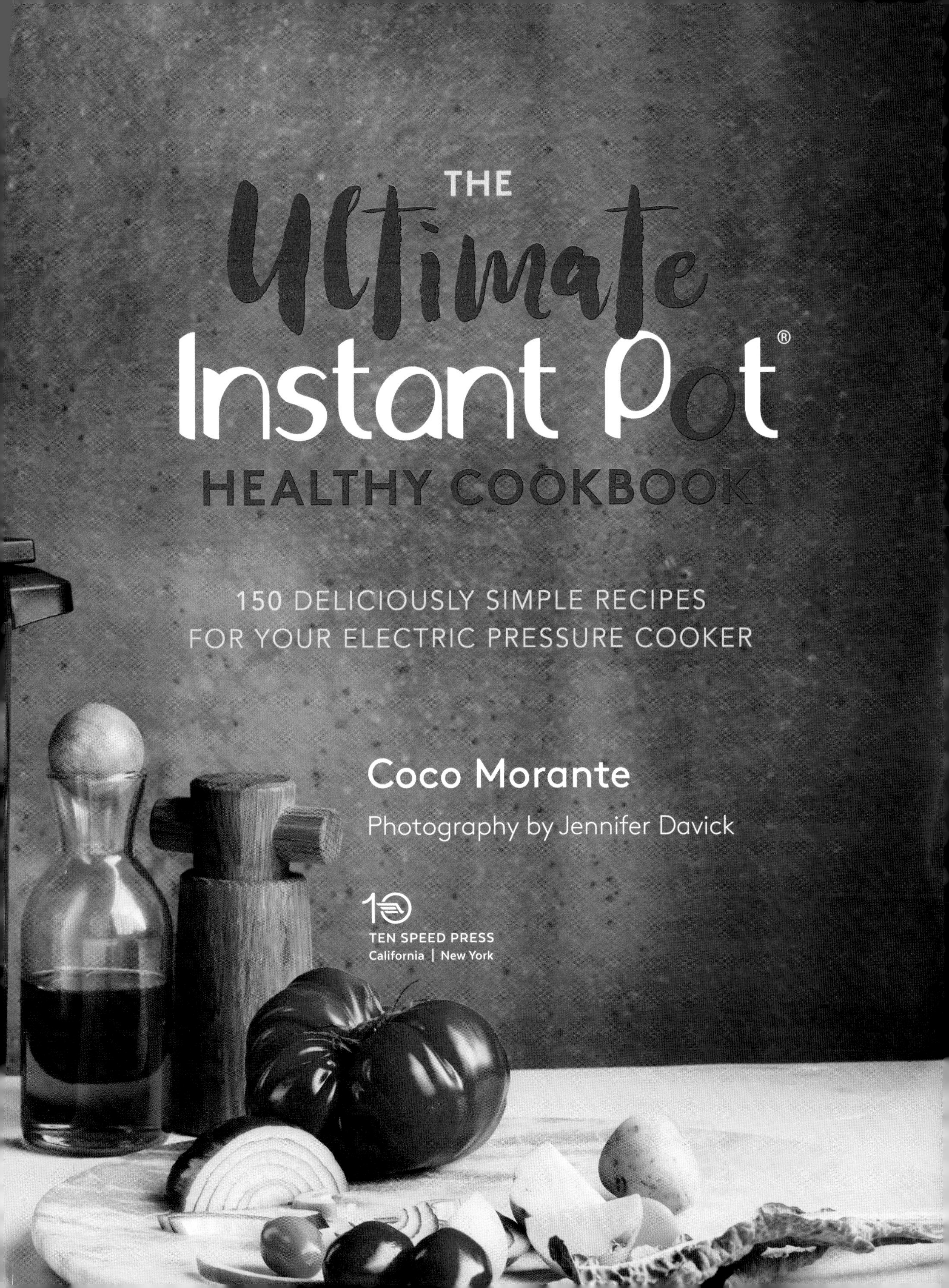

Contents

Introduction 1

How to Use the Instant Pot 2

CHAPTER 1: BREAKFAST

Butternut Squash Steel-Cut Oatmeal 19

Banana Oatmeal with Strawberry-Chia Jam 20

Barley Bowls with Sunny Eggs and Tamari 23

Quinoa Muesli Breakfast Bowls 24

Soft- or Hard-Boiled Eggs 25

Soft-Boiled Eggs in Yogurt Sauce 27

Corn and Zucchini Omelet with Smoked Salmon 28

Crustless Ham and Swiss Quiche 30

Sweet Potato and Arugula Frittata 31

Broccoli-Cheddar Egg Muffins 33

Yogurt 34

Yogurt Bowl with Ginger-Almond Granola 36

Chocolate and PB Yogurt Smoothie 37

Whole-Wheat Matzo Brei 38

Apple-Cinnamon French Toast Casserole 39

Yeasted Buckwheat Waffles 40

CHAPTER 2: BEANS, GRAINS, AND PASTAS

Basic Beans 44

Mixed-Bean Salad 45

Toasted Sesame Miso Hummus 47

Balsamic and Butter Lentils 48

Refried Black Beans 49

Basic Rice 50

Cajun-Spiced Red Beans and Rice 53

Spinach and Pea Risotto 54

Double Mushroom Risotto 55

Brown Rice Nori Rolls 56

Chickpea and Brown Rice Tabbouleh 58

Wild Rice Salad with Cranberries and Oranges 59

Basic Whole Grains 60

Sunshine Salad with Bulgur, Kale, and Mango 62

Quinoa with Pears and Walnuts 64

Farro Salad with Romaine, Raisins, and Almond Feta 65

Vegan Mac 'n' Greens 66

Winter White Pasta Salad 69

Whole-Wheat Penne Arrabbiata 70

CHAPTER 3: SOUPS AND CHILIS

Beet Borscht 75
Winter Squash Miso Soup 76
Cream of Zucchini Soup 77
Tomato–Red Pepper Bisque with Basil Oil 78
Green Minestrone 81
Pasta, Bean, and Sausage Soup 82
Red Lentil and Spinach Soup 83
Greek Lentil Soup 84
Hearty Multibean Soup 87
Sweet Potato Soup 88
Roasted Garlic and Potato Soup 89
Cabbage and Potato Soup 90
Vegan Red Pozole 91
Vegetable Beef Soup 92
Chicken Drumstick Soup 94
Chicken Pho 95
Vegan Soy Curls Chili 97
Tomatillo Chicken Chili 98
Tri-Tip and Bean Chili 99

CHAPTER 4: VEGETARIAN

Avocado Egg Salad Sandwiches 103
Seitan Chickpea Chorizo Sausages 104
Falafel-Spiced Chickpea Pita Pockets 107
Mixed-Vegetable Korma 108
BBQ Jackfruit Bowls with Alabama Sauce 110
Josephine's Special 112
Tamale Casserole 113
Vegan Salisbury Steak 114
Cheesy Loaded Potato Casserole 116
"Chick'n" and Brown Rice Pilaf 119
Black-Eyed Peas and Kale 120
Sesame Peanut Noodles with Seared Tofu 121
Korean Hot Pot with Tofu and Mushrooms 123
Garden Patch Jambalaya 124
Steamed Butternut or Spaghetti Squash 125
Spaghetti Squash Marinara with Vegan Parmesan 126

CHAPTER 5: SEAFOOD

Mussels with Tomatoes and White Wine Broth 131
Shrimp and Avocado Toast 132
Shrimp Ceviche with Sweet Potatoes and Corn 133
Cioppino Pasta 134
Seafood Risotto 136
New England Fish Chowder 137
Cod and Shrimp Stew with Tomatoes and Saffron 139
Fish Taco Salads with Fresh Mango Salsa 140
Salmon and Spinach Patties 142
Poached Salmon with Basil Vinaigrette 144
Thai Green Curry Tilapia 145

CHAPTER 6: POULTRY

Sweet and Spicy Chicken Wings 148
Honey Mustard Chicken Tenders and Slaw 149
Buffalo Chicken Lettuce Cups 150
Antipasto Chicken Chopped Salad 152
Za'atar-Spiced Chicken Salad with Tahini Dressing 153
Greek Chicken Meatballs 155
Dairy-Free Pesto Chicken Penne 156
Chicken, Chickpea, and Carrot Plov 157
Spicy Sesame Peanut Chicken 158
Salsa Chicken and Supercharged Rice 161
Southern Smothered Chicken 162
Chicken Cutlets in Tuscan Cream Sauce 165
Chicken and Mushroom Goulash 166
Whole Chicken in a Hurry 167
Tandoori-Spiced Chicken Thighs 168
Paella Turkey Meatballs 170
Chipotle Turkey Sloppy Joes 171

CHAPTER 7: PORK, LAMB, AND BEEF

Pork Chops Marsala 174
Pork Chops with Cumin and Coriander 176
Pork with Balsamic and Cherries 177
Crispy Pulled Pork Gyros 179
Ground Pork Bolognese 180
Honey-Dijon Baby Back Ribs 183
Spanish-Style Pork and White Beans 184
Braised Pork Shoulder with Chinese Black Bean Sauce 185
Pork Loin with Lemon, Capers, and Artichokes 186
Irish Lamb Stew 188
Cabbage Roll Casserole 189
Ground Beef Tostada Salads 190
Florentine Beef Meat Loaf 193
Beef Tips with Onion and Mushroom Gravy 194
Sweet Potato Cottage Pie 195
Shredded BBQ Pot Roast 196
Cincinnati Chili Mac 198
Beef and Spinach Lasagna 200
Indian-Style Beef Curry 202

CHAPTER 8: VEGETABLES AND SIDE DISHES

Pan-Grilled Artichokes with Curry Dip 206
Asparagus with Vegan Aioli 208
Baby Carrots with Honey Lemon Butter 209
Broccoli with Crispy Garlic Chips 210
Everything Brussels Sprouts 213
Cauliflower Carrot Mash 214
Cauliflower Florets with Herbed Butter 217
Celery Root Salad 218
Italian Braised Green Beans and Tomatoes 219
Chimichurri Corn on the Cob 220
Crunchy Vegetable Dip 222
Bacon-Braised Beets and Greens 223
Vegan Creamed Spinach 225
Giardiniera Salad 226
Zucchini with Olive Oil and Parsley 228
Steamed Potatoes (Regular and Sweet) 229
Beet, Carrot, and Potato Salad 231
Crispy Sriracha Potatoes 232
Mashed Sweet Potatoes 234
JoJo Potatoes 235

CHAPTER 9: DRINKS AND DESSERTS

Mulled Apple Cider with Oranges and Rosemary 238
Hot Cranberry Cocktail 239
Virgin Toddy Tonic 241
Frozen Yogurt Fudge Ice Pops 242
Coconut Bulgur Pudding 243
Wine-Poached Pears 244
Pink Applesauce 245
Dried Fruit Compote 246
Cinnamon Raisin Bread Pudding 248
Glazed Honey-Lemon Cake 251
Gluten-Free Chocolate Cake 253
Greek Yogurt Cheesecake 254
Flourless Chocolate Torte 256

CHAPTER 10: PANTRY

Low-Sodium Chicken Bone Broth 260
Low-Sodium Roasted Beef Bone Broth 260
Low-Sodium Vegetable Broth 261
Roasted Garlic 261
Salsa Picante 262
Tahini Dressing 262
Tzatziki 264
Basil Oil 264
Dill Pickle Chips 264
Cashew Sour Cream 265
Vegan Parmesan Cheese 265
Almond Feta Cheese 265

Cooking Charts 266
Dietary Chart 268
Acknowledgments 273
About the Author 274
Index 275

Rice
Porridge
Multigrain
Cake
Egg
Sterilize
Yogurt
Ultra
Start

Introduction

Preparing home-cooked meals is one of the best things you can do for your health, and using an Instant Pot makes it easy and convenient to incorporate cooking into any lifestyle. This electric, programmable pressure cooker has long been an indispensable tool in my kitchen, especially when it comes to healthy cooking.

Healthy cooking means different things to different people. For me, the most important part is starting out with wholesome ingredients, and this book takes the guesswork out of choosing the right groceries. Its recipes draw from a palette of mostly whole-food ingredients, including fresh, frozen, and canned vegetables and fruits; beans; whole grains and whole-grain flours; grass-fed dairy; lean proteins; healthy oils and fats; and moderate amounts of natural sweeteners. When cooking starts with good ingredients, you end up with good food.

You'll find that when you use the Instant Pot, there is always some built-in downtime. That's what I love most about this appliance: once you've closed the lid and selected a cooking program, you're free to get on with your day, tend to other kitchen tasks, or just relax for a bit while your meal cooks itself. It's changed the way I think about meal preparation and time management for the better, since there's so much more flexibility than with stove-top or oven recipes. Whether I've planned ahead or need to whip up dinner on the fly, the Instant Pot comes to he rescue.

In the chapters to come, you'll discover recipes for every meal of the day. Hearty breakfasts, vegetable-spiked rice and pasta dishes, and belly-warming soups are just the beginning. There's even a whole chapter of vegetarian main dishes (great if you eat a plant-based diet or you're just looking to incorporate some meatless Mondays into your routine), and some healthy spins on dessert favorites, such as cheesecake and chocolate cake brownies. And, of course, you'll find tried-and-true Instant Pot classics, including super-creamy mac 'n' cheese (surprise, it's vegan!), smothered chicken (full of flavor yet skinless to cut down on calories and saturated fat), and a rib-sticking steak and bean chili to satisfy big appetites.

Once you get comfortable with your Instant Pot and its possibilities, it can be a real joy to venture beyond the classics and try out flavor combinations from around the world. After all, many international cuisines are packed with healthy recipes if you just know where to look. Beet Borscht (page 75) is a light yet comforting soup, and it's absolutely loaded with vegetables. Italian Braised Green Beans and Tomatoes (page 219) takes advantage of a few fragrant spices and cooks in just minutes. Chicken and Mushroom Goulash (page 166) is the epitome of the one-pot meal, with protein and vegetables cooked together.

Before you jump into the recipe chapters, I encourage you to check out the rest of this introductory section. Whether you're an Instant Pot novice (welcome!) or an old pro, you'll find some new information here. I'll go over the basics of how to use your Instant Pot and all of its functions; review the best tools, accessories, and pantry staples; and chat about shortcuts and tricks for getting healthy food on the table.

The purchase of an Instant Pot often comes with the hope of preparing more healthful, home-cooked meals. In our modern, busy lives, this versatile appliance can truly help you to accomplish your nutritional goals and feed your household nourishing meals. I hope that this cookbook provides you with plenty of guidance and inspiration, and helps you to make healthy Instant Pot cooking part of your routine.

I wish you a rewarding pressure cooking journey!

How to Use the Instant Pot

When you first take your Instant Pot out of the box, do yourself a favor and immediately open the manual and turn to the diagrams. They'll help you get acquainted with the different parts of the Instant Pot, including all of the buttons and light-up indicators on the front and the mechanisms of the lid.

Next, consider joining one or both of these Facebook groups: Instant Pot Community and Instant Pot Recipes. The first is a lively gaggle of participants who will answer your beginner questions in a flash. The second is my page, where I regularly post my own recipes as well as those from my favorite bloggers and cooking websites.

I've tested the recipes in this cookbook in four slightly different 6-quart models of Instant Pot: the DUO60, DUO60 Plus, Smart Wi-Fi, and Ultra. These models are my favorites out of the whole Instant Pot line, as they all have a handy notch for resting the lid when the pot is open. They also include a setting for culturing yogurt, which the LUX models do not.

If you are primarily cooking for four people or fewer, I'd go with one of the 6-quart models. If you plan to cook larger pieces of meat (over 4 pounds) or serve a larger crowd on a regular basis, go with the DUO80, DUO80 Plus, or 8-quart Ultra, all of which have an 8-quart capacity. If you are cooking for only one or are extremely short on counter space, opt for one of the 3-quart pots.

No matter which model of Instant Pot you have, the panel on the front has settings for cooking different kinds of foods, adjusting the pot to High or Low Pressure, regulating the temperature of certain settings, and setting the cooking time. There is also a display that lets you know when the pot is on or off and how much time is left on the program setting once the pot reaches pressure.

You'll select a function key depending on what sort of food you are cooking. In Instant Pot terminology, this translates to pressing a function key to select a cooking program, or selecting a function with the universal dial on the Ultra models. For example, you'll select the Soup/Broth function key to cook a soup, the Rice key to steam a pot of rice, and so on. Each pressure-cooking program can be adjusted to High or Low Pressure, as well as Less, Normal, or More cooking time (shown in minutes on the LED display), with Normal being the default setting. You can also adjust the time up or down manually in any setting with the + and – buttons or with the dial, depending on the model. Here's a rundown of all the cooking program buttons.

Instant Pot Settings

Your Instant Pot has multiple cooking programs, or settings, which you'll select based on the type of dish you're preparing. While Instant Pot models vary in which settings are included, they all have a manual mode that can be used for most recipes. Following are descriptions of all of the Instant Pot settings:

Manual/Pressure Cook/Ultra You can cook any pressure cooker recipe on the Manual setting. If you're interested in using recipes written for stove-top pressure cookers, this setting is handy, as those recipes can easily be cooked in the Instant Pot. It opens up a whole world of recipes for you to explore, not just ones meant specifically for the Instant Pot. Stove-top cookers cook faster than the Instant Pot because they operate at slightly higher pressures, so you'll need to increase the cooking time by 15 percent. Depending on the model of Instant Pot you have, you'll use the Adjust or Pressure Level button or the universal dial to toggle between the Low Pressure and High Pressure settings.

Bean/Chili Whether you're cooking a basic pot of beans (page 44), Indian dal, or chili, use this cooking program. Adjust the cooking time to Less for just-done beans, Normal for soft beans, or More for very soft beans. See the chart on page 266 for exact cooking times for a variety of beans.

Cake Use the Less, Normal, and More settings according to the recipe you are making, from a delicate lemon sponge cake to a dense chocolate torte pound cake to cheesecake.

Egg When a recipe calls for eggs, use large eggs. You can cook soft-, medium-, or hard-boiled eggs (page 25). The Less, Normal, and More settings are timed for extra-large eggs, so you'll need to adjust the cooking times up or down as needed if your eggs are a different size.

Meat/Stew This one is self-explanatory. Adjust the time to Less, Normal, or More, depending on whether you like your meat cooked soft, very soft, or falling off the bone.

Multigrain The moderate, even heat of the Multigrain setting is perfect for brown rice and other long-cooking grains. The More setting includes a warm 45-minute presoak before an hour of pressure cooking and is well suited to mixtures of sturdy grains and beans.

Porridge Use this setting when making rice porridge, oatmeal, or a porridge made of any beans and/or other grains. Always use the natural release method when making porridge, and never fill the pot more than half full to avoid a spattered mess. Cooking porridge under pressure is perfectly safe as long as you stick to those guidelines. For a warm breakfast using this setting, try Butternut Squash Steel-Cut Oatmeal (page 19).

Rice Any type of white rice can be cooked on this setting. The Less, Normal, and More settings will yield just-tender, tender, and soft rice, respectively. The Ultra models have two automatic Rice program settings, for Low and High Pressure. Using Low Pressure will yield fluffier rice, while High Pressure will yield grains that are softer, with a greater tendency to stick together. For full instructions, see Basic Rice (page 50).

Sauté The Instant Pot allows you to simmer, sauté, and sear foods before or after cooking them under pressure, a feature that adds to its versatility. This is not a pressure setting, and you should never put the locking lid on when you're using it. You can use a tempered glass lid (either the one from Instant Pot or another one that fits snugly) on this setting to sweat vegetables or to get liquids to boil faster.

The Sauté setting behaves a little differently from the pressure settings, in that it doesn't display a countdown when it's on. While the pot is heating, it will display "On," and it will change to "Hot" once it is fully heated. The default Sauté level is Normal or Medium (it's labeled differently depending on your Instant Pot model), and this is the temperature level used for the recipes in this book, unless indicated otherwise. When I use the Sauté function in a recipe, I usually start cooking right away, without waiting for the pot to preheat. For instance, I put garlic and oil into the pot immediately after selecting Sauté, so the oil heats up at the same time as the pot. This saves a little time.

Slow Cook The Slow Cook function turns your Instant Pot into a slow cooker, with the Less, Normal, and More settings corresponding to the Low, Medium, and High settings on a slow cooker. Because the heating element in the Instant Pot is a focused source in the bottom of the pot, the heat distribution is a little different from that of a slow cooker, however. If you come across a great new slow cooker recipe or have some old favorites that you'd like to make, you can use the Slow Cook setting. When using the Instant Pot for slow cooking (or for any non-pressure setting), a tight seal is not required, so you can use an easy-to-clean tempered glass lid (either the one available from Instant Pot or any lid that fits snugly on the pot), rather than the pressure cooker lid.

Soup/Broth The heat ramps up a little more gently on this setting than on the previous setting, which makes it good for simmering soups and broths. Even better, broths turn out clear, not cloudy, when they're cooked under pressure. You'll find recipes for low-sodium beef bone broth, low-sodium chicken bone broth, and low-sodium vegetable broth in the Pantry chapter (pages 260 and 261).

Steam The Instant Pot comes with a wire metal steam rack that is used for raising foods off the bottom of the pot for steaming under pressure. You can also use any wire-mesh, silicone, or metal steamer basket. For 3- 6-, and 8-quart Instant Pots, use at least ½, 1, or 1½ cups of water on the Steam setting, respectively. The recipes in this book are written for the 6-quart Instant Pot, so you may need to add more or less liquid for steamed and pot-in-pot recipes (see page 9) if you have a 3- or 8-quart pot.

Sterilize The Normal setting sterilizes at about 230°F (110°C), and the More or High setting sterilizes at about 240°F (115°C). This program can be used for baby bottles, canning jars, or any other heatproof items you want to sterilize.

Yogurt This setting has two yogurt-related functions: it sterilizes milk on the More or High setting and then turns the milk into yogurt on the Normal setting. Homemade yogurt is easy to make and more economical than store-bought. You can even culture the yogurt right in a glass container inside the pot using my method on page 34. This is my preferred way to make yogurt, since the ingredients go from Instant Pot to fridge with zero cleanup. The Normal or Medium setting is also ideal for proofing bread doughs and batters, such as the batter for Yeasted Buckwheat Waffles (page 40). The LUX models do not have a yogurt setting.

Operation Keys

These are the buttons that adjust the pressure, cooking time, and, in certain cases, the heat level of whatever cooking program you've selected. Most Instant Pot models have an Adjust button that toggles among the Less, Normal, and More time and heat settings. For pressure settings, it adjusts the time, and for non-pressure settings, including Yogurt, Slow Cook, and Sauté, it adjusts the heat level. The + and – buttons adjust the cooking time up and down, respectively.

The DUO60 Plus has a dedicated Pressure level button instead of Adjust and/or Pressure buttons, and you press the appropriate function key more than once to toggle among the Less, Normal, and More time and heat settings. The LUX60 model pressure cooks at only High Pressure. It does not have a Low Pressure setting.

The Ultra has a universal dial that allows you to toggle among all of the cooking programs, pressure settings, heat levels, and cooking times on the Instant Pot, including a highly customizable Ultra setting.

Delay Start Many Instant Pot models allow you to delay the start of the cooking time for a recipe. You won't find lots of uses for this function, as you typically won't want to leave perishable foods in the Instant Pot for any length of time before cooking them. The one task I do like this function for is soaking and cooking beans and whole grains. I'll often put beans, water, and salt in the pot in the afternoon or evening; delay the time for 8 to 12 hours; and then wake up to perfectly cooked beans in the morning.

Mode and Function Indicators These are the lights that turn on to indicate what mode (Low or High Pressure) or function (aka cooking program) is currently selected on the Instant Pot. On models with a keypad interface, all of the function keys and mode indicators have a little white circle that lights up when they are selected. On models with a dial, the selected function is backlit.

Keep Warm/Cancel This multipurpose button has two separate functions: it cancels any cooking program, and it puts the pot on the Keep Warm setting, similar to the warming setting on a slow cooker. The DUO60, DUO60 Plus, and Ultra models have separate buttons for the Keep Warm and Cancel functions.

The Lid and Releasing Pressure

Now that you know the basic terminology for everything on the front panel of the pot, let's talk about the lid. The lids of the various Instant Pot models (LUX, DUO, Ultra, and SMART) all look slightly different, but they have similar mechanisms. The MAX has a wider range of pressure release modes, including an intermediate setting that allows for a gradual pressure release.

PRESSURE/STEAM RELEASE

The Pressure Release (PR), also called Steam Release on some models, can be set to two positions, Sealing or Venting. When the pot is closed and the Pressure Release is set to Sealing, the pot can come up to pressure. When the cooking program is finished, you can move the Pressure Release to Venting to release the steam from the pot, making it safe to open. And it's okay if the Pressure Release jiggles a bit or seems as if it is not fully secured. It's supposed to feel that way. You can remove it for cleaning as well.

PRESSURE RELEASES: QUICK, NATURAL, AND TIMED NATURAL

You can release the pressure on the Instant Pot in three different ways.

1. Quick Pressure Release (QPR) The moment the cooking program finishes, move the Pressure Release to Venting. This will cause a forceful plume of steam to issue forth, releasing the pressure from the Instant Pot. On the LUX, DUO, Ultra, and Smart models, you'll manually move the Pressure Release valve to the side, taking care to keep your fingers away from the hot steam. On the Ultra model, the lid has an extra safety mechanism: the Pressure Release button and valve are separate, ensuring your hand is nowhere near the steam. To be extra safe with any model of Instant Pot, use heat-resistant mitts when performing a quick pressure release.

Use the quick pressure release method for the following:

Steamed Vegetables Always release the pressure quickly (immediately after the cooking program ends) when cooking asparagus, broccoli, cauliflower, and any other vegetables you prefer lightly steamed or braised. I'll often set the cooking time to 0 (zero) minutes for these foods, which means they cook only for the time it takes for the pot to come up to pressure plus the time required for a quick pressure release. It's my favorite trick for asparagus, in particular, as it is so easy to overcook it on the stove top.

Soft- or Hard-Boiled Eggs The "set it and forget it" Instant Pot method for boiling eggs means you don't have to wait for and watch a pot of water as it heats on the stove top. A quick pressure release allows you to stop the cooking the moment the cooking program ends, so the yolks never end up with a grayish ring, the telltale sign of overcooked eggs. See page 25 for how to boil eggs.

Meals in Minutes If you are cooking a recipe with minimal liquid (1 cup or less), so the food won't create foam as it cooks, or the pot is less than half full, you can safely use the quick pressure release method before opening the pot immediately after the cooking program ends. The recipe for Ground Beef Tostada Salads (page 190) is a great example of this.

2. Natural Pressure Release (NPR) Rather than moving the Pressure Release, do nothing. Once a cooking program finishes, the pot will gradually lose pressure on its own as it cools. This can take anywhere from a few minutes to 30 minutes or more. That's because the pot retains more or less heat and pressure depending on the volume of food inside. The pot automatically defaults to its Keep Warm setting at the end of a cooking program, and you can leave it for up to 10 hours before it will shut off completely.

Use the natural pressure release method for the following:

Full Pots of Food If you've filled the Instant Pot to its maximum capacity (half or two-thirds full, depending on the type of food you're cooking), the safest way to open the pot after cooking is with a natural pressure release. This prevents messes that can result from food or liquid sputtering out of the pressure release valve.

Foamy Foods Beans, porridge, and cooked fruits such as applesauce, jams, and compotes have a tendency to sputter and spit if a quick release is used. That's because they typically foam up when boiled or otherwise expand when cooked. Although quick release can work with very small batches of these foods, it is generally safest to let the pressure release naturally, using a timed natural pressure release of at least 10 minutes.

Slow Cooker–Style Convenience The convenience of the Instant Pot lies not only in its ability to cook foods fast but also to hold them at temperature on the Keep Warm setting for up to 10 hours, much like a slow cooker. This means you can put the ingredients in the pot in the morning and set the cooking program. When the cooking is complete, the program will automatically switch to the Keep Warm setting, the pressure will release naturally, and you can come home to a piping-hot meal. Braises, roasts, soups, chilis, and stews hold up particularly well when left on the Keep Warm setting.

Egg Dishes and Cheesecakes Using a timed natural pressure release for at least 10 minutes allows fluffy egg dishes and cheesecakes to settle. In contrast, releasing the pressure quickly can cause these delicate foods to break apart and may make a mess inside the pot.

Delicate Fish Fillets After experimenting with many methods for cooking fish, I've determined my favorite: poach at low pressure and use a natural pressure release. This allows the fish to cook not just while it's under pressure but also from the residual heat on the Keep Warm setting as the pot cools down. Fish comes out evenly cooked and tender, not rubbery or tough, as it often does when the pressure is released quickly.

3. Timed Natural Pressure Release I often wait 10 or 15 minutes after the end of a cooking program, then move the Pressure Release to Venting to release a less geyser-like amount of steam from the pot.

The pressure release is given as QPR or NPR for each recipe in this book. When a recipe requires a timed natural pressure release, it's given as a timed NPR (for example, 10 minutes NPR). This means you'll let the pressure release naturally for the listed number of minutes before moving the Pressure Release to its Venting position. If a recipe notes that you should let the pressure release for "at least" a given number of minutes, you may leave the pot to release pressure naturally and stay on its default Keep Warm setting for up to 10 hours.

Use the timed natural release method for the following:

Pasta If you're cooking 1 pound or less of dried pasta (or 8 ounces or less in a 3-quart Instant Pot), the best way to get an al dente result is to set the cooking time for half the time recommended on the package, then let the pressure release naturally for 5 minutes before moving the Pressure Release to Venting and releasing the remaining pressure.

Half-Full Pots The time needed for the initial natural release will vary depending on the volume of food in the pot. It's difficult to come up with a hard-and-fast rule for how long you should wait before Venting. In recipes where I've stated that you should let the pressure release for "at least" a given amount of time, that means you should wait that long after the cooking program ends before manually venting (a timed natural pressure release), or you can leave the pot to release fully naturally. The amount of time required for a timed natural pressure release varies based not only on the volume of the food in the pot but also whether or not it's a food that has a tendency to foam, and whether or not you're trying to make use of the carryover heat, as in poached fish and seafood recipes.

If you're cooking a half batch of a recipe that would otherwise require a very long natural release, or if the pot is not filled to capacity, the pot will cool down and lose pressure much faster, and it will be safe to open in far less time than a very full pot. As long as you wait the minimum amount of time, you can open the pot whenever it is convenient. If you've doubled the recipe, though, it is safest to let the pressure release fully naturally.

Maximum Fill Levels

No matter what type of pressure cooker you are using, overfilling the pot can result in safety and performance issues, as food can end up clogging the valve and pressure release mechanisms in the lid.

Depending on what you are cooking, you can safely fill your Instant Pot half or two-thirds full. The inner pot in most models is stamped with half and two-thirds fill lines, so make sure the food doesn't come up past the line.

Fill the pot no more than half full for dried beans, grains, pastas, porridges, fruit sauces, and any other foods that can foam up when boiled or that expand when cooked.

Fill the pot no more than two-thirds full for stocks, broths, soups, stews, meaty main dishes, and steamed vegetables.

Instant Pot®

Pot-in-Pot Cooking and Steam Racks

You may have heard the term *pot-in-pot cooking* (see page 51) from Instant Pot aficionados. It's also sometimes referred to as PIP cooking. This simply means using an additional piece of cookware—cake pan, soufflé dish, Pyrex container, stacked stainless-steel pans (similar to an Indian tiffin carrier)—and nesting it inside the inner pot of the Instant Pot.

This method greatly expands the categories of food you can make in a pressure cooker. Foods that would otherwise scorch on the pot bottom because they include dairy; baked goods such as quiches and cheesecakes; and foods with too little liquid to get up to pressure can be prepared this way. With pot-in-pot cooking, the food is cooked by steam. You put a cup or two of water in the inner pot and the vessel containing the food sits on top of a steam rack.

In this book, I refer to three different kinds of steam racks: long-handled silicone steam rack, tall steam rack, and wire metal steam rack. See pages 10–11 for more information on each of these.

Preparation and Cooking Times

You'll notice that each recipe includes a chart with given times for preparation, cooking, and pressure release. The preparation, or prep time starts from the beginning of the recipe instructions, assuming that all of your ingredients are already ready to go as they are described in the ingredient list. Cooking time starts when you turn on the pot and includes any time spent sautéing, the time the pot takes to come up to pressure, and the time the food cooks under pressure. These times are estimates, meant to give you a rough idea of how long it will take to cook a recipe from start to finish—each home cook is different, of course, and variables such as the temperature of ingredients can affect the overall cooking time.

Tools and Accessories

You can absolutely start cooking in the Instant Pot without buying additional accessories or tools. If you're like me, though, you'll have fun outfitting your kitchen with a few extras that make Instant Pot cooking even more convenient and enjoyable. Some of these items will expand your recipe repertoire, allowing you to make many dishes that couldn't otherwise be prepared in a pressure cooker, such as Greek Yogurt Cheesecake (page 254) and the two-dish, one-pot Salsa Chicken and Supercharged Rice (page 161). Most of the items listed here are available at any well-stocked cookware store or can be purchased online.

Anti-Block Shield The little metal cap that fits on the inner part of the exhaust valve on the underside of the lid is the anti-block shield. It helps to keep foamy foods from blocking the valve. It's good practice to remove it and clean it after each use of the pot.

Extra Inner Pot If you plan on cooking two Instant Pot dishes in one night or covering the pot and storing it in the fridge, it's nice to have an extra inner pot ready to go. When storing the Instant Pot, I always make sure to leave the inner pot in the housing, in case anyone adds food or liquid to the pot without first checking if the inner pot is in place.

Sealing Ring The only part of the lid that you'll likely have to replace eventually is the silicone sealing ring, which is seated in a rack inside the perimeter of the lid. It has a life of 6 to 18 months, depending on how frequently you use your Instant Pot. The sealing ring needs to be seated properly in the lid for the pot to come up to pressure, so make sure to replace it securely in the sealing ring rack after you've cleaned it. I keep separate sealing rings for sweet and savory foods because the ring can retain strong odors. Using colored rings helps me remember which one to use for which purpose.

Fat Separator Tough cuts of meat well suited for pressure cooking often render a significant amount of fat, and a fat separator is an effective tool for defatting cooking liquids and stocks. My preferred models are from the brand OXO: they make a traditional fat separator with a pouring spout, as well as my new favorite: an ingenious spring-loaded version with a bottom spout.

Flexible Turner A flexible turner is ideal for getting under meat patties, chicken pieces, and other foods that can stick when seared in the pot. I'm once again partial to the OXO models, both in heat-resistant nylon and stainless steel.

Immersion Blender An immersion blender makes quick, low-mess work of blending sauces and gravies, pureeing fruits and vegetables, and emulsifying salad dressings and aioli. It's an indispensable tool in my kitchen, and it's much easier to clean than a countertop blender. Just remember safety first: be sure to unplug the blender and eject the blade assembly from the motor before cleaning.

Kitchen Thermometers An instant-read thermometer is handy for checking the temperature of meat or poultry to ensure it is cooked through. A probe thermometer with a remote display is useful when making yogurt, as you can set it to beep when it's time to add the culture to the cooled milk.

Kitchen Tongs Since everything in this book cooks in a deep pot, tongs are for turning and tossing ingredients. The OXO-brand 12-inch tongs are my favorite: they're made of sturdier metal than most and have a solid, well-made spring.

Bowls, Dishes, and Pans You'll find available a wide variety of bowls, pans, and dishes that fit into the 6-quart Instant Pot for pot-in-pot cooking (see page 9). My favorites are the Vollrath-brand 1½-quart stainless-steel bowl (both the thinner and thicker ones work well) and the Pyrex-brand 7-cup round tempered glass food storage dish. I use a 7-inch round springform or cheesecake pan for cheesecakes (these range from 2½ to 3 inches tall) and a 7 by 3-inch round cake pan for cakes, breads, and meat loaf. A 7-inch Bundt pan is also useful for cake making, with pretty, entertaining-friendly results. Ramekins with a 4-ounce (½-cup) capacity are ideal for coddling eggs or making individual omelets.

Jar Lifter and Jam Funnel These are especially useful for making yogurt and also for ladling jams, jellies, pickles, and chutneys into jars.

Long-Handled Silicone Steam Rack This is great for recipes requiring a soufflé dish, high-sided cake pan, or round tempered glass dish. I like the silicone steam rack from Instant Pot and the silicone pressure cooker sling made by OXO. Both have handles long enough that you can easily lower and lift a dish into and out of the pot, and they are easy to grip.

If you don't have a long-handled silicone steam rack, you can make a sling out of aluminum foil and use it to lower and lift the dish into and out of the pot. To make an aluminum foil sling, fold a 20-inch-long sheet of aluminum foil in half lengthwise, then in half again, creating a 3-inch-wide strip. Center it underneath the pan, dish, or other cooking vessel. Place the wire metal steam rack in the Instant Pot and pour in as much water as the recipe indicates. Firmly grasp the ends of the foil strip and use the strip as a sling to lower the cooking vessel into the pot, on top of the rack. Fold the ends of the sling so they fit into the pot. After cooking, use the sling to lift the cooking vessel out of the pot.

Sautéing Spatula A wooden or other stiff, heat-safe spatula is what I use when sautéing vegetables or other foods in the Instant Pot. Its slim profile also makes it great for scraping down the sides of the pot, nudging noodles underneath the cooking liquid, and stirring up a large amount of food without anything sloshing out of the pot.

Silicone Baking Cups and Mini Loaf Pans These small-capacity pans are great for cooking individual egg muffins (see page 33) as well as freezing foods, including leftovers, in small portions. For muffin-shaped egg bites, I use individual OXO-brand silicone baking cups or 7-inch round silicone egg bite molds, which are available from many brands. Each baking cup has a 2-ounce capacity, and you can fit up to 7 of them on the steam rack at one time.

Freezing staples such as broths and sauces in small portions makes for easy meal preparation, as they're quick to thaw, plus you can thaw only the quantity you need. For freezing foods in up to ¾-cup amounts, I portion the food into silicone loaf pans such as the Freshware-brand 6-cavity silicone mini loaf pans, which have a total capacity of 36 fluid ounces. Freeze the food until solid, then unmold, transfer to ziplock plastic freezer bags, label the bags with the date and contents, and store the bags in the freezer.

Silicone Mini Mitts Any time I refer to "heat-resistant mitts" in this book, I mean a pair of Instant Pot-brand silicone mini mitts. They protect your hands from steam when you vent the lid, and the thin, flexible silicone allows you to grip bowls, pans, and steam racks easily, so you can safely lift them out of the pot.

Spiralizer A tabletop or handheld vegetable spiralizer is the best, fastest way to make zucchini and sweet potato noodles. Serve vegetable noodles with any dish that calls for pasta for a low-calorie, gluten-free option.

Steamer Basket A wire-mesh, silicone, or expandable metal steamer basket is necessary for steaming vegetables in the Instant Pot. My favorite is a wire-mesh model from Instant Perrrt!, as it has easy-to-grasp, solidly attached handles. The fine mesh also makes this the most versatile type of steamer basket, as you can use it for steeping whole spices in mulled drinks such as Hot Cranberry Cocktail (page 239).

Tall Steam Rack This rack allows you to cook two things at once. I often use it to hold a bowl of rice and water above a meat or bean dish cooking directly in the inner pot. (I use a 1½-quart stainless-steel bowl with sloped sides to ensure the rice is submerged fully in liquid. This way, the rice always cooks evenly, even amounts as small as ½ cup.) It's a great hack for cooking other grains, too.

Many different companies make a tall steam rack. Just make sure to purchase one that's 2¾ to 3 inches tall, as it must stand high enough to use for pot-in-pot cooking (see page 9).

Tempered Glass Lid You can purchase a glass lid from Instant Pot, or you can use one from another pot in your kitchen, as long as it fits fairly snugly. I use a glass lid most often on the Sauté setting, usually to bring liquid to a boil quickly or to sweat vegetables. It is also useful for the Slow Cook setting.

Wire Metal Steam Rack This is the wire metal accessory that comes with your Instant Pot. In the manual, it is referred to simply as the "steam rack." It has arms that can be used to lift foods in and out of the pot. You can use the rack to steam vegetables and eggs, as well as ribs, whole chickens, and large roasts that would otherwise be difficult to lift out of the pot. Make sure to wear heat-resistant mitts when touching the rack, as it will be hot when you open the pot.

The Healthy Pressure Cooker Pantry

Pressure cooking is done in a hermetically sealed environment. A fair amount of liquid is needed for the pot to seal and come up to pressure, and very little moisture evaporates as the food cooks. This means that flavors don't concentrate in the same way as they would in a Dutch oven on the stove top. To compensate for this, I keep a few go-to ingredients in my pantry to amp up flavor and absorb moisture. Here are my favorites.

Broth Concentrates, Bone Broth, and Bouillon These are incredibly convenient ways to add flavor. When I don't have homemade broth on hand, I like to use the reduced-sodium broth concentrates from Better Than Bouillon and Savory Choice, bone broth concentrates from Kitchen Accomplice, and the vegetarian bouillon cubes from Edward & Sons.

I'll often use a blender to quickly combine broth concentrates and bouillons with water, even though the label recommends reconstituting the concentrate in boiling water before use.

Chia Seeds Tiny nutritional powerhouses, chia seeds are high in fiber, protein, omega-3 fatty acids, calcium, manganese, antioxidants, and more. They act as a natural thickener in Strawberry-Chia Jam (page 20), and a tablespoon or so added to your smoothie or yogurt bowl will boost your nutrient intake.

Coconut Butter More of a topping than a cooking ingredient, coconut butter has a strong, rich coconut flavor. Dollop it on oatmeal and waffles for a vegan alternative to butter. Nutiva makes a good organic coconut butter that it labels Coconut Manna.

Curry Paste and Other Spice Pastes Red, green, and *massaman* Thai curry pastes; Korean *gochujang*; Moroccan *harissa*—spice pastes are used in many different cuisines, and they add instant flavor. Thai curry paste makes Thai Green Curry Tilapia (page 145) a weeknight-friendly dinner, and *gochujang* adds its sweet and savory flavor to Korean Hot Pot (page 123).

Dried Fruits and Vegetables Dehydrated foods soak up excess liquid, so they're a no-brainer in pressure cooker recipes. Add a handful of raisins to the Coconut Bulgur Pudding (page 243), and it will thicken as it cools. Dried mushrooms are a great addition to soups and broths, and sun-dried tomatoes perk up pasta salads and frittatas.

Furikake A popular Japanese condiment, *furikake* is a dry seasoning sold in a variety of "flavors," from sesame, seaweed, fish, and egg to wasabi and shiso. It is typically sprinkled on cooked rice but is also good on noodles, fish, and vegetables.

Grains and Beans I make lots of one-pot dishes with chicken and grains, so I always keep a few different types of grain on hand. Oatmeal is a morning staple, which means steel-cut oats and old-fashioned rolled oats are in my pantry at all times. Dried beans are a popular choice in my kitchen, too. I usually have chickpeas on hand for my Toasted Sesame Miso Hummus (page 47), and I keep black beans, white beans, split peas, and lentils in the pantry for soups.

Jackfruit Canned in water or brine, this fruit is fairly neutral in flavor and has a meat-like texture, so it can be shredded like pulled pork. That means it lends itself for use as a replacement for meat in such dishes as BBQ Jackfruit Bowls with Alabama Sauce (page 110).

Miso Paste and Doenjang These fermented soybean pastes add salt and savory flavor to soups, stews, and even an Asian-inspired take on hummus (page 47). Japanese miso paste tends to have a mellower flavor than the funkier-flavored Korean *doenjang*.

Natural Sweeteners Use these in moderation when sweetening drinks and desserts. Agave nectar and brown rice syrup have the more neutral flavor, while coconut nectar has a toasted coconut flavor and the flavor of honey varies depending on the variety.

Nutritional Yeast If you're looking to add savory, cheesy flavor to a dairy-free dish, nutritional yeast is your go-to secret ingredient. In addition to being quite tasty, it contains B vitamins that can be tricky to find in other plant-based foods. Use it in Cashew Sour Cream (page 265) and Vegan Parmesan Cheese (page 265).

Oils and Fats Minimal processing is the key to high-quality, health-friendly cooking fats. When purchasing olive oil, look for extra-virgin oil with a production date printed somewhere on the label. For recipes that require a neutral oil, cold-pressed avocado oil is ideal. I'll also use moderate amounts of butter when its taste and texture are preferable to oil.

Peanut Powder With all the roasted peanut flavor of peanut butter but with much less fat, peanut powder is a great addition to smoothies like the Chocolate and PB Yogurt Smoothie (page 37). It can also be reconstituted with water to make a low-fat peanut butter alternative. PB2 and PBfit are two good brands.

Shirataki and Vegetable "Noodles" Found in the refrigerated section of grocery stores and natural foods stores, *shirataki* are noodles made from an extremely low-calorie, high-fiber Japanese yam. I like House Foods–brand *shirataki*, which blends yam flour and tofu flour, as they have a slightly more noodle-like flavor and texture than all-yam *shirataki*.

For another nutritious, lower-calorie alternative to pasta, use a spiralizer to transform zucchini and sweet potatoes into long strands. Zucchini noodles can be eaten raw or cooked, while sweet potato noodles benefit from a quick sauté. For an even easier option, look for already-spiralized vegetables in the produce section of the grocery store.

Spice and Herb Blends These blends are great for perking up pressure-cooked dishes. I use all types in my cooking, from common ones like chili powder and Old Bay to herbes de Provence, North African *ras el hanout*, Jamaican jerk seasoning, and Ethiopian *berbere*. I love shopping for these blends at natural foods stores that sell them in bulk. That way, I can buy only as much as I need. When I want to splurge on truly exceptional spice blends, I purchase them from Spice Hound at farmers' markets in the San Francisco Bay Area; Oaktown Spice Shop in Oakland, California; World Spice Merchants in Seattle, Washington; and Penzeys Spices, which has locations throughout the United States. All of these merchants also sell their spices online.

Soy Curls Available in natural foods stores and online, Butler Foods–brand Soy Curls are a gluten-free, vegan meat substitute made from whole soybeans and nothing else. The 8-ounce bags keep in the pantry for a long time, and each bag reconstitutes to yield about 2 pounds Soy Curls. Use them in Vegan Soy Curls Chili (page 97) or "Chick'n" and Brown Rice Pilaf (page 119).

Tamari and Coconut Aminos These are gluten-free alternatives to soy sauce. Tamari is made from soybeans and tends to have a strong flavor, while coconut aminos is made from coconut sap and has a mellower taste.

Tomato Paste This concentrated form of tomatoes adds body and depth of flavor to tomato-based dishes, so if you're using tomatoes (fresh or canned), double up on the flavor by adding a tablespoon of tomato paste as well. Because it can be difficult to get through a can of tomato paste before it goes bad, I buy it in a tube (it keeps a bit longer), or I freeze my canned tomato paste in 1-tablespoon dollops and thaw it as needed.

Vegan Buttery Spread Earth Balance makes a variety of spreads and baking sticks designed to replace butter and shortening. Its Original Buttery Spread can be used in place of butter in nearly any recipe. Just keep in mind that it does contain a bit of salt, so you may want to adjust any other salt in the recipe accordingly.

Vital Wheat Gluten A floury powder, vital wheat gluten is made by hydrating wheat flour and removing all the starch, leaving only the high-protein gluten. It's the main ingredient in seitan—aka wheat meat—a popular meat substitute. It adds chewy texture to the Seitan Chickpea Chorizo Sausages (page 104) and Vegan Salisbury Steak (page 114). I like to add cooked beans when using wheat gluten to yield a more tender, less bouncy texture.

Worcestershire Sauce and Other Strongly Flavored Condiments These are great when you need an umami flavor bomb to enhance a recipe. They'll improve chilis, stews, and braised meat dishes, making them extra savory. Dijon mustard is a go-to flavor enhancer for me, along with soy sauce, tamari, coconut aminos, fish sauce, miso paste, Sriracha sauce, and *sambal oelek*.

Shortcuts—Tips for Reducing Time until Dinner

Using the Instant Pot is already a great way to cut down on time in the kitchen, and you can make use of some other handy shortcuts to increase your efficiency even more. Here are a few of my favorite time-saving techniques and ingredients.

Better Than Bouillon Bases More often than not, I do not have homemade broths on hand to use in my recipes. In an ideal world, we'd all be cooking with bone broths all the time, but I don't know many people who can manage that feat. I'm not a fan of boxed and canned broths, as they tend to have a metallic aftertaste and take up tons of pantry space. My shortcut solution is to keep a few jars of Better Than Bouillon in my fridge at all times. They keep for months and months, and just a teaspoon of the concentrated paste reconstitutes to a cup of broth. I use the reduced-sodium versions of the vegetable, chicken, and beef varieties most often. I also reach for the lobster and clam bases when I'm making seafood dishes. You're technically supposed to mix the base with boiling water to reconstitute it, but when I'm in a hurry to get everything into the pot, I use the blender to combine tap water and a dollop of the base.

Skip Peeling Your Vegetables and Fruits The peels of carrots, potatoes, apples, pears, and even some kinds of winter squash are completely edible and contain lots of vitamins and fiber. When you're cutting up vegetables for a recipe, don't remove those nutritious skins. It'll save you time and effort, and you'll reap all those nutritional benefits.

The Keep Warm Setting When a cooking program ends, the Instant Pot automatically defaults to its Keep Warm setting. The food stays hot and ready to serve for up to 10 hours, which means you can cook any time of day that works for you. If you can find a few minutes in the morning to get some ingredients into the Instant Pot, your dish will cook through, then stay warm until dinnertime. Soup and chili recipes tend to be perfect for this method.

Canned and Frozen Vegetables I'll take a bag of frozen vegetables over out-of-season fresh vegetables 100 percent of the time. Frozen vegetables tend to be picked and processed at their peak ripeness, and my dietitian says they're just as nutritious as fresh vegetables. Just check the ingredients list and make sure that the vegetables are all that's in the bag.

Canned vegetables can be great, too, especially tomatoes. I use canned whole and diced tomatoes all the time, in everything from pasta sauces to soups and chilis. San Marzano and San Marzano–style tomatoes tend to be canned without added salt, and no-salt-added diced tomatoes are easy to track down in most grocery stores. I like to use low- or no-sodium canned vegetables so I can more easily season my food to taste (and they're a good option if you're watching your salt intake, as well).

Putting Together Healthy Meals

The word *healthy* means different things to different people, but dietitians agree on some basics across the board. Barring any medical conditions that preclude you from eating from specific food groups, here are some general rules to follow that will help you put together a healthy and balanced meal every time.

Build a Balanced Plate When you're thinking about what to eat for any meal, there's an ideal proportion of vegetables, starches, and protein to shoot for. Think of your plate as being divided into one half and two quarters, then fill the half with vegetables and one quarter with a starch and the other with a protein. Fats will end up interspersed throughout all of these categories—vinaigrette on salad, gravy on a meat dish, butter on potatoes, and so on. If you stick to these proportions, say, 80 percent of the time, you are likely doing a great job of eating a balanced diet.

Use Hand-Size Portion Control Each recipe in this book includes number of servings and nutrition information, but every person has individual energy needs, so you may find that you require more or less than one serving. One of the best tools to use for gauging serving sizes is your hand: it's always with you, and it's sized just right for your own personal use. A serving of protein is the size of your palm, a serving of starch is the size of your clenched fist, and a serving of cooked vegetables is an open handful. The portion size I most often need a reality check on is the starch, so whenever I'm eating grains, pasta, or mashed potatoes, I try to keep that fist-size serving in mind.

Keep Things Colorful and Healthy with Vegetables Many of the recipes in this book contain vegetable, protein, and starch all in one. If your main dish is largely meat and/or starch (is it mostly beige or brown?), chances are you'll want to pair it with a serving or two of vegetables. A colorful plate ensures that your meal is full of vitamins, minerals, and fiber. Make your plate or bowl vibrant with a couple of handfuls of cut-up crudités, steamed broccoli, or even a bag of frozen mixed vegetables, warmed in the microwave and drizzled with a little olive oil.

Have Healthy Treats on Hand Keep in-season fruits in the produce drawer of your fridge at all times. The dessert recipes in this book are meant to be "sometime foods," as Cookie Monster likes to say. When you're craving something sweet, try to choose fruit as your dessert of choice as often as you can. There's nothing like a silky ripe mango, a crisp fall apple, a juicy summer nectarine, or a bowl of berries.

1

Breakfast

This oatmeal gets its vibrant orange color from nutrient-packed butternut squash. Serve the sweet, spiced bowls of porridge with a pat of butter, a drizzle of syrup, and some chopped nuts for a satisfying breakfast. You'll need half of a medium-size squash or, for an easy shortcut, one 1-pound bag precut squash.

BUTTERNUT SQUASH STEEL-CUT OATMEAL

3 cups water

1 cup steel-cut oats

3 cups peeled and cubed butternut squash (about 1 pound)

1 teaspoon pumpkin pie spice

¼ teaspoon fine sea salt

Vegan buttery spread or salted butter, for serving

Pure maple syrup or honey, for serving

Chopped walnuts or pecans, for serving

Pomegranate arils or fresh berries, for serving

Ground cinnamon, for serving

PREP	0 MINUTES
COOK	25 MINUTES
PR	15 MINUTES NPR
SERVES	5

1 Combine the water, oats, squash, pumpkin pie spice, and salt in the Instant Pot and stir to combine, making sure all of the grains are submerged in the liquid.

2 Secure the lid and set the Pressure Release to **Sealing**. Select the **Porridge** setting and set the cooking time for 12 minutes at high pressure. (The pot will take about 10 minutes to come up to pressure before the cooking program begins.)

3 When the cooking program ends, let the pressure release naturally for 15 minutes, then move the Pressure Release to **Venting** to release any remaining steam. Open the pot and, wearing heat-resistant mitts, lift out the inner pot. Use a potato masher to mash the squash and mix it with the oatmeal, incorporating any extra liquid.

4 Ladle the oatmeal into bowls and serve topped with the buttery spread, maple syrup, walnuts, pomegranate or berries, and a dusting of cinnamon.

Nutrition Information

Per serving (oatmeal without toppings): 162 calories, 2 grams fat, 32 grams carbohydrates, 5 grams fiber, 5 grams protein

Here, hot cooked oatmeal is whisked with bananas so it's creamy and fluffy. Traditional jams contain lots of sugar, but this one has just enough agave nectar to satisfy your sweet tooth and requires no cooking. Chia seeds thicken the jam to its spreadable consistency after a couple of hours in the fridge. Make the jam the night before to speed up your breakfast routine.

BANANA OATMEAL WITH STRAWBERRY-CHIA JAM

Strawberry-Chia Jam

12 ounces fresh or thawed frozen strawberries, quartered

¼ cup agave nectar or honey

1 tablespoon chia seeds

Pinch of fine sea salt

Oatmeal

5 cups water

2 cups old-fashioned rolled oats

1 teaspoon ground cinnamon

½ teaspoon fine sea salt

2 large bananas, peeled and thinly sliced

PREP	5 MINUTES
COOK	20 MINUTES
PR	15 MINUTES NPR
CHILL	2 HOURS TO OVERNIGHT
SERVES	6 (WITH JAM LEFT OVER)

1 To make the jam: In a medium bowl, combine the strawberries, agave nectar, chia seeds, and salt. Use a potato masher to mash the strawberries and stir the mixture together until the berries are mostly mashed (it's fine if some chunky pieces remain) and the chia seeds are evenly distributed. Cover and transfer to the refrigerator to firm up for at least 2 hours or up to overnight. The jam will keep in an airtight container, refrigerated, for up to 1 week. Stir once more before serving.

2 To make the oatmeal: Combine the water, oats, cinnamon, and salt in the Instant Pot. Secure the lid and set the Pressure Release to **Sealing**. Select the **Porridge** setting and set the cooking time for 3 minutes at high pressure. (The pot will take about 15 minutes to come up to pressure before the cooking program begins.)

3 When the cooking program ends, let the pressure release naturally for 15 minutes, then move the Pressure Release to **Venting** to release any remaining steam. Open the pot and add the bananas. Vigorously whisk the bananas into the oatmeal, incorporating any liquid sitting on the surface. Most of the banana will be mashed and incorporated, but it's fine if some pieces remain evenly distributed throughout the oatmeal.

4 Spoon the oatmeal into bowls and spoon 2 tablespoons of the jam on top of each bowl. Serve warm.

Note: You can use any type of berry for the jam. Raspberries or blackberries are nice options—or even a blend.

Nutrition Information

Per serving of oatmeal: 138 calories, 2 grams fat, 29 grams carbohydrates, 4 grams fiber, 4 grams protein

Per serving of jam (2 tablespoons): 30 calories, 0 grams fat, 7 grams carbohydrates, 1 gram fiber, 0 grams protein

In this hearty breakfast bowl, chewy grains of pearl barley are crowned with fried eggs and a colorful mix of vegetables and Asian-inspired toppings. Tamari has a deeper, richer flavor than regular soy sauce, so just a teaspoon seasons the whole bowl, and a sprinkle of *furikake* (see page 12) on top adds a little texture and crunch. Make the barley ahead of time if your morning routine is a quick one. It will keep in the fridge for up to 4 days or in the freezer for up to 2 months.

BARLEY BOWLS WITH SUNNY EGGS AND TAMARI

1 cup water

1½ cups low-sodium vegetable broth (page 261)

1 cup pearl barley

2 tablespoons cold-pressed avocado oil

1 teaspoon toasted sesame oil

4 large eggs

2 green onions, green part only, sliced

1 cup cherry tomatoes, halved

4 teaspoons tamari

4 teaspoons furikake (optional)

PREP	0 MINUTES
COOK	35 MINUTES
PR	10 MINUTES NPR
SERVES	4

1 Pour the water into the Instant Pot and place a tall steam rack into the pot. Combine the broth and barley in a 1½-quart stainless-steel bowl and place the bowl on the rack. (The bowl should not touch the lid once the pot is closed.)

2 Secure the lid and set the Pressure Release to **Sealing**. Select the **Pressure Cook** or **Manual** setting and set the cooking time for 25 minutes at high pressure. (The pot will take about 10 minutes to come up to pressure before the cooking program begins.)

3 When the cooking program ends, let the pressure release naturally for at least 10 minutes, then move the Pressure Release to **Venting** to release any remaining steam. Open the pot and, wearing heat-resistant mitts, remove the bowl from the pot. Fluff the barley with a fork.

4 While the pressure is releasing, heat the avocado and sesame oils in a large skillet over medium-high heat. Crack the eggs and slip them into the pan. Fry for about 3 minutes, until the whites are set and a little crispy and browned around the edges and the yolks have thickened but are still runny.

5 Spoon the barley into bowls and top each bowl with a fried egg. Top with the green onions, tomatoes, tamari, and furikake (if using). Serve warm.

Nutrition Information

Per serving: 333 calories, 14 grams fat, 41 grams carbohydrates, 8 grams fiber, 12 grams protein

Try this sweetly spiced quinoa with all of the flavors and textures of a bowl of Switzerland's legendary apple-laced *Birchermüesli*. This recipe is gluten-free and vegan, so just about anyone can enjoy it. When you're buying quinoa, check the package to see if it requires rinsing. Nowadays, most brands don't require rinsing, but you'll want to make sure to avoid a bitter flavor.

QUINOA MUESLI BREAKFAST BOWLS

1¾ cups water
1½ cups quinoa
1 teaspoon ground cinnamon
¼ teaspoon ground cardamom
¼ teaspoon fine sea salt
2 large Granny Smith apples
1 tablespoon fresh lemon juice
Unsweetened almond milk, for serving
Chopped toasted walnuts, for serving
Raisins, for serving
Agave nectar or honey, for serving

PREP	0 MINUTES
COOK	10 MINUTES
PR	15 MINUTES NPR
SERVES	6

1 Combine the water, quinoa, cinnamon, cardamom, and salt in the Instant Pot. Secure the lid and set the Pressure Release to **Sealing**. Select the **Pressure Cook** or **Manual** setting and set the cooking time for 1 minute at high pressure. (The pot will take about 10 minutes to come up to pressure before the cooking program begins.)

2 While the quinoa is cooking, using a box grater or food processor, coarsely grate the apples. Add the lemon juice and toss to combine.

3 When the cooking program ends, let the pressure release naturally for 15 minutes, then move the Pressure Release to **Venting** to release any remaining steam. Open the pot and add the apples. Using a fork, incorporate the apples and fluff the quinoa.

4 Spoon the quinoa into bowls and top with the almond milk, walnuts, raisins, and agave nectar. Serve warm.

Note: Try different nuts—chopped toasted hazelnuts or almonds—and dried fruits—dried cranberries or cherries or chopped dried apricots—to switch up the flavors.

Nutrition Information

Per serving (without toppings): 198 calories, 3 grams fat, 38 grams carbohydrates, 5 grams fiber, 7 grams protein

Although these eggs are called "boiled," they are actually steamed under pressure in the Instant Pot. This technique results in evenly cooked, easy-to-peel soft- or hard-boiled eggs, and you can cook as many as you need at one time, from one or two up to a dozen.

You'll need a rack or steamer basket to keep the eggs above the water as they cook. If you're cooking only a few eggs at a time, the wire metal steam rack that comes with the Instant Pot works fine. For more than a half dozen eggs, I like to use the silicone or wire metal stackable steamer racks made especially for eggs because they hold the eggs upright, keeping the yolks centered. Don't be tempted to use a solid bowl, as the eggs will not cook as quickly or evenly.

SOFT- OR HARD-BOILED EGGS

Up to 12 large eggs, straight from the refrigerator

PREP	5 MINUTES
COOK	15 MINUTES
PR	QPR

1 Pour 1 cup water into the Instant Pot and place the wire metal steam rack, an egg rack, or a steamer basket into the pot. Gently place the eggs on the rack or in the basket, taking care not to crack them.

2 Secure the lid and set the Pressure Release to **Sealing**. Select the **Steam** setting and set the cooking time for 3 minutes at high pressure for soft-boiled eggs or 6 minutes at high pressure for hard-boiled eggs. (The pot will take about 10 minutes to come up to pressure before the cooking program begins. This will vary by a few minutes, depending on how many eggs you are cooking; the fewer the eggs, the shorter the time.)

3 While the eggs are cooking, prepare an ice bath.

4 When the cooking program ends, perform a quick release by moving the Pressure Release to **Venting**. Open the pot and, using tongs, transfer the eggs to the ice bath to cool.

5 The eggs will keep, refrigerated, for up to 1 week. Peel when ready to serve.

Note: For extra-large eggs, increase the cooking time to 4 minutes for soft-boiled or 7 minutes for hard-boiled eggs. For jumbo eggs, increase the cooking time to 5 minutes for soft-boiled or 8 minutes for hard-boiled eggs.

Nutritional Information

Per 1 large egg: 70 calories, 5 grams fat, 0 grams carbohydrates, 0 grams fiber, 6 grams protein

A Turkish-inspired breakfast kicks off your day with lots of protein, good fats, and whole grains. Traditionally, eggs in this dish are poached, but I find soft boiling them in the Instant Pot to be so much easier and hands-off. The garlicky yogurt sauce cuts the richness of the eggs, and everything is scooped up with flatbread.

SOFT-BOILED EGGS IN YOGURT SAUCE

Yogurt Sauce

1 cup plain 2 percent yogurt, homemade (page 34) or store-bought

2 garlic cloves, pressed or grated

½ teaspoon fine sea salt

½ teaspoon freshly ground black pepper

4 large eggs

Paprika Oil

2 tablespoons extra-virgin olive oil

1 teaspoon sweet paprika

Pinch of cayenne pepper

Whole-wheat flatbread, for serving

PREP	5 MINUTES
COOK	10 MINUTES
PR	QPR
COOL	3 MINUTES
SERVES	2

1 To make the yogurt sauce: In a small bowl, stir together the yogurt, garlic, salt, and pepper, mixing well.

2 Pour 1 cup water into the Instant Pot and place the wire metal steam rack, an egg rack, or a steamer basket into the pot. Gently place the eggs on the rack or in the basket, taking care not to crack them.

3 Secure the lid and set the Pressure Release to **Sealing**. Select the **Steam** setting and set the cooking time for 3 minutes at high pressure. (The pot will take about 5 minutes to come up to pressure before the cooking program begins.)

4 While the eggs are cooking, prepare an ice bath.

5 When the cooking program ends, perform a quick release by moving the Pressure Release to **Venting**. Open the pot and, using tongs, transfer the eggs to the ice bath. Let cool for about 3 minutes, until comfortable to handle.

6 While the eggs are cooling, make the paprika oil: In a small saucepan, combine the oil, paprika, and cayenne over low heat. Heat for about 2 minutes, until bubbling and fragrant, then remove from the heat.

7 To serve, peel the eggs and place two eggs in each bowl. Spoon the yogurt sauce over the eggs, then drizzle the paprika oil over the sauce. Serve with the flatbread.

Note: For a lower carb option, serve slices of bell pepper and cucumber instead of the flatbread.

Nutrition Information

Per serving: 341 calories, 25 grams fat, 10 grams carbohydrates, 1 gram fiber, 19 grams protein

This omelet is simple to throw together, but it comes out looking fancy—a perfect summertime brunch dish. Low-fat, high-fiber zucchini and corn are cooked into the omelet, which is then topped with a generous heap of silky smoked salmon and a dollop of creamy Greek yogurt.

CORN AND ZUCCHINI OMELET WITH SMOKED SALMON

6 large eggs

¼ teaspoon fine sea salt

¼ teaspoon freshly ground black pepper

1 cup fresh or thawed frozen corn kernels

One 5-ounce zucchini, diced (rounded 1 cup)

3 ounces thinly sliced cold-smoked salmon

3 tablespoons plain 2 percent Greek yogurt, homemade (page 34) or store-bought

1 tablespoon chopped fresh chives

PREP	5 MINUTES
COOK	35 MINUTES
PR	5 MINUTES NPR
REST	2 MINUTES
SERVES	3

1 Generously grease a 7-cup round heatproof glass dish with butter. Pour 1 cup water into the Instant Pot.

2 In a medium bowl, whisk together the eggs, salt, and pepper until well blended, then stir in the corn and zucchini.

3 Pour the egg mixture into the prepared dish and cover tightly with aluminum foil. Place the dish on a long-handled silicone steam rack, then, holding the handles of the steam rack, lower it into the Instant Pot. (If you don't have the long-handled rack, use the wire metal steam rack and a homemade sling as described on page 10.)

4 Secure the lid and set the Pressure Release to **Sealing**. Select the **Pressure Cook** or **Manual** setting and set the cooking time for 25 minutes at high pressure. (The pot will take about 10 minutes to come up to pressure before the cooking program begins.)

5 When the cooking program ends, let the pressure release naturally for 5 minutes, then move the Pressure Release to **Venting** to release any remaining steam. Open the pot and let the omelet sit for a minute or two, until it deflates and settles into its dish. Then, wearing heat-resistant mitts, grasp the handles of the steam rack and lift the dish out of the pot. Uncover the omelet, taking care not to get burned by the steam or to drip condensation onto the omelet.

6 Cut the omelet into wedges, top with the salmon, Greek yogurt, and chives, and serve right away.

Note: For a dairy-free version, substitute vegan buttery spread or extra-virgin olive oil for the butter and sliced avocado for the cream cheese.

Nutrition Information

Per serving: 280 calories, 16 grams fat, 11 grams carbohydrates, 2 grams fiber, 21 grams protein

Eggs, milk, salt, and pepper form the base for almost every quiche. Enjoy this high-protein ham and Swiss version, or use about 3 cups of any other filling of your choice, such as cooked sausage, green onions, and chopped bell pepper—it's up to you. Serve lightly dressed mixed salad greens on the side for a balanced and colorful brunch.

CRUSTLESS HAM AND SWISS QUICHE

6 large eggs

½ cup 2 percent milk

½ teaspoon fine sea salt

½ teaspoon freshly ground black pepper

1 small yellow onion, diced

1 cup chopped ham

1 cup firmly packed shredded Swiss cheese

PREP	5 MINUTES
COOK	40 MINUTES
PR	10 MINUTES NPR
REST	15 MINUTES
SERVES	6

1 Generously grease a 7-cup round heatproof glass dish with butter or nonstick cooking spray. Pour 1 cup water into the Instant Pot.

2 In a medium bowl, whisk together the eggs, milk, salt, and pepper until well blended, then stir in the onion, ham, and cheese.

3 Pour the egg mixture into the prepared dish and cover tightly with aluminum foil. Place the dish on a long-handled silicone steam rack, then, holding the handles of the steam rack, lower it into the Instant Pot. (If you don't have the long-handled rack, use the wire metal steam rack and a homemade sling as described on page 10.)

4 Secure the lid and set the Pressure Release to **Sealing**. Select the **Pressure Cook** or **Manual** setting and set the cooking time for 30 minutes at high pressure. (The pot will take about 10 minutes to come up to pressure before the cooking program begins.)

5 When the cooking program ends, let the pressure release naturally for 10 minutes, then move the Pressure Release to **Venting** to release any remaining steam. Open the pot and, wearing heat-resistant mitts, grasp the handles of the steam rack and lift the dish out of the pot. Uncover the quiche, taking care not to get burned by the steam or to drip condensation onto the quiche. Let the quiche rest for 15 minutes, giving it time to reabsorb some liquid and set up. It's fine if a couple of tablespoons of liquid remain in the dish.

6 Cut the quiche into wedges and serve warm or at room temperature.

Nutrition Information

Per serving: 189 calories, 11 grams fat, 4 grams carbohydrates, 0 grams fiber, 17 grams protein

This vegetarian frittata is packed with nutritious sweet potatoes and arugula. To make it vegan, use vegan cheese shreds, such as the ones from Daiya or Follow Your Heart, in place of the Parmesan. Cut the frittata into thirds for a light breakfast, or into halves to satisfy three-egg appetites.

SWEET POTATO AND ARUGULA FRITTATA

6 large eggs

1 tablespoon extra-virgin olive oil

½ teaspoon fine sea salt

½ teaspoon freshly ground black pepper

1 cup baby arugula

One 5-ounce sweet potato, peeled and coarsely grated (about 1 medium-large potato)

¼ cup grated Parmesan cheese, or ½ cup nondairy cheese shreds

PREP	5 MINUTES
COOK	35 MINUTES
PR	5 MINUTES NPR
REST	2 MINUTES
SERVES	3

1 Lightly grease a 7-cup round heatproof glass dish with butter or coat nonstick cooking spray. Pour 1 cup water into the Instant Pot.

2 In a bowl, whisk together the eggs, oil, salt, and pepper until well blended, then stir in the arugula, sweet potato, and cheese.

3 Pour the egg mixture into the prepared dish and cover tightly with aluminum foil. Place the dish on a long-handled silicone steam rack, then, holding the handles of the steam rack, lower it into the Instant Pot. (If you don't have the long-handled rack, use the wire metal steam rack and a homemade sling as described on page 10.)

4 Secure the lid and set the Pressure Release to **Sealing**. Select the **Pressure Cook** or **Manual** setting and set the cooking time for 25 minutes at high pressure. (The pot will take about 10 minutes to come up to pressure before the cooking program begins.)

5 When the cooking program ends, let the pressure release naturally for 5 minutes, then move the Pressure Release to **Venting** to release any remaining steam. Open the pot and let the frittata sit for a minute or two, until it deflates and settles into its dish. Then, wearing heat-resistant mitts, grasp the handles of the steam rack and lift the dish out of the pot. Uncover the frittata, taking care not to get burned by the steam or to drip condensation onto the surface.

6 Cut the frittata into three wedges and serve warm.

Nutrition Information

Per serving: 254 calories, 16 grams fat, 11 grams carbohydrates, 2 grams fiber, 16 grams protein

Here is a protein-and-vegetable-spiked way to start your day on mornings when you need to be out the door fast. These high-protein, three-bite muffins are adult and kid friendly, and you can substitute 1 cup of any chopped vegetable for the broccoli, if you like. For a portable meal, sandwich one in a toasted whole-wheat English muffin, wrap it in a napkin, and be on your way with breakfast in tow.

BROCCOLI-CHEDDAR EGG MUFFINS

3 large eggs

One ¾-ounce wedge Laughing Cow light Swiss cheese, or 1½ tablespoons cream cheese

1 cup broccoli florets, chopped

1 green onion, white and green parts, thinly sliced

¼ cup shredded Cheddar cheese

PREP	5 MINUTES
COOK	15 MINUTES
PR	5 MINUTES NPR
COOL	5 MINUTES
MAKES	7 MUFFINS

1 In a widemouthed 1-pint Mason jar, combine the eggs and Laughing Cow cheese. Using an immersion blender, blend for about 15 seconds, just until smooth.

2 Pour 1 cup water into the Instant Pot. Generously grease 7 silicone muffin cups with butter, making sure to coat all of the ridges well. Place the muffin cups on a long-handled silicone steam rack. (If you don't have the long-handled rack, use the wire metal steam rack and a homemade sling as described on page 10.)

3 Sprinkle the broccoli and green onions among the muffin cups, then pour in the egg mixture, dividing it evenly and filling each cup about half full. Sprinkle the cups evenly with the Cheddar cheese. Holding the handles of the steam rack, carefully lower the muffin cups into the pot. If necessary, clasp together the handles of the steam rack.

4 Secure the lid and set the Pressure Release to **Sealing**. Select the **Steam** setting and set the cooking time for 8 minutes at low pressure. (The pot will take about 5 minutes to come up to pressure before the cooking program begins.)

5 When the cooking program ends, let the pressure release naturally for 5 minutes, then move the Pressure Release to **Venting** to release any remaining steam. Open the pot. The egg muffins will have puffed up quite a bit during cooking, but they will deflate and settle as they cool. Wearing heat-resistant mitts, grasp the handles of the steam rack and lift the muffin cups out of the pot. Let the muffins cool for about 5 minutes, until you are able to comfortably handle them.

6 To unmold, pull the sides of the muffin cups away from the muffins and transfer the muffins to plates. Serve warm.

Nutrition Information

Per muffin: 57 calories, 4 grams fat, 1 gram carbohydrates, 0 grams fiber, 4 grams protein

When making yogurt from dairy milk, I find that the lowest-fat milk that still yields good results is 2 percent, also known as reduced-fat milk. If you want a richer yogurt, use whole milk.

It takes only two ingredients to make a batch of yogurt in the Instant Pot. Just make sure your Instant Pot has a Yogurt function before you start and you're good to go. The only ingredients are milk and a starter culture (fresh plain yogurt or freeze-dried starter culture will work). You can culture the yogurt right in the inner pot, but I like to use a glass container or jars that fit inside the inner pot. That way, the yogurt goes straight from the Instant Pot to the refrigerator without any additional cleanup required. The recipe yields 2 quarts, a generous amount, but you can make half as much by halving the ingredients and following the same instructions. Once the yogurt is cultured, it can be enjoyed as is or strained to make Greek yogurt (see step 5).

YOGURT

½ gallon 2 percent milk

¼ cup plain yogurt with live active cultures, or two 5-gram envelopes freeze-dried yogurt starter

PREP	5 MINUTES
COOK	8 HOURS 20 MINUTES
PR	N/A
COOL	30 MINUTES
SERVES	8

1 Pour the milk into the Instant Pot and cover with a tempered glass lid or leave the pot open. Select the **Yogurt** setting and adjust the heat level to **More** or **High**. This will heat the milk to 180°F, ensuring that it is free of bacteria that could keep it from culturing safely once the starter culture is added.

2 When the cooking program ends, remove the inner pot and set it on a trivet on the counter. Leave the milk to cool to 115°F. (A probe thermometer with a remote display is ideal for this step because you can leave the thermometer in the milk and set it to alert you when the milk has cooled to the proper temperature. Alternatively, you can test the milk periodically with an instant-read thermometer. If you don't have a thermometer, let the milk cool until lukewarm to the touch.) Add the yogurt to the cooled milk and whisk gently until fully incorporated.

3 Using a jam funnel, ladle the milk into four 1-pint jars or two 1-quart jars. Rinse out the inner pot, return it to the housing, and place the jars into the pot. Cover the pot with the glass lid and select the **Yogurt** program, making sure it is adjusted to its **Normal** or **Medium** setting.

Nutrition Information

Per 1 cup yogurt: 120 calories, 5 grams fat, 12 grams carbohydrates, 0 grams fiber, 8 grams protein

Per ½ cup Greek yogurt (drained for 12 hours): 85 calories, 2 grams fat, 4.5 grams carbohydrates, 0 grams fiber, 11 grams protein

The yogurt will begin to thicken after about 3 hours, but the flavor will be very mild at this point. For a moderately tart yogurt, let it culture for the full 8 hours of the default **Yogurt** program. If you like your yogurt somewhat tarter or very tart, adjust the program time to 10 or 12 hours, respectively.

4 Open the pot and remove the jars. Cover and refrigerate for at least 6 hours before serving. The yogurt will keep, refrigerated, for up to 2 weeks.

Variation: To make Greek yogurt, place a colander over a bowl. Line the colander with cheesecloth, a paper towel, or a clean kitchen towel. Pour the just-made yogurt into the prepared colander, transfer the bowl to the refrigerator, and allow the yogurt to drain until it reaches the desired thickness. This will take from 2 hours for a lightly drained yogurt to overnight for a very thick, spreadable consistency.

One of my favorite ways to serve my Instant Pot granola is with a handful of juicy sliced strawberries on top. This granola has a subtle gingery bite, so it's aromatic and just a little spicy. The recipe makes a fairly small batch of 3 cups, and it's easily doubled for a bigger crowd.

YOGURT BOWL WITH GINGER-ALMOND GRANOLA

Granola

¼ cup agave nectar or coconut nectar

¼ cup coconut oil or unsalted butter

1 teaspoon ground ginger

½ teaspoon ground cardamom

¼ teaspoon fine sea salt

2 cups old-fashioned rolled oats

1 cup sliced almonds, toasted

½ cup golden raisins

4 cups plain 2 percent yogurt, homemade (page 34) or store-bought

2 cups sliced fresh strawberries

PREP	0 MINUTES
COOK	35 MINUTES
PR	N/A
COOL	1 HOUR
SERVES	4

1 To make the granola: Preheat the oven to 300°F. Line a sheet pan with parchment paper or a silicone baking mat.

2 Select the **Sauté** setting on the Instant Pot, adjust the heat level to **Low**, and heat the agave nectar and coconut oil, stirring once or twice, for about 3 minutes, until the coconut oil has completely melted. Stir in the ginger, cardamom, and salt. Press the **Cancel** button to turn off the pot, then stir in the oats.

3 Using a silicone spatula, transfer the mixture to the prepared sheet pan, spreading it in an even layer. Bake, stirring every 10 minutes, for about 30 minutes, until the oats are evenly golden brown. Remove from the oven and let cool on the pan to room temperature (about 1 hour), then sprinkle with the almonds and raisins. Transfer to an airtight container and store at room temperature for up to 2 weeks.

4 To serve, spoon 1 cup of the yogurt into each bowl, followed by ¼ cup of the granola and ½ cup of the strawberries. Serve right away.

Note: To make this recipe strictly gluten-free, check the package of rolled oats to make sure it's labeled "gluten-free."

Nutrition Information

Per serving: 318 calories, 12 grams fat, 38 grams carbohydrates, 4 grams fiber, 14 grams protein

Granola only (¼ cup serving): 161 calories, 8 grams fat, 20 grams carbohydrates, 3 grams fiber, 3 grams protein

This smoothie is filling and high in protein thanks to the Greek yogurt. It's also not packed with added sugar and fat because the sweetness comes naturally from banana and the peanut powder is a light alternative to peanut butter. You can find the powder in natural foods stores and most grocery stores these days. Feel free to substitute real peanut butter if you're craving a richer smoothie.

CHOCOLATE AND PB YOGURT SMOOTHIE

½ cup water

1 cup plain 2 percent Greek yogurt, homemade (page 34) or store-bought

1 large banana, peeled

¼ cup peanut powder

2 tablespoons natural cocoa powder

PREP	5 MINUTES
COOK	0 MINUTES
PR	N/A
SERVES	2

1 In a blender, combine the water, yogurt, banana, peanut powder, and cocoa powder. Blend on high speed for about 30 seconds, until smooth, stopping to scrape down the sides as needed.

2 Pour into two glasses and serve right away.

Note: To add even more nutrition, blend in 2 packed cups baby spinach or a mix of greens (I like to use the Power Greens from Trader Joe's).

Nutrition Information

Per serving: 211 calories, 4 grams fat, 27 grams carbohydrates, 5 grams fiber, 18 grams protein

Matzo brei is usually cooked in a skillet, but when you make it in the Instant Pot, there's no tricky flipping required, and it'll stay warm until it's ready to serve. Whole-wheat matzo is easiest to find in the springtime around Passover, when it is usually carried in natural foods stores and well-stocked grocery stores. It turns this holiday treat of a breakfast into a whole-grain, wholesome dish.

WHOLE-WHEAT MATZO BREI

4 whole-wheat matzo crackers

1½ cups hot water

4 large eggs

¼ teaspoon fine sea salt

¼ teaspoon freshly ground black pepper

2 tablespoons salted butter or vegan buttery spread, for serving

¼ cup pure maple syrup, for serving

PREP	5 MINUTES
COOK	35 MINUTES
PR	10 MINUTES NPR
COOL	5 MINUTES
SERVES	4

1 Grease a 7-cup round heatproof glass dish with butter or nonstick cooking spray. Pour 1 cup water into the Instant Pot.

2 Place a colander in the sink. Break up the matzo crackers into 1-inch pieces and put them into a medium bowl. Pour the hot water over the crackers, let sit for 1 minute, and then drain the matzo in the colander.

3 In the same bowl, whisk together the eggs, salt, and pepper until well blended, then fold in the soaked matzo.

4 Pour the matzo mixture into the prepared dish and cover tightly with aluminum foil. Place the dish on a long-handled silicone steam rack, then, holding the handles of the steam rack, lower it into the Instant Pot. (If you don't have the long-handled rack, use the wire metal steam rack and a homemade sling as described on page 10.)

5 Secure the lid and set the Pressure Release to **Sealing**. Select the **Pressure Cook** or **Manual** setting and set the cooking time for 25 minutes at high pressure. (The pot will take about 10 minutes to come up to pressure before the cooking program begins.)

6 When the cooking program ends, let the pressure release naturally for 10 minutes, then move the Pressure Release to **Venting** to release any remaining steam. Open the pot and, wearing heat-resistant mitts, grasp the handles of the steam rack and lift the dish out of the pot. Uncover the matzo brei, taking care not to get burned by the steam or to drip condensation onto the surface. Let the matzo brei cool for 5 minutes, giving it time to deflate a bit and set up.

7 Cut the matzo brei into four wedges, top with butter and syrup, and serve warm.

Nutrition Information

Per serving: 273 calories, 11 grams fat, 36 grams carbohydrates, 3 grams fiber, 10 grams protein

For this warm breakfast casserole, be sure to use whole-grain bread and to leave the skins on the apples for more fiber. Maple syrup sweetens every bite, and the Instant Pot ensures the toast cooks up moist and tender.

APPLE-CINNAMON FRENCH TOAST CASSEROLE

4 large eggs

1 cup 2 percent milk

¼ cup pure maple syrup

¼ teaspoon fine sea salt

1 teaspoon ground cinnamon, plus more for serving

6 cups cubed whole-wheat French bread, in 1-inch cubes

1 large Fuji apple, quartered, cored and thinly sliced

PREP	15 MINUTES
REST	10 MINUTES TO 24 HOURS
COOK	45 TO 50 MINUTES
PR	10 MINUTES NPR
COOL	5 MINUTES
SERVES	6

1 Grease a 7-cup round heatproof glass dish with butter or nonstick cooking spray.

2 In a blender, combine the eggs, milk, maple syrup, salt, and cinnamon. Blend on low speed for about 30 seconds, until well mixed, stopping to scrape down the sides as needed.

3 Put the bread into a large bowl. Pour in the egg mixture and stir to combine, pressing down on the bread to make sure all of the pieces are moistened. Transfer one-third of the bread mixture to the prepared dish, spreading it in an even layer, then layer one-half of the apple slices evenly on top. Spread half of the remaining bread mixture over the apple, followed with a layer of the remaining apple slices. Finish with the remaining bread mixture, then pour any liquid remaining in the bowl over the top. Cover the dish tightly with aluminum foil. Let stand at room temperature for 10 minutes or refrigerate for up to 24 hours.

4 When you're ready to cook the casserole, pour 1 cup water into the Instant Pot. Place the dish on a long-handled silicone steam rack, then, holding the handles of the steam rack, lower it into the Instant Pot.

5 Secure the lid and set the Pressure Release to **Sealing**. Select the **Pressure Cook** or **Manual** setting and set the cooking time for 35 minutes at high pressure. (The pot will take about 10 minutes to come up to pressure from room temperature or 15 minutes from the fridge.)

6 When the cooking program ends, let the pressure release naturally for 10 minutes, then move the Pressure Release to **Venting** to release any remaining steam. Open the pot and lift the dish out. Uncover the casserole, taking care not to get burned by the steam or to drip condensation onto the surface. The casserole will have puffed up, but it will settle down into the dish as it cools. Let cool for 5 minutes.

7 Using a large spoon, scoop the casserole onto plates. Dust with cinnamon and serve warm.

Nutrition Information

Per serving: 222 calories, 5 grams fat, 35 grams carbohydrates, 3 grams fiber, 10 grams protein

Did you know you can use the Instant Pot's Yogurt setting for proofing batters and doughs? The warm, controlled environment produces a consistent, rapid rise, no matter what temperature your kitchen may be. It's perfect for making the batter for these fluffy, crisp waffles. They're soft on the inside, with the distinctive, heady aroma of buckwheat. You can make these waffles with milk and butter, or you can use nondairy milk and coconut oil for a dairy-free option. If you're keeping the waffles dairy-free, serve them with coconut butter, a delicious plant-based butter alternative made from dried coconut.

YEASTED BUCKWHEAT WAFFLES

1 cup buckwheat flour

1 cup whole-wheat pastry flour

1 teaspoon active dry yeast

½ teaspoon fine sea salt

2 cups 2 percent milk or nondairy milk

¼ cup unsalted butter or coconut oil, melted and cooled

1 tablespoon honey or coconut nectar

2 large eggs

Coconut butter, for serving

Coconut nectar or pure maple syrup, for serving

PREP	5 MINUTES
PROOF	1 HOUR
COOK	10 TO 20 MINUTES (DEPENDING ON SIZE OF WAFFLE IRON)
PR	N/A
MAKES	EIGHT 5-INCH SQUARE WAFFLES

1 Select the **Yogurt** setting on the Instant Pot and adjust the heat level to **Low**. Combine the buckwheat and pastry flours, yeast, and salt in the pot and, using a silicone spoon or spatula, stir until evenly mixed. Add the milk, butter, and honey and stir until all of the dry ingredients are evenly moistened, scraping around the sides and bottom of the pot to make sure you have not missed any pockets of dry ingredients. Cover the pot with a tempered glass lid and let the batter proof, for 1 hour.

2 After 1 hour, the batter should be bubbling and have a yeasty aroma. Remove the inner pot from the Instant Pot, then whisk the eggs into the flour mixture until no streaks of yolk are visible.

3 Preheat a waffle iron according to the manufacturer's instructions. Grease the waffle iron plates lightly with coconut oil, butter, or nonstick cooking spray. Measure out ½ cup of the batter and pour it onto the hot lower plate. Close the lid and cook for 5 to 6 minutes; the timing depends on the desired level of doneness and the waffle iron model. Transfer the finished waffle to a large heatproof plate or a sheet pan and keep warm in a low (200°F) oven while you cook the remaining batter.

4 Serve the waffles hot with coconut butter and coconut nectar. Alternatively, let the waffles cool to room temperature as they emerge from the waffle iron, then transfer them to ziplock plastic freezer bags and store in the freezer for up to 2 months. Toast in a toaster when ready to serve.

Note: For a gluten-free version, substitute 1 cup gluten-free flour blend (King Arthur or Cup4Cup brand is a good choice) for the whole-wheat pastry flour.

Nutrition information

Per waffle: 207 calories, 9 grams fat, 27 grams carbohydrates, 4 grams fiber, 7 grams protein

2

Beans, Grains, and Pastas

Dried beans are an economical and convenient pantry staple to keep on hand. They're an inexpensive source of protein, fiber, vitamins, and minerals, and they take up an impressively small amount of space on the shelf compared with canned beans. Once they are cooked, 1 pound dried beans is the equivalent of four 15-ounce cans, and you can flavor and season them however you like. The cooked beans will keep for up to 5 days in the fridge (perfect for weekend meal prep) or up to 6 months in the freezer.

In an ideal world, I'd always remember to soak my beans in salted water for 10 to 12 hours before cooking, as soaked beans typically hold their shape better during cooking. In contrast, unsoaked beans tend to split their skins and sometimes break apart, depending on the variety. Chickpeas are especially forgiving whether soaked or unsoaked, so they're a nice starter legume for those new to cooking beans. Refried beans (page 49) are another easy choice, since mashing them up after cooking disguises any imperfections.

BASIC BEANS

1 pound dried beans, any variety (about 2¼ cups)

8 cups water

2 teaspoons fine sea salt

SOAK	10 HOURS
PREP	10 MINUTES
COOK	VARIES
PR	30 MINUTES NPR
MAKES	ABOUT 6 CUPS

1 Combine the beans, water, and salt in the Instant Pot and stir to dissolve the salt. Secure the lid and set the Pressure Release to **Sealing**.

2 If soaking the beans, select the **Bean/Chili**, **Pressure Cook**, or **Manual** setting, then refer to the Soaked Cooking Time in the table on page 266 for setting the cooking time; use high pressure. Next, select the **Timer** or **Delay** function and set the time delay for 10 to 12 hours. (When the soaking time is complete, the pot will take about 20 minutes to come up to pressure before the cooking program begins.) If not soaking the beans, refer to the Unsoaked Cooking Time in the table on page 266 for setting the cooking time; use high pressure.

3 When the cooking program ends, let the pressure release naturally (this will take about 30 minutes). Open the pot and, wearing heat-resistant mitts, lift out the inner pot. If using the beans immediately, drain them in a colander. If refrigerating the beans, ladle the beans and their cooking liquid into airtight containers, let cool for about 1 hour, then cover and refrigerate for up to 5 days. If freezing the beans, drain them in a colander, let cool to room temperature, spoon 1½ cup portions into 1-quart ziplock plastic freezer bags, seal well, and freeze for up to 6 months.

Small red beans and black beans cook in the same amount of time, so you can save time by cooking them together in the Instant Pot. Mix the cooked beans with a garlicky mustard vinaigrette and some fresh crunchy vegetables and you've got a hearty, healthy salad. Serve it at a potluck or barbecue, or pack it into containers for a picnic dish.

MIXED-BEAN SALAD

Beans

1 cup dried black beans

1 cup dried small red beans

6 cups water

2 teaspoons fine sea salt

Vinaigrette

⅓ cup extra-virgin olive oil

3 tablespoons red wine vinegar

2 teaspoons Dijon mustard

1 garlic clove, minced or pressed

½ teaspoon dried oregano

½ teaspoon fine sea salt

¼ teaspoon freshly ground black pepper

1 red bell pepper, seeded and diced

1 cucumber, peeled, seeded, and diced

2 tablespoons chopped fresh flat-leaf parsley

SOAK	10 TO 12 HOURS
PREP	5 MINUTES
COOK	25 MINUTES
PR	35 MINUTES NPR
COOL	20 MINUTES
SERVES	8

1 To cook the beans: Combine the black and red beans, water, and salt in the Instant Pot and stir to dissolve the salt.

2 Secure the lid and set the Pressure Release to **Sealing**. Select the **Bean/Chili**, **Pressure Cook**, or **Manual** setting and set the cooking time for 8 minutes at high pressure. Next, select the **Timer** or **Delay** function and set the time delay for 10 to 12 hours. (When the soaking time is complete, the pot will take about 15 minutes to come up to pressure before the cooking program begins.)

3 When the cooking program ends, let the pressure release naturally (this will take about 35 minutes).

4 While the pressure is releasing, make the vinaigrette: In a jam jar or other tightly lidded container, combine the oil, vinegar, mustard, garlic, oregano, salt, and pepper. Cover and shake vigorously to combine.

5 When the pressure has fully released, open the pot and, wearing heatproof mitts, lift out the inner pot and drain the beans in a colander. Transfer the beans to a large bowl, add the vinaigrette, and toss to combine. Leave the beans to marinate and cool for 20 minutes.

6 Stir in the bell pepper, cucumber, and parsley. Serve the salad at room temperature or chilled. It will keep in an airtight container in the refrigerator for up to 3 days.

Nutrition Information

Per serving: 172 calories, 10 grams fat, 18 grams carbohydrates, 6 grams fiber, 6 grams protein

My friend Shinae gave me the idea for this Asian-inspired spin on hummus. It's got a savory-salty kick that you can't stop going back for, and omitting the traditional tahini makes it a lot lower in fat and calories than regular hummus. Scoop it up with fresh vegetables and rice crackers, or tuck it into nori rolls (page 56).

TOASTED SESAME MISO HUMMUS

4 cups water

1 cup dried chickpeas

1 teaspoon fine sea salt

3 tablespoons white miso paste

1 tablespoon toasted sesame oil, plus more for serving

1 tablespoon cold-pressed avocado oil

3 tablespoons fresh lemon juice

1 teaspoon toasted sesame seeds, for garnish

SOAK	10 TO 12 HOURS
PREP	5 MINUTES
COOK	30 MINUTES
PR	25 MINUTES NPR
MAKES	2⅔ CUPS

1 Combine the water, chickpeas, and salt in the Instant Pot.

2 Secure the lid and set the Pressure Release to **Sealing**. Select the **Bean/Chili**, **Pressure Cook**, or **Manual** setting and set the cooking time for 15 minutes at high pressure. Next, select the **Timer** or **Delay** function and set the time delay for 10 to 12 hours. (When the soaking time is complete, the pot will take about 15 minutes to come up to pressure before the cooking program begins.) Set a colander in a large bowl.

3 When the cooking program ends, let the pressure release naturally (this will take about 25 minutes). Open the pot and, wearing heat-resistant mitts, lift out the inner pot and drain the beans in the colander; reserve the cooking liquid in the bowl. Transfer the warm drained chickpeas to a food processor. Add ½ cup of the reserved cooking liquid, the miso, sesame and avocado oils, and lemon juice and process at medium speed for 2 to 3 minutes, until the mixture is smooth and creamy.

4 Serve the hummus warm or at room temperature, or let it cool to room temperature and store it in an airtight container in the refrigerator for up to 5 days. To serve, spoon the hummus into the center of a wide, shallow serving bowl and spread it in a thick circle. Sprinkle with the sesame seeds, then top with a few drops of sesame oil.

Note: After using ½ cup of the cooking liquid in the hummus, you can make aquafaba from the remaining cooking liquid. Pour it into a saucepan and boil over medium heat until reduced by half, watching it carefully to make sure it doesn't all boil away. It's the perfect egg substitute for the vegan aioli that accompanies asparagus on page 208. For a store-bought version of aquafaba, you can use the liquid from a can of chickpeas or white beans as is, without reducing it.

Nutrition Information

Per serving (2 tablespoons): 52 calories, 2 grams fat, 7 grams carbohydrates, 3 grams fiber, 2 grams protein

I love the way the small green French lentils hold their shape when cooked. Butter and balsamic vinegar play off of each other, with the richness of the butter cut the tangy vinegar. Serve these flavorful lentils alongside Poached Salmon with Basil Vinaigrette (page 144) or Whole Chicken in a Hurry (page 167) for a bistro-style dinner.

BALSAMIC AND BUTTER LENTILS

- 2 tablespoons unsalted butter or vegan buttery spread
- 2 garlic cloves, minced
- 1 large yellow onion, diced
- ¼ teaspoon fine sea salt
- ½ teaspoon freshly ground black pepper
- ½ teaspoon dried thyme
- 1 cup dried French (Puy) lentils
- 2 cups low-sodium vegetable broth (page 261) or chicken bone broth (page 260)
- 2 tablespoons aged balsamic vinegar

PREP	0 MINUTES
COOK	30 MINUTES
PR	10 MINUTES NPR
SERVES	4

1 Select the **Sauté** setting on the Instant Pot and melt 1 tablespoon of the butter. Add the garlic, onion, salt, pepper, and thyme, and sauté for about 4 minutes, until the onion softens and a little bit of browning is visible on the bottom of the pot. Stir in the lentils and broth, using a wooden spoon or spatula to nudge any browned bits from the bottom of the pot.

2 Secure the lid and set the Pressure Release to **Sealing**. Press the **Cancel** button to reset the cooking program, then select the **Pressure Cook** or **Manual** setting and set the cooking time for 20 minutes at high pressure. (The pot will take about 5 minutes to come up to pressure before the cooking program begins.)

3 When the cooking program ends, let the pressure release naturally for 10 minutes, then move the Pressure Release to **Venting** to release any remaining steam. Open the pot and stir in the remaining 1 tablespoon butter and the vinegar. Taste and adjust the seasoning with salt if needed.

4 Transfer the lentils to a serving bowl or ladle onto plates. Serve warm.

Note: An aged balsamic vinegar will really make this dish. It should be thicker than red wine vinegar and coat the sides of the bottle when it is shaken.

Nutrition Information

Per serving: 199 calories, 6 grams fat, 33 grams carbohydrates, 9 grams fiber, 10 grams protein

All beans are great for you: they're a natural probiotic, high in fiber, and an excellent vegetarian source of protein. Black beans are particularly nutritious because of their high antioxidant content, evidenced by their beautiful dark hue. Mash them up into refried beans for a side dish to go with any Mexican meal. To make this dish vegan, use vegan cheese shreds in place of the Cotija cheese.

REFRIED BLACK BEANS

1 ¼ cups dried black beans

4 cups water

1 teaspoon fine sea salt

2 tablespoons extra-virgin olive oil

2 garlic cloves

2 jalapeño chiles, seeded and diced

1 small yellow onion, diced

½ teaspoon ground cumin

2 tablespoons fresh lime juice

6 tablespoons shredded Cotija cheese or Monterey Jack cheese, for serving

2 tablespoons chopped fresh cilantro, for serving

Hot sauce (such as Cholula or Tapatío), for serving

PREP	0 MINUTES
SOAK	8 TO 12 HOURS (OPTIONAL)
COOK	30 (IF SOAKED) OR 45 MINUTES (IF UNSOAKED)
PR	25 MINUTES NPR
SERVES	6

1 Combine the beans, water, and salt in the Instant Pot and stir to dissolve the salt. Secure the lid and set the Pressure Release to **Sealing**.

2 If soaking the beans, select the **Bean/Chili**, **Pressure Cook**, or **Manual** setting and set the cooking time for 10 minutes at high pressure. Next, select the **Timer** or **Delay** function and set the time delay for 8 to 12 hours. (When the soaking time is complete, the pot will take about 10 minutes to come up to pressure before the cooking program begins.)

3 If cooking the beans right away, select the **Bean/Chili**, **Pressure Cook**, or **Manual** setting and set the cooking time for 25 minutes at high pressure. (The pot will take about 10 minutes to come up to pressure before the cooking program begins.) Set a colander in a large bowl.

4 When the cooking program ends, let the pressure release naturally (this will take about 25 minutes). Open the pot and, wearing heat-resistant mitts, lift out the inner pot and drain the beans in the colander; reserve the cooking liquid in the bowl. Rinse out the inner pot and return it to the housing.

5 Add the oil and garlic to the Instant Pot. Press the **Cancel** button to reset the cooking program, then select the **Sauté** setting and sauté for 1 minute, until the garlic begins to bubble. Add the jalapeños and onion and sauté for about 4 minutes, until the onion begins to soften. Add the cumin and sauté for about 1 more minute, until the cumin is fragrant. Add the beans and ½ cup of the reserved cooking liquid and stir to combine. Press the **Cancel** button to turn off the pot. Using an immersion blender, puree the beans, adding more cooking liquid if you like refried beans with a looser consistency. Stir in the lime juice. Taste and adjust the seasoning with salt if needed.

6 Scoop the beans into bowls or onto plates and top with the cheese and cilantro. Serve warm, with the hot sauce on the side.

Nutrition Information

Per serving: 121 calories, 5 grams fat, 16 grams carbohydrates, 4 grams fiber, 5 grams protein

Cooking rice couldn't be easier than with the Instant Pot, and you can prepare anywhere from a couple of servings to enough for a crowd. For pleasantly firm, separate grains of rice, use a 1:1 ratio of water or broth to rice, no matter the variety. For softer rice, use a little more liquid. (For risotto, you'll need even more liquid, as in the recipes on pages 54 and 55). Just be sure not to fill the pot more than half full with liquid. Grains and beans can foam, expand, and spatter when they cook. Keeping the pot no more than half full prevents the pressure valve from clogging.

BASIC RICE

PREP	5 MINUTES
COOK	VARIES
PR	10 MINUTES NPR

1 Measure the rice into a wire-mesh strainer, then rinse under running cold water for 10 seconds, swishing the grains around. Set the strainer over a bowl and let the rice drain well, which should take about 1 minute. If cooking a small amount of rice, use the pot-in-pot method (see Notes). Otherwise, remove the inner pot from the Instant Pot housing and pour the rice and water or broth into the inner pot (see the headnote for the ratio of liquid to rice). Jiggle the pot back and forth on the countertop so the rice settles in an even layer, then return the inner pot to the housing.

2 Secure the lid in the **Sealing** position. For white rice or quick-cooking brown rice, select the **Rice** setting. The pot will adjust the cooking time automatically. For brown rice, select the **Multigrain**, **Pressure Cook**, or **Manual** setting and set the cooking time for 25 minutes at high pressure.

3 When the cooking program ends, let the pressure release naturally for 10 minutes, then move the Pressure Release to **Venting** to release any remaining steam. Open the pot and, wearing heat-resistant mitts, lift out the inner pot. Use a rice paddle to scoop the rice out of the pot. Serve warm or freeze for later use.

4 To freeze single or double portions of rice, spread the hot rice in a thin layer on a sheet pan, then let cool for about 20 minutes, until room temperature. Scoop the cooled rice into small ziplock plastic bags in single or double portions and seal closed. Slip the bags into 1-quart or 1-gallon ziplock plastic freezer bags, seal them closed, and freeze the bags flat. Rice will keep in the freezer for up to 2 months. When you're ready to eat the rice, transfer it, still frozen, to a bowl, cover the bowl with a reusable silicone lid or plastic wrap, and heat it in the microwave for 2 to 3 minutes, until piping hot.

Notes: For small amounts of rice (less than 1 cup in the 3-quart Instant Pot, less than 1½ cups in the 6-quart pot, or less than 2 cups in the 8-quart pot), use the pot-in-pot method: Place a steam rack into the pot, pour water into the pot (1 cup water for a 3- or 6-quart pot, or 1½ cups water for an 8-quart pot), then place a stainless-steel bowl on top of the steam rack. Add your rinsed rice and cooking liquid to the bowl, give the bowl a shake so the rice and liquid settle in an even layer, and proceed with the recipe from the point at which you secure the lid. This method works for other grains, too.

Minute brand carries a quick-cooking brown rice that cooks in about the same time as white rice, so you can use the **Rice** cooking program for it. If using sprouted brown rice, choose the **Multigrain**, **Pressure Cook**, or **Manual** setting and set the cooking time for 20 minutes.

You may find that you need to tweak cooking times and the ratio of liquid to rice, as the texture of rice often comes down to personal preference. More liquid and longer cooking times will yield softer grains, while less liquid and shorter cooking times will yield firmer grains. Also, the cooking times in the basic recipe are for unsoaked rice. If you soak the rice, the cooking time will be shorter.

Cooked beans and quick-cooking brown rice make this recipe come together much faster than if you start with dried beans and traditional brown rice. Serve a green salad on the side for a balanced meal. This is a recipe that's also easily doubled for a crowd.

CAJUN-SPICED RED BEANS AND RICE

2 tablespoons extra-virgin olive oil

2 garlic cloves, minced

1 cup Minute brand quick-cooking brown rice

1 ½ teaspoons Cajun spice blend, or 2 teaspoons Old Bay seasoning and ⅛ teaspoon cayenne pepper

1 ½ cups drained cooked kidney beans (page 44), or one 15-ounce can kidney beans, rinsed and drained

1 ¼ cups water

1 green onion, white and green parts, thinly sliced, for serving

Hot sauce (such as Frank's RedHot or Tabasco), for serving

PREP	0 MINUTES
COOK	20 MINUTES
PR	20 MINUTES NPR
SERVES	6

1 Select the **Sauté** setting on the Instant Pot and heat the oil and garlic for 3 minutes, until the garlic is golden but not browned. Add the rice and Cajun spice blend and sauté for 1 more minute, until the rice is coated with the oil and the spices are fragrant. Add the beans and water and stir to combine, using a wooden spoon or spatula to nudge any browned bits from the bottom of the pot.

2 Secure the lid and set the Pressure Release to **Sealing**. Press the **Cancel** button to reset the cooking program, then select the **Pressure Cook** or **Manual** setting and set the cooking time for 10 minutes at high pressure. (The pot will take about 5 minutes to come up to pressure before the cooking program begins.)

3 When the cooking program ends, let the pressure release naturally (this will take about 20 minutes). Open the pot and stir the rice and beans.

4 Spoon the rice and beans into bowls. Sprinkle with the green onion and serve warm with the hot sauce on the side.

Note: Add skillet-seared rounds of Seitan Chickpea Chorizo Sausage (page 104) or other sausage for a hearty main dish.

Nutrition Information

Per serving: 200 calories, 6 grams fat, 34 grams carbohydrates, 6 grams fiber, 6 grams protein

A small amount of cheese makes a big difference here, adding creaminess to this risotto. I like to use a wedge of Laughing Cow brand light Swiss cheese, or a dollop of cream cheese if I have it on hand. Spinach and peas lend some green color and nutrition, and the brown rice means you'll be getting a good dose of fiber. Serve the risotto as part of a meal that both vegetarians and omnivores can enjoy.

SPINACH AND PEA RISOTTO

2 tablespoons extra-virgin olive oil

2 garlic cloves, minced

1 yellow onion, minced

1½ cups medium-grain brown rice

⅓ cup dry white wine

3 cups low-sodium vegetable broth (page 261)

½ cup grated Parmesan cheese

One ¾-ounce wedge Laughing Cow light Swiss cheese, or 1½ tablespoons cream cheese

3 cups firmly packed baby spinach

1½ cups frozen peas, thawed

¼ teaspoon freshly ground black pepper

Fine sea salt

PREP	0 MINUTES
COOK	50 MINUTES
PR	10 MINUTES NPR
REST	2 MINUTES
SERVES	8

1 Select the **Sauté** setting on the Instant Pot and heat the oil and garlic for 2 minutes, until the garlic is bubbling but not browned. Add the onion and sauté for about 4 minutes, until softened. Stir in the rice and sauté for 1 more minute. Pour in the wine and cook for about 2 minutes, until the liquid has evaporated and the rice begins to sizzle. Stir in the broth, then scrape down the sides of the pot to make sure all of the grains are submerged in the broth.

2 Secure the lid and set the Pressure Release to **Sealing**. Press the **Cancel** button to reset the cooking program, then select the **Pressure Cook** or **Manual** setting and set the cooking time for 30 minutes at high pressure. (The pot will take about 10 minutes to come up to pressure before the cooking program begins.)

3 When the cooking program ends, let the pressure release naturally for 10 minutes, then move the Pressure Release to **Venting** to release any remaining steam. Open the pot and stir in the Parmesan and Laughing Cow cheeses, spinach, peas, and pepper. Let sit for 2 minutes to allow the spinach to wilt thoroughly, then stir once more. Taste and adjust the seasoning with salt if needed.

4 Spoon the risotto into bowls and serve right away.

Nutrition Information

Per serving: 242 calories, 6 grams fat, 37 grams carbohydrates, 4 grams fiber, 7 grams protein

Risotto is a blank canvas for seasonal ingredients, and in the fall, my favorite additions are savory cremini and shiitake mushrooms, which lend lots of earthy flavor to this creamy side dish. Sprouted rice takes a few minutes less to cook than regular brown rice, and it releases starch more easily to make a creamier risotto.

DOUBLE MUSHROOM RISOTTO

2 tablespoons extra-virgin olive oil

1 large shallot, minced

8 ounces cremini mushrooms, sliced

4 ounces shiitake mushrooms, stemmed and sliced

½ teaspoon fine sea salt

¼ teaspoon dried thyme

¼ teaspoon dried sage

1½ cups sprouted brown rice

½ cup dry white wine

3 cups low-sodium chicken bone broth (page 260) or vegetable broth (page 261)

½ cup grated Pecorino Romano cheese

¼ teaspoon freshly ground black pepper

PREP	0 MINUTES
COOK	45 MINUTES
PR	10 MINUTES NPR
SERVES	6

1 Select the **Sauté** setting on the Instant Pot and heat the oil and shallot for 4 minutes, until the shallot has softened. Add the cremini and shiitake mushrooms and salt and sauté for 5 more minutes, until the mushrooms are wilted and beginning to give up their liquid. Stir in the thyme, sage, and rice and sauté for 1 more minute. Pour in the wine and cook for about 3 minutes, until the liquid has evaporated and the rice begins to sizzle. Stir in the broth, then scrape down the sides of the pot to make sure all of the grains are submerged in the broth.

2 Secure the lid and set the Pressure Release to **Sealing**. Press the **Cancel** button to reset the cooking program, then select the **Pressure Cook** or **Manual** setting and set the cooking time for 22 minutes at high pressure. (The pot will take about 10 minutes to come up to pressure before the cooking program begins.)

3 When the cooking program ends, let the pressure release naturally for 10 minutes, then move the Pressure Release to **Venting** to release any remaining steam. Open the pot and stir in the pecorino and pepper.

4 Spoon the risotto into bowls and serve right away.

Note: If you like your risotto with a looser texture, stir in an additional ¼ cup broth just before serving.

Nutrition Information

Per serving: 285 calories, 10 grams fat, 42 grams carbohydrates, 3 grams fiber, 8 grams protein

Sushi rolls look fancy and celebratory, and they're easy to make. Here, toasted nori sheets are rolled with brown rice, hummus, and vegetables for a nutritious, bite-size snack. Tuck this recipe into your back pocket to serve as an appetizer at your next get-together.

BROWN RICE NORI ROLLS

1 cup medium-grain brown rice

1 cup water

½ teaspoon fine sea salt

1 tablespoon rice vinegar

1 tablespoon brown rice syrup or agave nectar

3 sheets roasted nori seaweed, each about 7½ by 8½ inches

6 tablespoons Toasted Sesame Miso Hummus (page 47) or store-bought hummus

1 carrot, shredded

½ cucumber, peeled, seeded, and cut into 8 by ¼-inch strips

¾ avocado, peeled and sliced lengthwise

1 teaspoon toasted sesame seeds

PREP	15 MINUTES
COOK	35 MINUTES
PR	10 MINUTES NPR
COOL	20 MINUTES
MAKES	24 PIECES

1 Pour 1 cup water into the Instant Pot and place a tall steam rack in the pot. Combine the rice, the 1 cup water, and the salt in a 1½-quart stainless-steel bowl and stir to dissolve the salt. Place the bowl on the rack. (The bowl should not touch the lid once the pot is closed.)

2 Secure the lid and set the Pressure Release to **Sealing**. Select the **Pressure Cook** or **Manual** setting and set the cooking time for 25 minutes at high pressure. (The pot will take about 10 minutes to come up to pressure before the cooking program begins.)

3 When the cooking program ends, let the pressure release naturally for 10 minutes, then move the Pressure Release to **Venting** to release any remaining steam.

4 Open the pot and, wearing heat-resistant mitts, remove the bowl from the pot. Add the vinegar and rice syrup to the rice and stir gently to combine thoroughly. Let the rice cool until it is just slightly above room temperature, about 20 minutes, fluffing it every once in a while to help it cool more quickly. (For quicker cooling, spread the rice on a sheet pan.) If you haven't yet shredded and sliced the vegetables, you can use this time to prepare them.

5 To make the sushi rolls, place a nori sheet, smooth side down and with a long side facing you, on a sushi rolling mat. Spread one-third of the rice on the nori, leaving a 1¼-inch-wide border uncovered at the top edge. Spread 2 tablespoons of the hummus in a 2-inch-wide horizontal stripe across the middle of the rice, then, using one-third of each vegetable, place rows of carrot, cucumber, and avocado on top of the hummus. Starting at the edge nearest you, lift the nori and fold it over the filling, then continue to roll, using the mat to tighten the roll and keep it uniform. When you reach the bare border at the top of the nori sheet, dab a little water on the nori (to help seal the roll) and complete the roll. Set the roll aside, seam side down. Repeat with the remaining nori sheets and filling.

Nutrition Information

Per serving: 165 calories, 4 grams fat, 32 grams carbohydrates, 4 grams fiber, 4 grams protein

6 At this point, you can wrap the rolls tightly in plastic wrap and refrigerate for up to 1 day before serving. To serve right away, wait a few minutes for the rolls to set up a little, then, using a sharp knife, slice each roll into eight pieces. Arrange on a serving plate, sprinkle with the sesame seeds, and serve.

Notes: To double this recipe, cook the rice directly in the inner pot of the Instant Pot rather than in a bowl.

Brown rice sushi can be a little more delicate and difficult to slice than white rice sushi. Make sure to choose a very sharp knife, to use slicing rather than pushing motions, and to wipe the knife blade clean before each cut if needed.

For a spicy version, mix a little Sriracha sauce into the hummus and drizzle more Sriracha on top.

For easier cleanup, cover your bamboo sushi mat with plastic wrap before using. Or for an even simpler option, use my favorite sushi mat, which is made by Silpat. It is easy to wipe clean or to throw in the dishwasher.

Cook the chickpeas and brown rice together in the Instant Pot, which saves time. They make a hearty salad when tossed with fresh vegetables, olive oil, and lemon juice for a classically flavored tabbouleh. The original recipe uses bulgur wheat and is a side dish. This tabbouleh makes a good light centerpiece for a meal.

CHICKPEA AND BROWN RICE TABBOULEH

1 cup dried chickpeas

5 cups water

1½ teaspoons fine sea salt

1 cup medium-grain brown rice (regular or a sprouted blend)

2 cups cherry or grape tomatoes, quartered

4 Persian cucumbers, diced

One 3-ounce bunch flat-leaf parsley, stemmed and chopped

¼ cup extra-virgin olive oil

¼ cup fresh lemon juice

PREP	5 MINUTES
SOAK	10 TO 12 HOURS
COOK	30 MINUTES
PR	15 MINUTES NPR
SERVES	8

1 Combine the chickpeas, 4 cups of the water, and 1 teaspoon of the salt in the Instant Pot and stir to dissolve the salt.

2 Place a tall steam rack into the Instant Pot, making sure all of its legs are resting firmly on the bottom. Combine the rice and the remaining 1 cup water and ½ teaspoon salt in a 1½-quart stainless-steel bowl and stir to dissolve the salt. Place the bowl on the rack. (The bowl should not touch the lid once the pot is closed.)

3 Secure the lid and set the Pressure Release to **Sealing**. Select the **Pressure Cook** or **Manual** setting and set the cooking time for 15 minutes at high pressure. Next, select the **Timer** or **Delay** function and set the time delay for 10 to 12 hours. (When the soaking time is complete, the pot will take about 15 minutes to come up to pressure before the cooking program begins.)

4 When the cooking program ends, let the pressure release naturally for at least 15 minutes, then move the Pressure Release to **Venting** to release any remaining steam. Open the pot and, wearing heat-resistant mitts, lift the bowl out of the pot and transfer the rice to a large bowl. Then remove the rack, lift out the inner pot, and drain the chickpeas in a colander. Transfer the chickpeas to the bowl with the rice. Add the tomatoes, cucumbers, parsley, oil, and lemon juice and stir to mix well. Taste and adjust the seasoning with salt if needed.

5 Serve the tabbouleh in bowls at room temperature or chilled. It will keep in an airtight container in the refrigerator for up to 2 days.

Note: In place of regular brown rice, I like to use sprouted rice blends, such as brown, red, and black, for their mix of textures and colors.

Nutrition Information

Per serving: 255 calories, 9 grams fat, 39 grams carbohydrates, 10 grams fiber, 6 grams protein

This hearty salad made from fragrant, earthy wild rice, crisp celery and apples, tart-sweet oranges and cranberries, and crunchy almonds and pecans is great to serve any time of the year. It's especially nice around the winter holidays, however, when you're tired of heavier side dishes and looking for some texture and crunch. You can serve it on its own or you can offer it alongside nearly any protein, such as Whole Chicken in a Hurry (page 167).

WILD RICE SALAD WITH CRANBERRIES AND ORANGES

Salad

1 cup wild rice

1⅓ cups water

¼ teaspoon fine sea salt

4 celery stalks, diced

1 large Fuji or Gala apple, cored and chopped

2 navel oranges or 4 tangerines, peeled and chopped or separated into segments

½ cup dried cranberries

¼ cup toasted slivered almonds

¼ cup chopped toasted pecans

Vinaigrette

¼ cup extra-virgin olive oil

2 tablespoons red wine vinegar

1 small garlic clove, minced or pressed

½ teaspoon chopped fresh thyme leaves

¼ teaspoon freshly ground black pepper

¼ teaspoon fine sea salt

PREP	5 MINUTES
COOK	35 MINUTES
PR	10 MINUTES NPR
SERVES	8

1 To make the salad: Pour 1 cup water into the Instant Pot and place a tall steam rack into the pot. Combine the wild rice, the 1⅓ cups water, and the salt in a 1½-quart stainless-steel bowl and stir to dissolve the salt, making sure all of the grains are submerged. Place the bowl on the rack. (The bowl should not touch the lid once the pot is closed.)

2 Secure the lid and set the Pressure Release to **Sealing**. Select the **Steam** setting and set the cooking time for 30 minutes at high pressure. (The pot will take about 5 minutes to come up to pressure before the cooking program begins.)

3 While the rice is cooking, in a large bowl, combine the celery, apple, oranges, cranberries, almonds, and pecans and stir to mix.

4 To make the vinaigrette: In a jam jar or other tightly lidded container, combine the oil, vinegar, garlic, thyme, pepper, and salt. Cover and shake vigorously to combine.

5 When the cooking program ends, let the pressure release naturally for 10 minutes, then move the Pressure Release to **Venting** to release any remaining steam. Open the pot and, wearing heat-resistant mitts, lift out the bowl and drain the rice in a colander to rid it of any remaining water.

6 Transfer the drained rice to the large bowl with the other salad ingredients. Shake the vinaigrette once more, then pour it over the salad and toss to combine.

7 Serve the salad warm or chilled. It will keep in an airtight container in the refrigerator for up to 3 days.

Nutrition Information

Per serving: 250 calories, 12 grams fat, 26 grams carbohydrates, 4 grams fiber, 3 grams protein

Whole grains are a big part of what I consider a healthy diet. They're full of fiber, and each one boasts its own unique profile of vitamins and minerals. Although pearl barley, kasha, and quinoa are not technically whole grains, their cooking method is the same as for whole grains, so they are found in this table. Quick-cooking (Minute or other brand) brown rice *is* considered a whole grain, and it's one of my favorites: you get all of the nutritional advantages of brown rice with a faster cooking time. You'll find it in the table here, as well as in recipes sprinkled throughout this book.

BASIC WHOLE GRAINS

COOK	VARIES
PR	10 MINUTES NPR

1 For less than 1½ cups uncooked grain, use the grain-to-water ratio, cooking time, and pressure indicated in the table at right and cook according to the pot-in-pot cooking method. Season with salt if you like, using ¼ to ½ teaspoon fine sea salt for each cup.

2 For 1½ cups or more uncooked grain, combine the grain and water in the Instant Pot. Season with fine sea salt if you like, using ¼ teaspoon for each ½ cup.

3 Secure the lid and set the Pressure Release to **Sealing**, then refer to the table for setting the cooking time and pressure.

4 When the cooking program ends, let the pressure release naturally for 10 minutes, then move the Pressure Release to **Venting** to release any remaining steam. Open the pot and fluff the grains with a fork if desired.

5 Serve or use immediately, or let cool to room temperature (to cool the grains quickly, spread them on a sheet pan), then transfer to an airtight container and refrigerate for up to 4 days or freeze for up to 2 months.

Grain	Grain-to-Water Ratio	Cooking Time (in minutes)	Pressure
Barley, pearl	1:1½ to 2	25 to 30	High
Barley, pot	1:3 to 4	25 to 30	High
Brown rice (short, medium, or long grain)	1:1 to 1¼	20 to 25	High
Brown rice (quick cooking)	1:1	10 to 15	High
Bulgur (coarse)	1:1½	10 to 15	Low
Freekeh (cracked)	1:1½	10 to 15	Low
Kasha (roasted buckwheat)	1:1½	10 to 15	Low
Millet	1:1⅔	10 to 12	High
Oats, old-fashioned (rolled)	1:1⅔	6	High
Oats (steel-cut)	1:3	10 to 12	High
Oats (whole groats)	1:3	25 to 30	High
Quinoa (rinsed and drained)	1:1 to 1¼	8	Low
Wheat berries, rye berries, spelt, farro, and kamut	1:1½ to 2	25 to 30	High
Rice, wild	1:1⅓ to 1½	25 to 30	High

Note: Use the **Multigrain**, **Pressure Cook**, or **Manual** setting when cooking 1½ cups or more grain; for smaller amounts, use the **Steam** setting and the pot-in-pot method (see page 51). After adding the grain and water to the pot, make sure the pot is no more than half full to prevent excessive foaming and/or bubbling and blocking of the mechanisms in the lid. If the grain-to-water ratio in the table contains a range for the amount of water, use less if you like your grains with a firmer texture or more if you prefer them softer and more tender. The shorter cooking time will result in firmer grains, and the longer cooking time will result in softer grains.

Mango, kale, and hazelnuts make an unusual and delicious combination. Chewy grains of bulgur wheat add substance to this salad, making it work on its own, as a side dish, or as the base of a bowl topped with skillet-seared tofu, chicken, or salmon. This dish is a nutrient powerhouse, with whole grains, healthy fats, and dark leafy greens all in one.

SUNSHINE SALAD WITH BULGUR, KALE, AND MANGO

Bulgur

½ cup coarse bulgur wheat

½ cup water

¼ teaspoon fine sea salt

Salad

One 6-ounce bunch curly kale, stemmed and cut into ¼-inch-wide ribbons

1 large mango, peeled, pitted, and cut into ½-inch cubes

½ cup hazelnuts or pecans, toasted and coarsely chopped

2 tablespoons extra-virgin olive oil

2 tablespoons raw cider vinegar

1 tablespoon agave nectar or honey

¼ teaspoon fine sea salt

¼ teaspoon freshly ground black pepper

PREP	5 MINUTES
COOK	10 MINUTES
PR	QPR
COOL	10 MINUTES
SERVES	6

1 To cook the bulgur: Pour 1 cup water into the Instant Pot. Combine the bulgur, the ½ cup water, and the salt in a 1½-quart stainless-steel bowl and stir to dissolve the salt, making sure all of the grains are submerged. Place the bowl on the wire metal steam rack and, holding the arms of the steam rack, lower the bowl into the pot.

2 Secure the lid and set the Pressure Release to **Sealing**. Select the **Steam** setting and set the cooking time for 5 minutes at high pressure. (The pot will take about 5 minutes to come up to pressure before the cooking program begins.)

3 When the cooking program ends, perform a quick pressure release by moving the Pressure Release to **Venting**. Open the pot and, wearing heat-resistant mitts, grasp the arms of the steam rack and lift the bowl out of the pot. Using a fork, fluff the bulgur, then let it cool for 10 minutes.

4 To make the salad: In a large bowl, combine the kale, mango, and nuts and toss briefly to mix. Add the bulgur, oil, vinegar, agave nectar, salt, and pepper and toss for about 2 minutes, until the ingredients are evenly distributed. (At this point, the salad can be covered and refrigerated for up to 1 day.)

5 Spoon the salad into bowls and serve at room temperature or chilled.

Note: For a nut-free version, substitute toasted unsweetened dried coconut flakes for the chopped nuts. Sprinkle them into the salad at the last minute so they stay crunchy.

Nutrition Information

Per serving: 197 calories, 12 grams fat, 23 grams carbohydrates, 4 grams fiber, 4 grams protein

Although it's both vegan and gluten-free, this simple autumn side dish will satisfy any omnivorous tablemates. Quinoa is a particularly nutritious choice for vegetarians, as it's a complete protein. Here, I've added toasted walnuts and diced pears for crunch and raisins for sweetness, and I've dressed the quinoa with a simple mix of lemon juice, tamari, and olive oil that harks back to the dressings I made during my vegan college days. I still love this unusual combination of flavors.

QUINOA WITH PEARS AND WALNUTS

1 cup quinoa

1 cup water

¼ teaspoon fine sea salt

1 ripe D'Anjou or Bartlett pear

2 tablespoons fresh lemon juice

1 tablespoon tamari, coconut aminos, or soy sauce

1 tablespoon extra-virgin olive oil

2 tablespoons chopped fresh flat-leaf parsley

¼ cup chopped toasted walnuts

¼ cup raisins

PREP	0 MINUTES
COOK	15 MINUTES
PR	10 MINUTES NPR
SERVES	4

1 Pour 1 cup water into the Instant Pot and place a tall steam rack into the pot. Combine the quinoa, the 1 cup water, and the salt in a 1½-quart stainless-steel bowl and stir to dissolve the salt, making sure all of the grains are submerged. Place the bowl on the rack.

2 Secure the lid and set the Pressure Release to **Sealing**. Select the **Steam** setting and set the cooking time for 8 minutes at high pressure. (The pot will take about 5 minutes to come up to pressure before the cooking program begins.)

3 While the quinoa is cooking, dice the pear, then toss with the lemon juice in a small bowl.

4 When the cooking program ends, let the pressure release naturally for 10 minutes, then move the Pressure Release to **Venting** to release any remaining steam. Open the pot and, wearing heat-resistant mitts, lift out the bowl. Fluff the quinoa with a fork, then fold in the pear, tamari, oil, and parsley.

5 Spoon the quinoa onto plates, top with the walnuts and raisins, and serve warm. Alternatively, let cool, cover and refrigerate, and serve chilled.

Note: To get your greens, serve the quinoa on a bed of arugula or baby spinach.

Nutrition Information

Per serving: 285 calories, 11 grams fat, 45 grams carbohydrates, 4 grams fiber, 8 grams protein

Whole-grain salads are nutritious and filling, and this farro version is no exception. Chewy, wheaty grains of farro are a great foil for crunchy romaine and tangy, salty bites of homemade vegan feta cheese. You can serve this salad year-round, as a side or a main dish.

FARRO SALAD WITH ROMAINE, RAISINS, AND ALMOND FETA

Farro

1 cup pearled farro

1½ cups water

½ teaspoon fine sea salt

Salad

1 head romaine lettuce, shredded

1 large Fuji apple, chopped

¼ cup firmly packed chopped fresh mint

⅓ cup raisins

2 tablespoons extra-virgin olive oil

2 tablespoons red wine vinegar

6 tablespoons Almond Feta Cheese (page 265)

PREP	0 MINUTES
COOK	35 MINUTES
PR	10 MINUTES NPR
COOL	10 MINUTES
SERVES	6

1 To cook the farro: Pour 1 cup water into the Instant Pot. Combine the farro, the 1½ cups water, and the salt in a 1½-quart stainless-steel bowl and stir to dissolve the salt. Place the bowl on the wire metal steam rack and, holding the arms of the steam rack, lower the bowl into the pot.

2 Secure the lid and set the Pressure Release to **Sealing**. Select the **Pressure Cook** or **Manual** setting and set the cooking time for 25 minutes at high pressure. (The pot will take about 10 minutes to come up to pressure before the cooking program begins.)

3 When the cooking program ends, let the pressure release naturally for 10 minutes, then move the Pressure Release to **Venting** to release any remaining steam. Open the pot and, wearing heat-resistant mitts, grasp the arms of the steam rack and lift the bowl out of the pot. Spoon the farro out onto a plate, spread it in an even layer, and let cool for about 10 minutes, until no longer piping hot.

4 To make the salad: In a large bowl, combine the romaine, apple, mint, raisins, oil, vinegar, and farro and stir to mix evenly. (At this point, the salad can be covered and refrigerated for up to 3 days.)

5 Spoon the salad into bowls and top each serving with 1 tablespoon of the cheese, spooning it on in ½-teaspoon dollops. Serve at room temperature or chilled.

Note: If you eat dairy, feel free to substitute regular crumbled feta for the almond feta.

Nutrition Information

Per serving: 280 calories, 11 grams fat, 38 grams carbohydrates, 5 grams fiber, 7 grams protein

Here's to nutritious recipes that taste like the best comfort food. Steamed butternut squash is blended with cashews to make a super-creamy "cheese" sauce that covers the noodles and greens. Just before serving, steamed broccoli and chard and peas are mixed in to create this vegetable-filled pasta bowl.

VEGAN MAC 'N' GREENS

Sauce

3 cups peeled and cubed butternut squash (about 1 pound)

½ cup raw whole cashews, soaked in water to cover for 2 hours and drained

¾ cup unsweetened nondairy milk

1½ tablespoons fresh lemon juice

2 tablespoons nutritional yeast

1 teaspoon Tabasco sauce

½ teaspoon fine sea salt

¼ teaspoon garlic powder

½ teaspoon cayenne pepper (optional)

8 ounces broccoli crowns, cut into bite-size florets

1 bunch chard, stemmed and cut crosswise into 1-inch-wide ribbons (to yield 4¾ ounces)

8 ounces whole-wheat elbow pasta

2 cups water

½ teaspoon fine sea salt

1 cup frozen peas, thawed

1 To make the sauce: Pour 1 cup water into the Instant Pot and place a steamer basket into the pot. Arrange the squash evenly in the steamer basket.

2 Secure the lid and set the Pressure Release to **Sealing**. Select the **Steam** setting and set the cooking time for 3 minutes at high pressure. (The pot will take about 10 minutes to come up to pressure before the cooking program begins.)

3 When the cooking program ends, perform a quick pressure release by moving the Pressure Release to **Venting**. Open the pot and, using tongs, transfer the squash to a plate or cutting board. Let cool for about 5 minutes, or until it can be handled, and transfer to a blender.

4 Add the cashews, nondairy milk, lemon juice, nutritional yeast, Tabasco, salt, garlic powder, and cayenne (if using) to the blender. Blend at high speed for 1 to 2 minutes, until smooth, stopping to scrape down the sides as needed. Set aside.

5 The steamer basket and some cooking liquid should still be in the Instant Pot. Add ½ cup water to the pot, then add the broccoli and chard to the steamer basket. Secure the lid and set the Pressure Release to **Sealing**. Press the **Cancel** button to reset the cooking program, then select the **Steam** setting and set the cooking time for 0 (zero) minutes at low pressure. (The pot will take about 5 minutes to come up to pressure before the cooking program begins.)

6 When the cooking program ends, perform a quick pressure release by moving the Pressure Release to **Venting**. Open the pot and, wearing heat-resistant mitts, remove the steamer basket and set aside with the vegetables. Lift out the inner pot, pour out the cooking liquid, and return the pot to the housing.

Nutrition Information

Per serving: 262 calories, 8 grams fat, 44 grams carbohydrates, 9 grams fiber, 12 grams protein

PREP	5 MINUTES
COOK	30 MINUTES
PR	QPR FOR VEGETABLES, 5 MINUTES NPR FOR PASTA
COOL	5 MINUTES
REST	3 MINUTES
SERVES	6

7 Combine the pasta, the 2 cups water, and the salt in the Instant Pot. Secure the lid and set the Pressure Release to **Sealing**. Press the **Cancel** button to reset the cooking program, then select the **Pressure Cook** or **Manual** setting and set the cooking time for 6 minutes at high pressure. (The pot will take about 5 minutes to come up to pressure before the cooking program begins.)

8 When the cooking program ends, let the pressure release naturally for 5 minutes, then move the Pressure Release to **Venting** to release any remaining steam. Open the pot and stir in the sauce, the steamed chard and broccoli, and the peas. Let stand for 3 minutes to allow the vegetables and sauce to warm through. Stir once more.

9 Ladle the pasta into bowls and serve warm.

Note: To cut down on the time a bit, while the squash and vegetables are steaming, cook the pasta in a pot on the stove top, according to the package directions.

The mostly monochromatic look of this salad is pretty and unexpected. With whole-grain pasta and a generous amount of cauliflower and fennel, it's much more nutritious than your typical pasta salad. It makes a lovely side dish in the winter, when you're craving some fresh, crunchy vegetables. Serve it as an accompaniment to a main course or over salad greens for a light lunch.

WINTER WHITE PASTA SALAD

8 ounces whole-wheat elbow pasta

2 cups water

¾ teaspoon fine sea salt

½ medium-size cauliflower, thinly sliced

1 medium-size fennel bulb, trimmed and thinly sliced crosswise, with fronds reserved for garnish

3 tablespoons extra-virgin olive oil

2 tablespoons fresh lemon juice

½ cup crumbled feta cheese

¼ cup pine nuts, toasted

Freshly ground black pepper

PREP	5 MINUTES
COOK	15 MINUTES
PR	5 MINUTES NPR
SERVES	8

1 Combine the pasta, water, and ½ teaspoon of the salt in the Instant Pot, spreading the pasta in as even a layer as possible. It's fine if a few pieces are sticking up out of the water.

2 Secure the lid and set the Pressure Release to **Sealing**. Select the **Pressure Cook** or **Manual** setting and set the cooking time for 5 minutes at high pressure. (The pot will take about 10 minutes to come up to pressure before the cooking program begins.)

3 When the cooking program ends, let the pressure release naturally for 5 minutes, then move the Pressure Release to **Venting** to release any remaining steam. Open the pot and, wearing heat-resistant mitts, lift out the inner pot. Stir in the cauliflower and fennel. Pour the oil and lemon juice over the pasta and vegetables, then sprinkle in the remaining ¼ teaspoon salt. Stir to mix thoroughly and to coat all of the ingredients evenly.

4 Spoon the pasta into bowls and garnish each bowl with the feta, pine nuts, and a couple of small fennel fronds. Top with a grind or two of pepper and serve warm or chilled.

Notes: A mandoline makes quick work of slicing the vegetables. It's my preferred tool to use when I want superthin slices of dense, firm vegetables like fennel.

For a vegan variation, use Almond Feta Cheese (page 265) in place of the feta cheese.

Nutrition Information

Per serving: 217 calories, 11 grams fat, 26 grams carbohydrates, 4 grams fiber, 7 grams protein

Whole-wheat pasta stands up well to this spicy tomato sauce. The generous kick of heat from pickled peppers and red pepper flakes is a nice change from the usual marinara sauce. Serve a big green salad alongside this pasta for an easy and balanced vegetarian meal.

WHOLE-WHEAT PENNE ARRABBIATA

3 tablespoons extra-virgin olive oil

3 garlic cloves, minced

1 small yellow onion, diced

One 28-ounce can whole San Marzano tomatoes and their liquid

4 pickled hot chiles or pepperoncini, minced

2 teaspoons Italian seasoning

½ teaspoon red pepper flakes

1 teaspoon fine sea salt

3½ cups water

1 pound whole-wheat penne

Vegan Parmesan Cheese (page 265) or grated Parmesan cheese, for serving

PREP	0 MINUTES
COOK	35 MINUTES
PR	5 MINUTES NPR
SERVES	8

1 Select the **Sauté** setting on the Instant Pot and heat the oil and garlic for 2 minutes, until the garlic is bubbling but not browned. Add the onion and sauté for about 3 minutes, until softened. Add the tomatoes and their liquid, crushing the tomatoes with your hands as you add them to the pot. Stir in the chiles, Italian seasoning, red pepper flakes, and salt and cook, stirring occasionally, for about 6 more minutes, until thickened.

2 At this point, you can use the sauce as is, let it cool and store it in an airtight container in the refrigerator for up to 1 week or in the freezer for up 6 months, or continue with the recipe, adding the water and penne directly to the sauce and cooking it under pressure for a one-pot dish.

3 To continue, pour the water into the sauce and stir well. Add the penne and then use a wooden spoon to nudge it under the liquid, making sure all of the pasta is submerged. Secure the lid and set the Pressure Release to **Sealing.** Press the **Cancel** button to reset the cooking program, then select the **Pressure Cook** or **Manual** setting and set the cooking time for 6 minutes at high pressure. (The pot will take about 15 minutes to come up to pressure before the cooking program begins.)

4 When the cooking program ends, let the pressure release naturally for 5 minutes, then move the Pressure Release to **Venting** to release any remaining steam. Open the pot and give the pasta and sauce a good stir.

5 Spoon the pasta into bowls and sprinkle with the Parmesan. Serve right away.

Nutrition Information

Per serving: 284 calories, 7 grams fat, 47 grams carbohydrates, 6 grams fiber, 9 grams protein

3

Soups and Chilis

This soup is absolutely packed with diced and grated vegetables, including the vibrant red beets that give it its color. It's light on calories, yet hearty enough to get you through any cold-weather snap. A little lemon juice is stirred in at the end to brighten it up, and then it's topped with fresh dill and with tangy yogurt in place of the traditional sour cream.

BEET BORSCHT

- 2 tablespoons extra-virgin olive oil
- 2 garlic cloves, minced
- 1 yellow onion, diced
- 1 teaspoon fine sea salt
- ½ teaspoon freshly ground black pepper
- 1 bay leaf
- 1 tablespoon tomato paste
- 4 cups low-sodium roasted beef bone broth (page 260) or vegetable broth (page 261)
- 2 carrots, grated
- 12 ounces beets, peeled and grated
- 1 parsnip, peeled and grated
- ¼ head green cabbage, chopped
- One 8-ounce zucchini, diced (about 1¾ cups)
- 1 red bell pepper, seeded and diced
- 8 ounces Yukon gold or other waxy potatoes, diced
- 2 tablespoons fresh lemon juice
- ⅔ cup plain 2 percent Greek yogurt, homemade (page 34) or store-bought, or Cashew Sour Cream (page 265), for serving
- ¼ cup chopped fresh dill, for serving

1 Select the **Sauté** setting on the Instant Pot and heat the oil and garlic for 2 minutes, until the garlic is bubbling but not browned. Add the onion, salt, pepper, and bay leaf and sauté for about 3 minutes, until the onion begins to soften. Add the tomato paste and sauté for about 2 more minutes, until the tomato paste is aromatic and beginning to stick to the bottom of the pot.

2 Add the broth and use a wooden spoon or spatula to nudge any browned bits from the bottom of the pot. Add the carrots, beets, parsnip, cabbage, zucchini, bell pepper, and potatoes and stir to combine. The liquid will not cover the vegetables completely.

3 Secure the lid and set the Pressure Release to **Sealing**. Press the **Cancel** button to reset the cooking program, then select the **Pressure Cook** or **Manual** setting and set the cooking time for 5 minutes at high pressure. (The pot will take about 15 minutes to come up to pressure before the cooking program begins.)

4 When the cooking program ends, let the pressure release naturally for 15 minutes, then move the Pressure Release to **Venting** to release any remaining steam. Open the pot and remove and discard the bay leaf. Stir in the lemon juice.

5 Ladle the soup into bowls and top with the yogurt and dill. Serve piping hot.

PREP	0 MINUTES
COOK	30 MINUTES
PR	15 MINUTES NPR
SERVES	10

Nutrition Information

Per serving (soup only): 104 calories, 3 grams fat, 19 grams carbohydrates, 4 grams fiber, 3 grams protein

A simple sipper of a soup, I love this one as a low-calorie, nutrient-rich afternoon snack on snowy days. You can use any winter squash you prefer. My favorite is the sweet, dense flesh of the Red Kuri, but kabocha or butternut will work well in this soup, too.

WINTER SQUASH MISO SOUP

1 tablespoon cold-pressed avocado oil

1 yellow onion, diced

2 carrots, diced

½ teaspoon fine sea salt

One 2-pound Red Kuri, kabocha, or butternut squash, peeled, seeded, and diced

3 cups water

1 tablespoon white miso paste

2 tablespoons rice vinegar

2 green onions, green part only, thinly sliced

PREP	0 MINUTES
COOK	25 MINUTES
PR	10 MINUTES NPR
SERVES	6

1 Select the **Sauté** setting on the Instant Pot and heat the oil for 1 minute. Add the onion, carrots, and salt and sauté for about 5 minutes, until the onion has softened but not browned. Add the squash and water.

2 Secure the lid and set the Pressure Release to **Sealing**. Press the **Cancel** button to reset the cooking program, then select the **Pressure Cook** or **Manual** setting and set the cooking time for 3 minutes at high pressure. (The pot will take about 15 minutes to come up to pressure before the cooking program begins.)

3 When the cooking program ends, let the pressure release naturally for at least 10 minutes, then move the Pressure Release to **Venting** to release any remaining steam. Open the pot, add the miso paste and vinegar, and use an immersion blender to puree the soup until smooth.

4 Ladle the soup into bowls or cups, sprinkle the green onions on top, and serve hot.

Nutrition Information

Per serving: 116 calories, 3 grams fat, 22 grams carbohydrates, 3 grams fiber, 2 grams protein

A comforting, creamy vegetable soup that's thickened with a secret ingredient: a couple of tablespoons of masa harina. The flour adds a subtle corn flavor that pairs nicely with the zucchini and adds body and richness, so no cream is required. Serve this soup as a first course or alongside a quesadilla or sandwich at lunchtime.

CREAM OF ZUCCHINI SOUP

1 tablespoon extra-virgin olive oil

1 garlic clove, minced

1 small yellow onion, diced

¼ teaspoon fine sea salt

¼ teaspoon freshly ground black pepper

1 pound zucchini, halved lengthwise and thinly sliced into half-moons

2 cups low-sodium vegetable broth (page 261) or chicken bone broth (page 260)

2 tablespoons masa harina

½ cup 2 percent milk or unsweetened nondairy milk

PREP	0 MINUTES
COOK	25 MINUTES
PR	10 MINUTES NPR
SERVES	5

1 Select the **Sauté** setting on the Instant Pot and heat the oil and garlic for 2 minutes, until the garlic is bubbling but not browned. Add the onion, salt, and pepper and sauté for about 4 minutes, until the onion has softened but not browned. Add the zucchini and sauté for about 3 more minutes, until warmed through. Pour in the broth and stir to combine.

2 Secure the lid and set the Pressure Release to **Sealing**. Press the **Cancel** button to reset the cooking program, then select the **Pressure Cook** or **Manual** setting and set the cooking time for 3 minutes at high pressure. (The pot will take about 5 minutes to come up to pressure before the cooking program begins.)

3 When the cooking program ends, let the pressure release naturally for 10 minutes, then move the pressure release to **Venting** to release any remaining steam.

4 In a small bowl, stir together the masa harina and milk. Open the pot and stir in the mixture. Press the **Cancel** button to reset the cooking program, then select the **Sauté** setting. Let the soup cook for about 4 minutes, stirring occasionally, until the broth has thickened slightly. Press the **Cancel** button to turn off the pot. Using an immersion blender, puree the soup until smooth.

5 Ladle the soup into bowls and serve piping hot.

Nutrition Information

Per serving: 79 calories, 4 grams fat, 9 grams carbohydrates, 2 grams fiber, 4 grams protein

The tomato soup with basil oil served at the Tender Greens chain of restaurants is so simple and so good that it inspired me to make this Instant Pot version, with red bell pepper added for even more flavor and an additional dose of vitamin C. It's warm and comforting in a mug or bowl, with whole-grain toast or crackers alongside. The soup is good on its own, but it's even better with a topping of bright green basil oil. You'll use about half of a batch of the oil for the soup. Save the remainder for drizzling on fish, salads, and steamed vegetables.

TOMATO–RED PEPPER BISQUE WITH BASIL OIL

- 2 tablespoons extra-virgin olive oil
- 2 garlic cloves, minced
- 1 yellow onion, diced
- 2 carrots, diced
- 2 celery stalks, diced
- 1 red bell pepper, seeded and diced
- 1 teaspoon fine sea salt
- One 28-ounce can whole San Marzano–style tomatoes and their liquid
- 4 ounces new potatoes, diced
- 2½ cups low-sodium vegetable broth (page 261)
- 1½ teaspoons Italian seasoning
- ¼ cup half-and-half or vegan half-and-half (such as Ripple brand)
- ¼ cup Basil Oil (page 264)

PREP	0 MINUTES
COOK	20 MINUTES
PR	15 MINUTES NPR
SERVES	8

1 Select the **Sauté** setting on the Instant Pot and heat the oil and garlic for 2 minutes, until the garlic is bubbling but not browned. Add the onion, carrots, celery, bell pepper, and salt and sauté for about 5 minutes, until the onion has softened but not browned. Add the tomatoes and their liquid, crushing the tomatoes with your hands as you add them to the pot. Stir in the potatoes, broth, and Italian seasoning.

2 Secure the lid and set the Pressure Release to **Sealing**. Press the **Cancel** button to reset the cooking program, then select the **Pressure Cook** or **Manual** setting and set the cooking time for 5 minutes at high pressure. (The pot will take about 10 minutes to come up to pressure before the cooking program begins.)

3 When the cooking program ends, let the pressure release naturally for 15 minutes, then move the Pressure Release to **Venting** to release any remaining steam. Open the pot, add the half-and-half, and, using an immersion blender, puree the soup until smooth.

4 Ladle the soup into mugs or bowls, drizzle each serving with 1½ teaspoons basil oil, and serve piping hot.

Nutrition Information

Per serving (1 cup soup plus 1½ teaspoons Basil Oil): 140 calories, 10 grams fat, 10 grams carbohydrates, 2 grams fiber, 2 grams protein

In this beautiful green take on one of my favorite comforting soups, potatoes take the place of the traditional noodles, so the soup keeps better in the fridge. For a richer bowl, add a dollop of pesto to each serving.

GREEN MINESTRONE

- 2 tablespoons extra-virgin olive oil
- 3 garlic cloves, minced
- 1 yellow onion, diced
- 2 celery stalks, diced
- ½ teaspoon fine sea salt
- 1 teaspoon Italian seasoning
- ½ teaspoon red pepper flakes (optional)
- 1 bunch Lacinato or curly kale, stemmed and cut into ¼-inch-wide ribbons
- ½ head cauliflower or romanesco, cut into bite-size florets
- 1 small zucchini, halved lengthwise and sliced into half-moons
- 12 ounces russet potatoes, diced
- 1 cup frozen peas, thawed
- 4 cups low-sodium vegetable broth (page 261)
- 1 bay leaf
- Pesto (page 156), for serving (optional)
- Grated Parmesan or Vegan Parmesan Cheese (page 265), for serving

PREP	0 MINUTES
COOK	25 MINUTES
PR	15 MINUTES NPR
SERVES	8

1 Select the **Sauté** setting on the Instant Pot and heat the olive oil and garlic for 3 minutes, until the garlic is bubbling but not browned. Add the onion, celery, and salt and sauté for about 4 minutes, until the onion begins to soften. Add the Italian seasoning and red pepper flakes and sauté for 1 minute. Stir in the kale and sauté for 1 more minute, until it wilts. Add the cauliflower, zucchini, potatoes, peas, broth, and bay leaf and stir well. It's fine if the vegetables are not fully submerged, as they will release their own liquid as they cook.

2 Secure the lid and set the pressure release to **Sealing**. Press the **Cancel** button to reset the cooking program, then select the **Pressure Cook** or **Manual** setting and set the cooking time for 2 minutes at high pressure. (The pot will take about 15 minutes to come up to pressure before the cooking program begins.)

3 When the cooking program ends, let the pressure release naturally for 15 minutes, then move the Pressure Release to **Venting** to release any remaining steam. Open the pot and remove and discard the bay leaf.

4 Ladle the soup into bowls and top with a dollop of pesto and a sprinkle of Parmesan. Serve piping hot.

Note: Feel free to swap in different green vegetables. Options include green beans, broccoli, cabbage, chard, and escarole.

Nutrition Information

Per serving (soup only): 135 calories, 4 grams fat, 23 grams carbohydrates, 4 grams fiber, 5 grams protein

What sets this recipe apart from many other pasta-based soups is that a whole bag of baby spinach is stirred in at the end—a delicious way to get a big dose of healthy greens! The spinach wilts in just a few minutes, mixing with the pasta, sausage, and beans. Tote this soup in a thermos for a school or work lunch, as it's a great complete meal.

PASTA, BEAN, AND SAUSAGE SOUP

2 tablespoons extra-virgin olive oil

2 garlic cloves, minced

1 yellow onion, diced

2 carrots, diced

2 celery stalks, diced

1 pound fresh Italian chicken sausage, casings removed

4 cups low-sodium chicken bone broth (page 260)

1½ teaspoons Italian seasoning

½ teaspoon freshly ground black pepper

1¼ cups whole-wheat elbow pasta

1½ cups drained cooked kidney or cannellini beans (page 44), or one 15-ounce can kidney beans, rinsed and drained

One 14½-ounce can diced tomatoes and their liquid

One 6-ounce bag baby spinach

PREP	0 MINUTES
COOK	30 MINUTES
PR	10 MINUTES NPR
REST	1 MINUTE
SERVES	8

1 Select the **Sauté** setting on the Instant Pot and heat the olive oil and garlic for 2 minutes, until the garlic is bubbling but not browned. Add the onion, carrots, and celery and sauté for 5 minutes, until the onion has softened. Add the sausage and sauté, breaking it up with a wooden spoon as it cooks, for about 5 minutes, until it is in small pieces and no streaks of pink remain.

2 Stir in the broth, Italian seasoning, pepper, and pasta, using the spoon to nudge any browned bits from the bottom of the pot and making sure all of the pasta is submerged in the liquid. Pour in the kidney beans and then the tomatoes. Do not stir them in.

3 Secure the lid and set the Pressure Release to **Sealing**. Press the **Cancel** button to reset the cooking program, then select the **Pressure Cook** or **Manual** setting and set the time for 3 minutes at high pressure. (The pot will take about 15 minutes to come up to pressure before the cooking program begins.)

4 When the cooking program ends, let the pressure release naturally for 10 minutes, then move the Pressure Release to **Venting** to release the remaining pressure. Open the pot, add the spinach, and stir to combine. At first, it may look like it won't fit, but it will wilt dramatically as you stir. Let the soup sit for 1 minute to allow the spinach to cook through, then stir once more.

5 Ladle the soup into bowls and serve right away.

Note: For a gluten-free variation, substitute chickpea or brown rice elbow pasta for the whole-wheat pasta. Lower the cooking time to 2 minutes at low pressure.

Nutrition Information

Per serving: 292 calories, 14 grams fat, 25 grams carbohydrates, 7 grams fiber, 16 grams protein

Balsamic vinegar adds a little sweet-sour kick to this satisfying soup, which boasts nutrient-rich red lentils and spinach. For a filling meal, accompany the soup with a slice of avocado toast.

RED LENTIL AND SPINACH SOUP

- 3 tablespoons extra-virgin olive oil
- 2 garlic cloves, minced
- 1 yellow onion, diced
- 2 carrots, diced
- ½ teaspoon fine sea salt
- 1 teaspoon Italian seasoning
- 1 cup dried red lentils
- 4 cups low-sodium vegetable broth (page 261) or chicken bone broth (page 260)
- One 14½-ounce can diced tomatoes and their liquid
- 3 cups firmly packed baby spinach
- 1 tablespoon aged balsamic vinegar
- Freshly ground black pepper, for serving

PREP	0 MINUTES
COOK	25 MINUTES
PR	15 MINUTES NPR
REST	2 MINUTES
SERVES	8

1 Select the **Sauté** setting on the Instant Pot and heat the oil and garlic for 2 minutes, until the garlic is bubbling but not browned. Add the onion, carrots, and salt and sauté for about 4 minutes, until the onion has softened. Add the Italian seasoning and sauté for 1 more minute. Add the lentils, broth, and tomatoes and stir to combine.

2 Secure the lid and set the Pressure Release to **Sealing**. Press the **Cancel** button to reset the cooking program, then select the **Pressure Cook** or **Manual** setting and set the cooking time for 5 minutes at high pressure. (The pot will take about 15 minutes to come up to pressure before the cooking program begins.)

3 When the cooking program ends, let the pressure release naturally for 15 minutes, then move the Pressure Release to **Venting** to release any remaining steam. Open the pot and stir in the spinach and vinegar. Let the soup sit for 2 minutes, then stir once more.

4 Ladle the soup into bowls, top with a few grinds of pepper, and serve right away.

Note: If you are using another variety of lentils, you will need to adjust the cooking time. Refer to the chart on page 267 for lentil cooking times.

Nutrition Information

Per serving: 175 calories, 5 grams fat, 23 grams carbohydrates, 9 grams fiber, 8 grams protein

A favorite light lunch, this lentil soup, known as *fakes* in Greece, is seasoned with oregano and includes a dollop of tomato paste. The lentils and vegetables become meltingly soft, making every bowl pure comfort food.

GREEK LENTIL SOUP

3 tablespoons extra-virgin olive oil

3 garlic cloves, minced

1 large yellow onion, diced

2 carrots, diced

2 celery stalks, diced

1 teaspoon fine sea salt

1 teaspoon dried oregano

½ teaspoon freshly ground black pepper

1 cup dried green or brown lentils

4 cups low-sodium chicken bone broth (page 260) or vegetable broth (page 261)

2 tablespoons tomato paste

2 tablespoons red wine vinegar, for serving

2 tablespoons fresh chopped fresh flat-leaf parsley, for serving

PREP	6 MINUTES
COOK	45 MINUTES
PR	15 MINUTES NPR
SERVES	6

1 Select the **Sauté** setting on the Instant Pot and heat 2 tablespoons of the oil and the garlic for 2 minutes, until the garlic is bubbling but not browned. Add the onion, carrots, celery, and salt and sauté for about 3 minutes, until the onion has softened. Add the oregano and pepper and sauté for 1 more minute. Add the lentils and broth and stir to combine. Add the tomato paste in a dollop on top. Do not stir it in.

2 Secure the lid and set the pressure release to **Sealing**. Press the **Cancel** button to reset the cooking program, then select the **Pressure Cook** or **Manual** setting and set the cooking time for 25 minutes at high pressure. (The pot will take about 10 minutes to come up to pressure before the cooking program begins.)

3 When the cooking program ends, let the pressure release naturally for at least 15 minutes, then move the Pressure Release to **Venting** to release any remaining steam. Open the pot, then stir the soup to incorporate the tomato paste.

4 Ladle the soup into bowls, drizzle with the remaining 1 tablespoon oil and the vinegar, and sprinkle with the parsley. Serve right away.

Notes: The more vegetables, the merrier. For example, add chopped bell pepper or parsnip.

If you're using the last few stalks of celery (near the heart) from a head, chop the leaves and add them, too.

Nutrition Information

Per serving: 208 calories, 8 grams fat, 26 grams carbohydrates, 12 grams fiber, 9 grams protein

Whether your store-bought blend has nine, thirteen, fifteen, or some other number of different bean varieties, it'll work perfectly in this soup. The thirteen-bean blend from Bob's Red Mill is the one I have on hand most often. Whichever mix you choose, you'll end up with a pot of soup high in fiber and protein and enjoyable as a side or main event.

HEARTY MULTIBEAN SOUP

2 tablespoons extra-virgin olive oil

2 garlic cloves, minced

1 leek, white part only, halved lengthwise and sliced crosswise

1 carrot, diced

2 celery stalks, diced

1 teaspoon fine sea salt

1½ teaspoons Old Bay seasoning

¼ teaspoon cayenne pepper (optional)

¼ teaspoon freshly ground black pepper

1 bay leaf

1 cup dried bean soup mix

One 14½-ounce can diced tomatoes and their liquid

4 cups low-sodium vegetable broth (page 261)

PREP	0 MINUTES
COOK	55 MINUTES
PR	35 MINUTES NPR
SERVES	6

1 Select the **Sauté** setting on the Instant Pot and heat the oil and the garlic for 2 minutes, until the garlic is bubbling but not browned. Add the leek, carrot, celery, and salt and sauté for about 5 minutes, until the leek is beginning to soften. Add the Old Bay, cayenne pepper (if using), black pepper, bay leaf, beans, tomatoes and their liquid, and broth and stir to combine.

2 Secure the lid and set the pressure release to **Sealing**. Press the **Cancel** button to reset the cooking program, then select the **Pressure Cook** or **Manual** setting and set the cooking time for 35 minutes at high pressure. (The pot will take about 10 minutes to come up to pressure before the cooking program begins.)

3 When the cooking program ends, let the pressure release naturally (this will take about 35 minutes). Open the pot and remove and discard the bay leaf.

4 Ladle the soup into bowls and serve hot.

Note: If you like, substitute a medium-size yellow onion for the leek.

Nutrition Information

Per serving: 137 calories, 5 grams fat, 24 grams carbohydrates, 10 grams fiber, 7 grams protein

This not-too-sweet potato soup includes fire-roasted tomatoes. To lighten it up (and make it dairy-free), omit the yogurt garnish or substitute a dairy-free yogurt or Cashew Sour Cream (page 265).

SWEET POTATO SOUP

2 tablespoons cold-pressed avocado oil

1 yellow onion, diced

2 carrots, diced

2 garlic cloves, chopped

½ teaspoon fine sea salt

2 pounds sweet potatoes, peeled and cubed

4 cups low-sodium vegetable broth (page 261) or chicken bone broth (page 260)

One 14½-ounce can no-salt-added diced fire-roasted tomatoes and their liquid

⅔ cup plain 2 percent Greek yogurt, homemade (page 42) or store-bought, for serving

2 tablespoons chopped fresh cilantro, for serving

Lime wedges, for serving

PREP	0 MINUTES
COOK	25 MINUTES
PR	10 MINUTES NPR
SERVES	10

1 Select the **Sauté** setting on the Instant Pot and heat the oil for 2 minutes. Add the onion, carrots, garlic, and salt and sauté for about 5 minutes, until the onion has softened but not browned. Add the sweet potatoes and broth and stir to combine. Pour the tomatoes and their liquid on top. Do not stir them in.

2 Secure the lid and set the Pressure Release to **Sealing**. Press the **Cancel** button to reset the cooking program, then select the **Pressure Cook** or **Manual** setting and set the cooking time for 5 minutes at low pressure. (The pot will take about 15 minutes to come up to pressure before the cooking program begins.)

3 When the cooking program ends, let the pressure release naturally for at least 10 minutes, then move the Pressure Release to **Venting** to release any remaining steam. Open the pot and use an immersion blender to puree the soup until smooth.

4 Ladle the soup into bowls or mugs. Swirl about 1 tablespoon of the yogurt into each bowl, then sprinkle the cilantro on top. Serve warm, with the lime wedges on the side.

Nutrition information

Per serving: 162 calories, 5 grams fat, 25 grams carbohydrates, 4 grams fiber, 4 grams protein

Whole cloves of roasted garlic are blended into this creamy yet dairy-free potato soup. You can either roast the garlic ahead of time, or make it right before you cook the potatoes. A generous squeeze of lemon juice perks up the flavors in this soup, making it comforting yet bright. Low in calories but big on flavor, this is a favorite of mine when I'm feeling under the weather.

ROASTED GARLIC AND POTATO SOUP

2 pounds Yukon Gold potatoes, cut into ½-inch cubes

4 cups low-sodium vegetable broth (page 261)

3 heads roasted garlic cloves (page 261)

2 tablespoons unsalted butter or vegan buttery spread

2 tablespoons fresh lemon juice

PREP	0 MINUTES
COOK	15 MINUTES
PR	15 MINUTES NPR
SERVES	8

1 Add the potatoes and broth to the Instant Pot.

2 Secure the lid and set the Pressure Release to **Sealing**. Press the **Cancel** button to reset the cooking program, then select the **Pressure Cook** or **Manual** setting and set the cooking time for 1 minute at high pressure. (The pot will take about 15 minutes to come up to pressure before the cooking program begins.)

3 When the cooking program ends, let the pressure release naturally for at least 15 minutes, then move the Pressure Release to **Venting** to release any remaining steam.

4 Open the pot and add the garlic and butter to the potatoes. Using an immersion blender, puree the soup until smooth. Blend in the lemon juice. Taste and adjust the seasoning with salt if needed.

5 Ladle the soup into bowls and serve hot.

Nutrition Information

Per serving: 130 calories, 5 grams fat, 23 grams carbohydrates, 2 grams fiber, 3 grams protein

This recipe has its roots in Mollie Katzen's *The Enchanted Broccoli Forest* cookbook. I loved making her Swedish Cabbage Soup as a kid, and this Instant Pot version is even easier to whip up. The ingredient list is short, but it comes out so delicious and comforting. My recipe makes a smaller, more potato-packed batch of soup than Mollie's does, and it cooks for just 1 minute under pressure. The caraway adds a distinctly Scandinavian flavor, reminiscent of rye bread. The soup is light on fat and calories, but the potato and cabbage make it filling and satisfying. Serve it as a first course or heat up a bowl to enjoy midmorning or in the afternoon on chilly days.

CABBAGE AND POTATO SOUP

1 tablespoon unsalted butter or vegan buttery spread

1 large yellow onion, diced

¾ teaspoon fine sea salt

1 teaspoon caraway seeds

3 cups low-sodium vegetable broth (page 261) or chicken bone broth (page 260)

1 pound russet potatoes, cut into ½-inch cubes

½ head green cabbage, shredded

PREP	0 MINUTES
COOK	25 MINUTES
PR	15 MINUTES NPR
SERVES	6

1 Select the **Sauté** setting on the Instant Pot and melt the butter for 2 minutes. Add the onion and salt and sauté for about 4 minutes, until the onion has softened. Add the caraway and sauté for 1 more minute, until fragrant. Add the broth and the potatoes and stir to combine. Add the cabbage on top in an even layer. Do not stir it in.

2 Secure the lid and set the Pressure Release to **Sealing**. Press the **Cancel** button to reset the cooking program, then select the **Pressure Cook** or **Manual** setting and set the cooking time for 1 minute at high pressure. (The pot will take about 15 minutes to come up to pressure before the cooking program begins.)

3 When the cooking program ends, let the pressure release naturally for at least 15 minutes, then move the Pressure Release to **Venting** to release any remaining steam. Open the pot and stir the soup.

4 Ladle the soup into bowls and serve hot.

Nutrition Information

Per serving: 117 calories, 2 grams fat, 21 grams carbohydrates, 4 grams fiber, 3 grams protein

The broth for this pozole gets its richness and red color from dried chiles and diced tomatoes, which are whirled in a blender along with broth, garlic, onion, and seasonings. It is the base for this simple soup, which features soft beans rich in protein and chewy hominy for a satisfying bite. Don't leave off the crunchy toppings of cabbage and radish, and definitely squeeze in some lime at the table. For those who like a spicier soup, have some red pepper flakes on hand.

VEGAN RED POZOLE

4 dried guajillo chiles, stemmed and seeded

2 cups water

4 cups low-sodium vegetable broth (page 261)

One 14½-ounce can no-salt-added diced fire-roasted tomatoes and their liquid

4 garlic cloves, peeled

1 small yellow onion, diced

1 teaspoon dried oregano

½ teaspoon ground cumin

¼ teaspoon smoked paprika

1 teaspoon fine sea salt

2 tablespoons extra-virgin olive oil

One 25-ounce can hominy, drained

1½ cups cooked pinto beans (page 44), or one 15-ounce can pinto beans, drained and rinsed

3 cups firmly packed shredded green cabbage

1 bunch radishes, sliced

2 limes, cut into wedges, for serving

Red pepper flakes, for serving

PREP	5 MINUTES
SOAK	15 MINUTES
COOK	40 MINUTES
PR	15 MINUTES NPR
SERVES	6

1 Place the guajillo chiles into the Instant Pot, then pour in the water. Cover the pot with a tempered glass lid, select the **Sauté** setting, and set the cooking time for 6 minutes. When the timer goes off, let the chiles soak in the water for an additional 15 minutes to soften.

2 Open the pot and, using tongs, transfer the soaked chiles to a blender. Using heat-resistant mitts, lift out the inner pot, discard the soaking water, wipe out the pot, and return it to the housing. Add 1 cup of the broth, the tomatoes, garlic, onion, oregano, cumin, paprika, and salt to the blender. Blend on high speed for about 1 minute, until smooth.

3 Select the **Sauté** setting on the Instant Pot and heat the oil for 2 minutes. Pour in the chile puree, stir to combine with the oil, and bring to a simmer (this will take about 2 minutes), then let simmer for 3 minutes. Don't stir the puree while it's simmering, as it will spatter. Pour in the remaining 3 cups broth, add the hominy and beans, and stir to combine.

4 Secure the pressure cooking lid and set the Pressure Release to **Sealing**. Press the **Cancel** button to reset the cooking program, then select the **Pressure Cook** or **Manual** setting and set the cooking time for 10 minutes at high pressure. (The pot will take about 15 minutes to come up to pressure before the cooking program begins.)

5 When the cooking program ends, let the pressure release naturally for at least 15 minutes, then move the Pressure Release to **Venting** to release any remaining steam. Open the pot and stir the pozole.

6 Ladle the pozole into bowls and top each bowl with ½ cup of the cabbage and the radishes. Serve piping hot, with the lime wedges and red pepper flakes on the side.

Nutrition Information

Per serving: 219 calories, 6 grams fat, 35 grams carbohydrates, 9 grams fiber, 7 grams protein

Hearty soups like this one are ideal for chilly nights when I want to make a one-pot dish that everyone will like. With its tomatoey broth packed with beef, potatoes, and other vegetables, this soup is meant to be the whole meal, and each serving is enough to fill a big bowl. It's also nutritionally well balanced, taking all of the guesswork out of a healthy dinner.

VEGETABLE BEEF SOUP

2 tablespoons extra-virgin olive oil

2 garlic cloves, minced

1 large yellow onion, diced

1 carrot, diced

2 celery stalks, diced

½ teaspoon fine sea salt

½ teaspoon ground black pepper

1½ pounds beef stew meat or sirloin tips, cut into ½-inch pieces

4 cups low-sodium roasted beef bone broth (page 260) or vegetable broth (page 261)

One 14½-ounce can diced tomatoes and their liquid

1 pound Yukon Gold potatoes, cut into ½-inch pieces

8 ounces green beans, trimmed and cut into ½-inch pieces

1 cup frozen corn, thawed

1 cup frozen peas, thawed

1 teaspoon Italian seasoning

1 bay leaf

PREP	0 MINUTES
COOK	45 MINUTES
PR	20 MINUTES NPR
SERVES	8

1 Select the **Sauté** setting on the Instant Pot and heat the oil and garlic for 2 minutes, until the garlic is bubbling but not browned. Add the onion, carrot, celery, salt, and pepper and sauté for about 5 minutes, until the onion has softened. Add the beef and sauté for 3 more minutes, until the beef is mostly opaque on the outside. It does not have to be cooked all the way through. Add the broth, tomatoes and their liquid, potatoes, green beans, corn, peas, Italian seasoning, and bay leaf and stir to combine.

2 Secure the lid and set the Pressure Release to **Sealing**. Press the **Cancel** button to reset the cooking program, then select the **Pressure Cook** or **Manual** setting and set the cooking time for 10 minutes at high pressure. (The pot will take about 25 minutes to come up to pressure before the cooking program begins.)

3 When the cooking program ends, let the pressure release for at least 20 minutes, then move the Pressure Release to **Venting** to release any remaining steam. Open the pot and remove and discard the bay leaf.

4 Ladle the soup into bowls and serve piping hot.

Nutrition Information

Per serving: 273 calories, 7 grams fat, 26 grams carbohydrates, 4 grams fiber, 25 grams protein

Drumsticks are my favorite chicken parts for making a fast, flavorful soup. They are less expensive than thighs, the bones give lots of flavor to the broth, and it's extremely easy to remove the meat from the bones and add it back to the soup, rather than having to bone a whole chicken. I make this soup whenever someone in my family is sick—it's a comforting cure-all.

CHICKEN DRUMSTICK SOUP

2 pounds bone-in chicken drumsticks, skinned

2 celery stalks, diced

2 carrots, diced

1 parsnip, peeled and diced

1 rutabaga, peeled and diced

1 yellow onion, diced

12 flat-leaf parsley sprigs

3 dill sprigs

2 bay leaves

1½ teaspoons fine sea salt

6 cups water

1 tablespoon raw cider vinegar

Freshly ground black pepper, for serving

Lemon wedges, for serving

PREP	0 MINUTES
COOK	45 MINUTES
PR	30 MINUTES NPR
SERVES	6

1 Combine the chicken, celery, carrots, parsnip, rutabaga, and onion in the Instant Pot. Arrange the parsley, dill, and bay leaves on top of the chicken and vegetables, then sprinkle with the salt. Pour in the water and vinegar.

2 Secure the lid and set the Pressure Release to **Sealing**. Select the **Soup/Broth** setting and set the cooking time for 15 minutes at high pressure. (The pot will take about 30 minutes to come up to pressure before the cooking program begins.)

3 When the cooking program ends, let the pressure release naturally for at least 30 minutes, then move the Pressure Release to **Venting** to release any remaining steam. Open the pot and remove and discard the parsley, dill, and bay leaves. Using tongs, transfer the chicken to a plate. Remove the chicken meat from the bones and discard the bones. Use a pair of forks to shred the meat into bite-size pieces. Stir the meat into the soup.

4 Ladle the soup into bowls, top each bowl with a grind or two of pepper, and serve piping hot, with the lemon wedges on the side.

Note: For a heartier soup, you can add hot cooked noodles or rice to each bowl. If you are not serving all of the soup, store the noodles or rice separately from the leftover soup. That way, they won't absorb too much liquid and become soggy.

Nutrition Information

Per serving: 212 calories, 5 grams fat, 15 grams carbohydrates, 4 grams fiber, 26 grams protein

Many recipes for pho involve separate steps of charring the ginger and spices, preparing a broth, and cooking the chicken. For this simplified Instant Pot version, I have created a flavorful chicken broth, tender meat, and crunchy toppings with fewer steps. A small amount of fat renders out of the chicken skin, adding a bit of richness and a nice mouthfeel. If you prefer a leaner soup, skin the chicken before cooking.

CHICKEN PHO

Broth

2 pounds bone-in, skin-on chicken parts (mix of dark and light meat)

2-inch piece fresh ginger, peeled and cut into ⅛-inch-thick slices

4 green onions, white and green parts, cut into 2-inch lengths

½ bunch cilantro

8 cups low-sodium chicken bone broth (page 260)

1 tablespoon fish sauce

1 teaspoon brown rice syrup or agave nectar

One 8-ounce package mai fun brown rice noodles, cooked

½ cup chopped fresh cilantro

½ cup chopped green onions, white and green parts

2 tablespoons store-bought fried shallots (optional)

For Serving

2 cups mung bean sprouts

4 fresh Thai basil sprigs

1 jalapeño chile, thinly sliced

Lime wedges

Sriracha sauce

PREP	10 MINUTES
COOK	40 MINUTES
PR	20 MINUTES NPR
COOL	10 MINUTES
SERVES	4

1 To make the broth: Place a steamer basket into the Instant Pot. Add the chicken, ginger, green onions, and cilantro to the steamer basket. Pour in the broth.

2 Secure the lid and set the Pressure Release to **Sealing**. Select the **Soup/Broth** setting and set the cooking time for 15 minutes at high pressure. (The pot will take about 25 minutes to come up to pressure before the cooking program begins.)

3 When the cooking program ends, let the pressure release naturally for 20 minutes, then move the Pressure Release to **Venting** to release any remaining steam. While the pressure is releasing, prepare an ice bath.

4 Open the pot and, using tongs, transfer the chicken to the ice bath. Wearing heat-resistant mitts, lift the steamer basket out of the pot and discard the cilantro, green onions, and ginger. Let the chicken cool in the ice bath for 10 minutes.

5 Remove the chicken from the ice bath and transfer to a dish or cutting board. Discard the skin and bones, then, using two forks or your hands, shred the meat into bite-size pieces.

6 The broth in the Instant Pot should still be piping hot on the **Keep Warm** setting. Stir the fish sauce and brown rice syrup into the broth. Taste for seasoning, adding more fish sauce if needed.

7 Divide the cooked noodles among four large bowls. Place the shredded chicken on top of the noodles. Ladle 2 cups of the broth over the noodles and chicken in each bowl, then top with the cilantro, green onions, and shallots.

8 Serve immediately, with the mung bean sprouts, basil, jalapeño, lime wedges, and Sriracha sauce at the table.

Nutrition Information

Per serving: 406 calories, 8 grams fat, 55 grams carbohydrates, 6 grams fiber, 31 grams protein

Here is a simple plant-based recipe for chili that's perfect to serve a crowd of vegans, omnivores, and everyone in between. A chopped chipotle adds smoke and spice, and the meaty texture from chopped Soy Curls and hearty kidney beans makes for an extra-satisfying bowl. Serve it with crunchy tortilla chips and a dollop of Cashew Sour Cream.

VEGAN SOY CURLS CHILI

- 4 ounces Butler Soy Curls (see page 13)
- 2 cups boiling water
- 2 tablespoons extra-virgin olive oil
- 2 garlic cloves, minced
- 1 large yellow onion, diced
- 2 carrots, diced
- 2 tablespoons chili powder
- 1 teaspoon dried oregano
- 2 cups low-sodium vegetable broth (page 261)
- 1½ cups drained cooked kidney beans (page 44), or one 15-ounce can kidney beans, rinsed and drained
- One 14½-ounce can diced tomatoes and their liquid
- One 4-ounce can diced green chiles
- 1 chipotle chile in adobo sauce, diced
- 2 tablespoons tomato paste
- Chopped fresh cilantro, for serving
- Cashew Sour Cream (page 265), for serving
- Tortilla chips, for serving
- Hot sauce (such as Cholula or Tapatío), for serving

SOAK	10 MINUTES
PREP	5 MINUTES
COOK	25 MINUTES
PR	15 MINUTES NPR·
SERVES	6

1 Put the Soy Curls into a medium heatproof bowl, pour in the boiling water, and stir to combine. Let the curls soak for 10 minutes. Drain the curls in a colander, pushing out any excess liquid with the back of a spoon. Transfer the curls to a cutting board and chop them into about ½-inch pieces.

2 Select the **Sauté** setting on the Instant Pot and heat the oil and garlic for 2 minutes, until the garlic is bubbling but not browned. Add the onion and carrots and sauté for about 4 minutes, until the onion begins to soften. Add the chili powder and oregano and sauté for 1 more minute. Pour in the broth and use a wooden spoon or spatula to nudge any browned bits from the bottom of the pot. Pour the chopped curls, kidney beans, tomatoes, green chiles, chipotle, and tomato paste on top. Do not stir them in.

3 Secure the lid and set the pressure release to **Sealing**. Press the **Cancel** button to reset the cooking time, then select the **Pressure Cook** or **Manual** setting and set the cooking time for 5 minutes at high pressure. (The pot will take about 10 minutes to come up to pressure before the cooking program begins.)

4 When the cooking program ends, let the pressure release naturally for at least 15 minutes, then move the Pressure Release to **Venting** to release any remaining steam. Open the pot and stir the chili.

5 Ladle the chili into bowls and sprinkle the cilantro on top. Serve hot, with the sour cream, tortilla chips, and hot sauce on the side.

Nutrition Information

Per serving (chili only): 237 calories, 8 grams fat, 17 grams carbohydrates, 5 grams fiber, 8 grams protein

Here, chicken thighs become fall-apart tender after cooking for just 15 minutes under pressure in a freshly made tomatillo salsa. At the grocery store, tomatillos resemble little paper lanterns, but when you peel away their outer husk, you're left with something that looks like a green tomato and has a tangy, fresh flavor. They're the main ingredient in salsa verde, which is the base for this protein-packed recipe.

TOMATILLO CHICKEN CHILI

1 tablespoon cold-pressed avocado oil

1 small yellow onion, sliced

1 garlic clove, peeled

1 serrano chile, seeded and diced

1 jalapeño chile, seeded and diced

1 pound tomatillos, husked, well rinsed, and quartered

½ cup water

¾ teaspoon fine sea salt

½ bunch cilantro, bottom 4 inches of stems discarded

1½ pounds boneless, skinless chicken thighs

1½ cups drained cooked white beans or pinto beans (page 44), or one 15-ounce can white beans or pinto beans, rinsed and drained

Warmed corn tortillas or cooked brown rice (page 50) or cauliflower rice, for serving

PREP	5 MINUTES
COOK	45 MINUTES
PR	20 MINUTES NPR
SERVES	6

1 Select the high **Sauté** setting on the Instant Pot and heat the oil for 2 minutes. Add the onion, garlic, and serrano and jalapeño chiles and sauté for about 5 minutes, until the onion softens and begins to brown. Add the tomatillos, water, and salt and stir to combine.

2 Secure the lid and set the Pressure Release to **Sealing**. Press the **Cancel** button to reset the cooking program, then select the **Pressure Cook** or **Manual** setting and set the cooking time for 5 minutes at high pressure. (The pot will take about 5 minutes to come up to pressure before the cooking program begins.)

3 When the cooking program ends, let the pressure release naturally for at least 10 minutes, then move the Pressure Release to **Venting** to release any remaining steam. Open the pot and add the cilantro. Wearing heatproof mitts, lift the inner pot out of the Instant Pot and transfer it to a trivet on the counter. Using an immersion blender, puree the mixture until smooth, tilting the pot so the head of the blender is submerged. Return the inner pot to the housing.

4 Add the chicken and white beans to the Instant Pot and stir to combine. Secure the lid and set the Pressure Release to **Sealing**. Press the **Cancel** button to reset the cooking program, then select the **Pressure Cook** or **Manual** setting and set the cooking time for 15 minutes at high pressure. (The pot will take about 10 minutes to come up to pressure before the cooking program begins.)

5 When the cooking program ends, let the pressure release naturally for at least 10 minutes, then move the Pressure Release to **Venting** to release any remaining steam. Open the pot and, using two forks, shred the chicken into bite-size pieces.

6 Ladle the chili into bowls and serve hot, with the tortillas on the side.

Nutrition Information

Per serving: 250 calories, 11 grams fat, 19 grams carbohydrates, 7 grams fiber, 26 grams protein

Great on its own, over rice, or with cornbread, this chili of tender tri-tip bites and a colorful mix of black beans, tomatoes, and corn is a healthy one-bowl meal. Don't skip offering the toppings of onion, cilantro, and tortilla chips, as they deliver both flavor and crunch. If spicy chili is not your thing, omit the cayenne.

TRI-TIP AND BEAN CHILI

- 1½ tablespoons extra-virgin olive oil
- 4 garlic cloves, minced
- 1 large yellow onion, diced, plus more for serving
- 1 red bell pepper, seeded and diced
- 2 jalapeño chiles, seeded and diced
- 2 pounds tri-tip steak or roast, cut into ¾-inch cubes
- ¼ cup chili powder
- 1 tablespoon ground cumin
- 1 tablespoon ground coriander
- 2 teaspoons dried oregano
- ½ teaspoon cayenne pepper
- 1 teaspoon fine sea salt
- 2 cups low-sodium roasted beef bone broth (page 260)
- 1½ cup drained cooked black beans (page 44), or one 15-ounce can black beans, rinsed and drained
- One 14½-ounce can petite diced tomatoes and their liquid
- 2 cups frozen corn, thawed
- Chopped fresh cilantro, for serving
- Tortilla chips, for serving
- Hot sauce (such as Cholula or Tapatío), for serving

1 Select the **Sauté** setting on the Instant Pot and heat the oil and garlic for 2 minutes, until the garlic is bubbling but not browned. Add the onion, bell pepper, and jalapeños and sauté for about 4 minutes, until the onion begins to soften. Add the tri-tip and sauté for about 3 minutes, until the meat is mostly opaque on the outside (it does not have to be cooked through). Add the chili powder, cumin, coriander, oregano, cayenne, and salt and sauté for 1 more minute. Pour in the broth and stir to combine, using a wooden spoon or spatula to nudge any browned bits from the bottom of the pot. Pour the beans, tomatoes, and corn on top in even layers. Do not stir them in.

2 Secure the lid and set the Pressure Release to **Sealing**. Press the **Cancel** button to reset the cooking program, then select the **Pressure Cook** or **Manual** setting and set the cooking time for 20 minutes at high pressure. (The pot will take about 15 minutes to come up to pressure before the cooking program begins.)

3 When the cooking program ends, let the pressure release naturally for at least 20 minutes, then move the Pressure Release to **Venting** to release any remaining steam. Open the pot and stir the chili.

4 Ladle the chili into bowls and serve piping hot, with the onion, cilantro, tortilla chips, and hot sauce on the side.

Note: If you prefer a thicker chili, simmer and reduce it for 15 minutes on the **Sauté** setting after cooking. Do not stir it while it is simmering, and let it stand for 5 minutes after the program finishes to avoid sputtering.

PREP	0 MINUTES
COOK	45 MINUTES
PR	20 MINUTES NPR
SERVES	8

Nutrition Information

Per serving (without toppings): 324 calories, 10 grams fat, 24 grams carbohydrates, 6 grams fiber, 28 grams protein

4

Vegetarian

This fast and fresh lunch dish was inspired by my friend Lizzie, who makes a version of these sandwiches all the time. Serve the sandwiches open-faced with Greek Lentil Soup (page 84) alongside for a filling, vegetarian meal. Or for a lighter spin, leave out the bread and spoon the salad onto leaves of endive or romaine lettuce.

AVOCADO EGG SALAD SANDWICHES

6 large eggs

1 avocado, pitted and peeled

2 green onions, white and green parts, chopped

1 tablespoon fresh lemon juice

1 teaspoon Dijon mustard

¼ teaspoon fine sea salt

¼ teaspoon freshly ground black pepper, plus more for finishing

4 slices whole-grain or gluten-free bread, toasted

2 radishes, thinly sliced

2 tablespoons chopped fresh chives or cilantro

4 lemon wedges, for finishing

Flaky sea salt, for finishing

PREP	5 MINUTES
COOK	10 MINUTES
PR	5 MINUTES NPR
COOL	10 MINUTES
SERVES	4

1 Pour 1 cup water into the Instant Pot and place the wire metal steam rack, an egg rack, or a steamer basket into the pot. Gently place the eggs on the rack or in the basket, taking care not to crack them. Secure the lid and set the Pressure Release to **Sealing**. Select the **Steam** setting and set the cooking time for 5 minutes at high pressure. (The pot will take about 5 minutes to come up to pressure before the cooking program begins.)

2 While the eggs are cooking, prepare an ice bath.

3 When the cooking program ends, let the pressure release naturally for 5 minutes, then move the Pressure Release to **Venting** to release any remaining steam. Open the pot and, using tongs, transfer the eggs to the ice bath to cool for 10 minutes.

4 Peel the eggs, then cut them in half and tip the egg yolks into a medium bowl. Chop the whites and reserve.

5 Add the avocado to the egg yolks and, using a fork, mash them together until smooth. Add the green onions, lemon juice, mustard, fine sea salt, pepper, and chopped egg whites and stir to mix well.

6 Spoon one-fourth of the egg salad onto each bread slice and spread it in an even layer. Top with the radishes and chives. Finish each sandwich with a squeeze of lemon juice, a pinch of flaky salt, and a grind or two of black pepper. Serve right away.

Note: For a portable, closed sandwich, use whole-grain sandwich thins or English muffins.

Nutrition Information

Per serving (salad only): 169 calories, 13 grams fat, 5 grams carbohydrates, 3 grams fiber, 10 grams protein

Seitan-based sausages are vegan, and high in protein, with a satisfyingly chewy texture nearly everyone will like. Crisp up whole sausages in a skillet with a little olive oil and serve them in buns with grainy mustard, or slice them and add them to a pasta, paella, or bean dish. They're inspired by Spanish chorizo, which has a milder and more versatile flavor profile than the more heavily spiced Mexican chorizo. You can use them in place of andouille, kielbasa, or any smoky, spicy sausage.

SEITAN CHICKPEA CHORIZO SAUSAGES

¾ cup drained cooked chickpeas (page 44), or one-half 15-ounce can chickpeas, rinsed and drained

2 tablespoons nutritional yeast

1 tablespoon extra-virgin olive oil

1 tablespoon tomato paste

1 teaspoon smoked paprika

½ teaspoon red pepper flakes

¾ teaspoon fine sea salt

½ teaspoon freshly ground black pepper

1 cup vital wheat gluten

¾ cup low-sodium vegetable broth (page 261)

PREP	10 MINUTES
COOK	25 MINUTES
PR	10 MINUTES NPR
MAKES	4 SAUSAGES

1 In a food processor, combine the chickpeas, nutritional yeast, oil, tomato paste, paprika, red pepper flakes, salt, and black pepper. Process using about ten 1-second pulses, until the mixture is fairly smooth, stopping to scrape down the sides as needed. Add the wheat gluten and broth and pulse about fifteen more times, until a ball of dough forms.

2 Turn the dough out onto a work surface and divide it into four equal pieces. Roll one piece into a 6-inch-long log and place it on top of an 8-inch square of parchment paper. Roll up the log in the parchment and tie the ends with kitchen twine. Repeat with the remaining dough to make three more sausages.

3 Pour 1 cup water into the Instant Pot and place the wire metal steam rack into the pot. Place the sausages in a single layer on the rack. Secure the lid and set the Pressure Release to **Sealing**. Select the **Steam** setting and set the cooking time for 20 minutes at high pressure. (The pot will take about 5 minutes to come up to pressure before the cooking program begins.)

4 When the cooking program ends, let the pressure release naturally for 10 minutes, then move the Pressure Release to **Venting** to release any remaining steam. Open the pot and, wearing heat-resistant mitts, grasp the handles of the steam rack and lift the sausages out of the pot. Let the sausages cool to room temperature.

5 Unwrap the cooled sausages and use them right away, or store them in an airtight container in the refrigerator for up to 4 days or in the freezer for up to 3 months.

Nutrition Information

Per sausage link: 315 calories, 5 grams fat, 39 grams carbohydrates, 1 gram fiber, 27 grams protein

Falafel is traditionally deep-fried, but here I pressure-cook the chickpeas, then sauté them in a falafel-inspired mix of spices for a much healthier result. The chickpeas come out of the skillet a little crisp, a little chewy, and totally delicious when tucked into pita pockets full of vegetables and creamy tahini dressing. Top the chickpeas with whatever spicy condiment you like best. My favorites are Moroccan *harissa* (a complex, dark red spice paste) Middle Eastern *zhoug* (a piquant, bright green cilantro-chile blend), and Indonesian *sambal oelek* (aka chile paste).

FALAFEL-SPICED CHICKPEA PITA POCKETS

1 cup dried chickpeas
4 cups water
1 teaspoon fine sea salt
1 tablespoon extra-virgin olive oil
½ teaspoon cumin
½ teaspoon coriander
½ teaspoon onion powder
¼ teaspoon garlic powder
¼ teaspoon fine sea salt
¼ teaspoon freshly ground black pepper
4 Persian cucumbers, sliced
1 head romaine lettuce, shredded
2 tomatoes, thinly sliced
½ small red onion, thinly sliced
6 whole-wheat pitas, warmed and split
¾ cup tahini dressing (page 262), for serving
Harissa, zhoug, or sambal oelek, for serving (optional)

SOAK	10 TO 12 HOURS
PREP	10 MINUTES
COOK	35 MINUTES
PR	15 MINUTES NPR
SERVES	6

1 Combine the chickpeas, water, and salt in the Instant Pot and stir to dissolve the salt. Secure the lid and set the Pressure Release to **Sealing**. Select the **Bean/Chili**, **Pressure Cook**, or **Manual** and set the cooking time for 15 minutes at high pressure. Next, select the **Timer** or **Delay** function and set the time delay for 10 to 12 hours. (When the soaking time is complete, the pot will take about 10 minutes to come up to pressure before the cooking program begins.)

2 When the cooking program ends, let the pressure release for at least 15 minutes, then move the Pressure Release to **Venting** to release any remaining steam. Open the pot and, wearing heat-resistant mitts, lift out the inner pot and drain the chickpeas in a colander, then transfer them to a medium bowl.

3 Add 1½ teaspoons of the oil, the cumin, coriander, onion powder, garlic powder, salt, and pepper and toss to coat the chickpeas evenly with the oil and spices.

4 Heat the remaining 1½ teaspoons oil in a skillet over medium-high heat. Add the chickpeas and sauté for 8 to 10 minutes, until the chickpeas are slightly browned and the spices are aromatic and toasted but not burned. Remove from the heat.

5 Tuck the cucumbers, lettuce, tomatoes, and onion into the pitas, then spoon ½ cup of the warm chickpeas into each pocket. Drizzle each filled pita with 2 tablespoons tahini dressing and with hot sauce to taste. Serve the pita pockets while the chickpeas are warm.

Nutrition Information

Per serving (pita, vegetables, chickpeas, and tahini sauce): 363 calories, 15 grams fat, 58 grams carbohydrates, 18 grams fiber, 14 grams protein

Korma is an Indian stew of vegetables swimming in a creamy, tomato-based sauce. This vegan version is heavy on the vegetables, with a sauce that's rich but not overly so. Guaranteed to satisfy vegans, vegetarians, and omnivores alike, it pairs perfectly with rice or naan for a traditional accompaniment or with cauliflower rice for a healthier alternative.

MIXED-VEGETABLE KORMA

- 1 tablespoon cold-pressed avocado oil
- ½ cup raw whole cashews
- 1 red onion, diced
- 3 garlic cloves, minced
- 1-inch piece fresh ginger, peeled and minced
- ½ cup water
- 1 teaspoon fine sea salt
- One 14½ ounce can diced tomatoes and their liquid
- 2 carrots, sliced on the diagonal
- 1 red bell pepper, seeded and cut into 1-inch pieces
- 8 ounces broccoli crowns, cut into 1-inch florets
- 8 ounces green beans, trimmed and cut into 1-inch pieces
- 1 medium zucchini, halved lengthwise and sliced
- 1 cup frozen peas, thawed
- 1 cup frozen corn, thawed
- ½ cup coconut cream
- 2 teaspoons garam masala
- ⅛ teaspoon cayenne pepper
- 2 tablespoons golden raisins
- 2 tablespoons chopped fresh cilantro
- Cooked rice or cauliflower rice or naan, for serving

1 Select the **Sauté** setting on the Instant Pot and heat the oil for 2 minutes. Add the cashews and sauté for about 3 minutes, until lightly toasted. Scoop out half of the cashews and set them aside for garnish. Add the onion, garlic, and ginger to the pot and sauté for about 3 minutes, until the onion is beginning to soften. Add the water and salt, using a wooden spoon or spatula to nudge any browned bits from the bottom of the pot. Pour in the tomatoes and their liquid. Do not stir them in.

2 Secure the lid and set the Pressure Release to **Sealing**. Press the **Cancel** button to reset the cooking program, then select the **Pressure Cook** or **Manual** setting and set the cooking time for 5 minutes at high pressure. (The pot will take about 10 minutes to come up to pressure before the cooking program begins.)

3 When the cooking program ends, perform a quick pressure release by moving the Pressure Release to **Venting**, or let the pressure release naturally (this will take about 20 minutes). Open the pot and, wearing heat-resistant mitts, lift out the inner pot. Transfer the mixture to a blender. Blend the mixture at high speed for about 1 minute, until smooth and creamy. Set aside. Rinse out the inner pot and return it to the Instant Pot housing.

4 Pour 1 cup of water into the Instant Pot and place a steamer basket into the pot. Add the carrots, bell pepper, broccoli, green beans, and zucchini to the steamer basket. Press the **Cancel** button to reset the cooking program, then select the **Steam** setting and set the cooking time for 1 minute at low pressure. (The pot will take about 10 minutes to come up to pressure before the cooking program begins.)

5 When the cooking program ends, perform a quick pressure release by moving the Pressure Release to **Venting**. Open the pot and, wearing heat-resistant mitts, lift out the steamer basket and pour the steamed

Nutrition Information

Per serving (stew only): 178 calories, 8 grams fat, 23 grams carbohydrates, 5 grams fiber, 5 grams protein

PREP	5 MINUTES
COOK	35 MINUTES
PR	QPR OR NPR
SERVES	8

vegetables into the pot with their steaming liquid. Add the thawed peas and corn, the blended sauce, coconut cream, garam masala, and cayenne to the pot and stir to combine. Press the **Cancel** button to reset the cooking program, then select the **Sauté** setting. Stir the mixture together and bring to a simmer for 1 minute, then press the **Cancel** button to turn off the pot.

6 Transfer the korma to a serving bowl. Garnish with the reserved cashews, the raisins, and the cilantro. Serve warm with rice.

Note: If you made the korma sauce ahead of time and are cooking the vegetables in a cold pot, reduce the steaming time to 0 (zero) minutes.

Jackfruit takes the place of pulled pork or beef in this vegan bowl, and it cooks at the same time as the rice in the Instant Pot. The Alabama sauce, which takes just a minute to make in a blender, is a cashew-based take on the classic southern condiment that's usually made with mayonnaise, and it's every bit as tangy and delicious as the original. Serve some of the sauce on these bowls and enjoy the rest spread onto sandwiches, drizzled on top of grilled sausages, or as a vegetable and chip dip.

BBQ JACKFRUIT BOWLS WITH ALABAMA SAUCE

Alabama Sauce

1 cup raw whole cashews, soaked in water to cover for 2 hours and drained

½ cup water

2 tablespoons raw cider vinegar

1 tablespoon prepared white horseradish

½ teaspoon fine sea salt

½ teaspoon freshly ground black pepper

½ teaspoon garlic powder

⅛ teaspoon cayenne pepper

Rice and Jackfruit

1 cup Minute brand quick-cooking brown rice

1¾ cups water

¾ teaspoon fine sea salt

Two 20-ounce cans green jackfruit, packed in brine

1 tablespoon cold-pressed avocado oil

3 garlic cloves, minced

1 yellow onion, sliced

1 tablespoon chili powder

½ teaspoon freshly ground black pepper

1 To make the Alabama sauce: In a blender or mini blender, combine the cashews, water, vinegar, horseradish, salt, black pepper, garlic powder, and cayenne. Blend on high speed for about 1 minute, until very smooth. Transfer to an airtight container and store in the refrigerator for up to 1 week. If the dip becomes too thick, add a splash of water and stir.

2 To make the rice and jackfruit: Combine the rice, 1 cup of the water, and ¼ teaspoon of the salt in a 1½-quart stainless-steel bowl and stir to dissolve the salt.

3 Place the jackfruit into a colander and rinse under cold running water. Drain well, then transfer to a cutting board. Cut off and chop up the tougher cores and seeds from the jackfruit pieces, then use your hands to pull the stringy parts of the jackfruit into thin shreds.

4 Select the **Sauté** setting on the Instant Pot and heat the oil and garlic for 2 minutes, until the garlic is bubbling but not browned. Add the onion and sauté for about 5 minutes, until it has softened and is just beginning to brown. Add the chili powder, black pepper, the remaining ½ teaspoon salt, and the remaining ¾ cup water and, using a wooden spoon or spatula, nudge any browned bits from the bottom of the pot. Stir in the jackfruit.

5 Place a tall steam rack into the pot, making sure all of its legs are resting firmly on the bottom. Place the bowl of rice on the rack. (The bowl should not touch the lid once the pot is closed.)

Nutrition Information

Per serving: 438 calories, 16 grams fat, 77 grams carbohydrates, 13 grams fiber, 10 grams protein

1½ cups frozen corn, thawed

⅓ cup barbecue sauce of choice (I like Stubb's brand Original or Spicy)

1 head romaine lettuce, shredded

½ small head red cabbage, shredded

Pickle slices, homemade (page 264) or store-bought, for serving

1 tablespoon chopped fresh flat-leaf parsley, for serving

PREP	10 MINUTES
COOK	30 MINUTES
PR	10 MINUTES NPR
SERVES	4

6 Secure the lid and set the Pressure Release to **Sealing**. Press the **Cancel** button to reset the cooking program, then select the **Pressure Cook** or **Manual** setting and set the cooking time for 10 minutes at high pressure. (The pot will take about 10 minutes to come up to pressure before the cooking program begins.)

7 When the cooking program ends, let the pressure release naturally for at least 10 minutes, then move the Pressure Release to **Venting** to release any remaining steam. Open the pot and, wearing heat-resistant mitts, remove the bowl of rice and then remove the rack. Use a fork to fluff the rice and fold in the corn.

8 Press the **Cancel** button to reset the cooking program, then select the **Sauté** setting. Add the barbecue sauce to the jackfruit mixture and stir to combine. Let simmer, stirring occasionally, for about 5 minutes, until slightly thickened. Press the **Cancel** button to turn off the pot.

9 To serve, divide the lettuce and cabbage evenly among four bowls and spoon the rice and jackfruit on top. Top each serving with a few pickle slices and 2 tablespoons Alabama sauce and sprinkle with the parsley. Serve right away.

This is a vegan spin on Joe's Special, one of my favorite dinners when I was growing up. It was served at Original Joe's restaurant in San Francisco and was a jumble of sautéed ground beef, scrambled eggs, spinach, and Parmesan cheese. In this plant-based remake, crumbled tofu takes the place of the scrambled eggs and cremini mushrooms stand in for the ground beef. It's cooked entirely on the Sauté setting in under 20 minutes, perfect for nights when you need to whip up dinner on the fly. Warm slices of toasted sourdough bread are a mandatory accompaniment.

JOSEPHINE'S SPECIAL

3 tablespoons nutritional yeast

½ teaspoon Italian seasoning

½ teaspoon ground turmeric

¼ teaspoon ground cumin

¼ teaspoon freshly ground black pepper

⅛ teaspoon ground nutmeg

1 tablespoon fresh lemon juice

1 teaspoon vegan Worcestershire sauce

½ teaspoon Tabasco sauce

2 tablespoons extra-virgin olive oil

4 garlic cloves, minced

1 yellow onion, diced

8 ounces cremini mushrooms, sliced

1 teaspoon fine sea salt

One 14-ounce block firm tofu, drained and crumbled

One 6-ounce bag baby spinach

Vegan Parmesan Cheese (page 265), for serving

Whole-wheat sourdough bread, toasted, for serving

PREP	5 MINUTES
COOK	20 MINUTES
PR	N/A
SERVES	4

1 In a small bowl, stir together the nutritional yeast, Italian seasoning, turmeric, cumin, pepper, and nutmeg. In another small bowl, stir together the lemon juice, Worcestershire, and Tabasco. Set both bowls near the Instant Pot.

2 Select the **Sauté** setting on the Instant Pot and heat the oil and garlic for 2 minutes, until the garlic is bubbling but not browned. Add the onion and sauté for about 3 minutes, until it begins to soften. Add the mushrooms and salt and sauté for about 6 minutes, until the mushrooms have wilted and given up their liquid. Stir in the tofu and the nutritional yeast mixture and sauté for about 5 more minutes, until the tofu is warmed through and beginning to brown on the bottom of the pot.

3 Add the lemon juice mixture and use a wooden spoon or spatula to nudge any browned bits from the bottom of the pot. Add the spinach and sauté for about 2 minutes, until wilted. Press the **Cancel** button to turn off the pot.

4 Spoon onto plates and sprinkle with the vegan Parmesan. Serve right away, with the toasted sourdough on the side.

Nutrition Information

Per serving: 208 calories, 12 grams fat, 14 grams carbohydrates, 6 grams fiber, 14 grams protein

Rather than using the masa harina called for in traditional tamale recipes, most tamale casseroles (including this one) are made with a topping of American-style cornbread. Here, a filling of seitan sausages, beans, and vegetables rests underneath jalapeño cornbread. If you want to gild the lily, add a topping of shredded cheese and a spoonful of sour cream.

TAMALE CASSEROLE

¾ cup cornmeal

⅓ cup gluten-free flour blend

1 teaspoon baking powder

½ teaspoon fine sea salt

1 large egg

1 tablespoon honey or agave nectar

2 tablespoons unsalted butter or vegan buttery spread, melted

½ cup buttermilk or unsweetened nondairy milk

1 jalapeño chile, seeded and diced (optional)

⅔ cup salsa picante, homemade (page 262) or store-bought

2 Seitan Chickpea Chorizo Sausages (page 104) or other vegetarian sausage links, sliced

1 zucchini, cut into small dice

1 cup drained cooked black beans (page 44), or two-thirds 15-ounce can black beans, rinsed and drained or canned

1 cup frozen corn kernels, thawed

1 teaspoon chili powder

½ cup shredded Cheddar cheese or vegan cheese shreds (optional)

Lime wedges, for serving

PREP	15 MINUTES
COOK	1 HOUR 5 MINUTES
PR	10 MINUTES NPR
REST	5 MINUTES
SERVES	4

1 Grease a 7-cup round heatproof glass dish with butter or vegan buttery spread.

2 In a medium bowl, whisk together the cornmeal, flour, baking powder, and salt. Make a well in the center of the dry ingredients and add the egg, honey, butter, buttermilk, and jalapeño. Whisk the wet ingredients together until there are no streaks of egg yolk, then stir in the dry ingredients from the sides of the bowl, just until they are fully incorporated.

3 In another medium bowl, stir together the salsa, sausages, zucchini, beans, corn, and chili powder. Pour the mixture into the prepared dish. Pour the cornmeal batter on top of the sausage mixture and use a rubber spatula to spread it in an even layer. Cover the dish tightly with aluminum foil and place it on a long-handled silicone steam rack.

4 Pour 1 cup water into the Instant Pot. Holding the handles of the steam rack, lower the dish into the pot.

5 Secure the lid and set the Pressure Release to **Sealing**. Select the **Pressure Cook** or **Manual** setting and set the cooking time for 55 minutes at high pressure. (The pot will take about 10 minutes to come up to pressure before the cooking program begins.)

6 When the cooking program ends, let the pressure release naturally for 10 minutes, then move the Pressure Release to **Venting** to release any remaining steam. Open the pot and, wearing heat-resistant mitts, grasp the handles of the steam rack, lift the dish out of the pot, and set the dish on a cooling rack. Uncover the casserole, taking care not to get burned by the steam or to drip condensation onto the surface. Sprinkle the cheese on top, if using, and let sit for 5 minutes to melt.

7 Using a serving spoon, scoop the casserole onto plates. Serve hot, with the lime wedges on the side.

Nutrition Information

Per serving (without cheese or sour cream): 440 calories, 11 grams fat, 67 grams carbohydrates, 9 grams fiber, 20 grams protein

These hearty, high-protein patties made from beans and wheat gluten are toothsome and boast a wealth of B vitamins and iron. They're cooked right in a savory mushroom sauce for an easy, one-pot vegan main dish. Serve them over spiralized vegetable noodles for a light dinner or over whole-grain noodles for a more substantial meal.

VEGAN SALISBURY STEAK

Seitan Steaks

- ¾ cup drained cooked white beans (page 44), or one-half 15-ounce can white beans, rinsed and drained
- 2 tablespoons nutritional yeast
- 2 tablespoons extra-virgin olive oil
- 1 tablespoon tomato paste
- ½ teaspoon garlic powder
- ¾ teaspoon fine sea salt
- ½ teaspoon freshly ground black pepper
- 1 cup vital wheat gluten
- ¾ cup low-sodium vegetable broth (page 261)

Mushroom Sauce

- 1 tablespoon extra-virgin olive oil
- 1 small yellow onion, sliced
- 1 garlic clove, chopped
- 8 ounces cremini mushrooms, sliced
- ½ teaspoon fine sea salt
- 2 tablespoons tomato paste
- 1½ teaspoons yellow mustard
- 2 cups low-sodium vegetable broth (page 261)
- 2 teaspoons cornstarch

- 2 tablespoons chopped fresh flat-leaf parsley (optional)
- Cooked whole-grain noodles or spiralized vegetable noodles, for serving

1 To make the seitan steaks: In a food processor, combine the beans, nutritional yeast, 1 tablespoon of the oil, the tomato paste, garlic powder, salt, and pepper. Process using about ten 1-second pulses, until the mixture is fairly smooth, stopping to scrape down the sides as needed. Add the wheat gluten and broth and pulse about fifteen more times, until a ball of dough forms.

2 Turn the dough out onto a work surface and divide it into four equal pieces. Place one piece of the dough between two squares of parchment paper and, using a rolling pin, roll it out into an oval about ½ inch thick. Repeat with the remaining dough to make three more patties.

3 Heat the remaining 1 tablespoon oil in a large nonstick skillet over medium heat. Add the patties to the skillet and sear about for 3 minutes, until browned, then flip them over and sear for 3 minutes on the second side. Remove from the heat.

4 To make the sauce: Select the **Sauté** setting on the Instant Pot and heat the oil for 2 minutes. Add the onion and garlic and sauté for about 3 minutes, until the onion begins to soften. Add the mushrooms and salt and sauté for 6 more minutes, until the mushrooms have wilted and given up their liquid.

5 Add the tomato paste, mustard, and 1½ cups of the broth and stir with a wooden spoon or spatula, nudging any browned bits from the bottom of the pot. Add the seitan patties to the pot in a single layer, spooning a bit of the sauce over each one.

6 Secure the lid and set the Pressure Release to **Sealing**. Press the **Cancel** button to reset the cooking program, then select the **Pressure Cook** or **Manual** setting and set the cooking time for 20 minutes at high pressure. (The pot will take about 5 minutes to come up to pressure before the cooking program begins.)

Nutrition Information

Per serving: 302 calories, 12 grams fat, 22 grams carbohydrates, 5 grams fiber, 28 grams protein

PREP	10 MINUTES
COOK	45 MINUTES
PR	10 MINUTES NPR
SERVES	4

7 When the cooking program ends, let the pressure release naturally for 10 minutes, then move the Pressure Release to **Venting** to release any remaining steam. Open the pot and, using a slotted spatula, transfer the patties to a serving plate.

8 Press the **Cancel** button to reset the cooking program, then select the **Sauté** setting. In a small bowl, stir together the cornstarch and the remaining ½ cup vegetable broth. When the sauce comes to a simmer, stir in the cornstarch mixture and let it boil for 1 minute, until the sauce has thickened, then press the **Cancel** button to turn off the pot.

9 Spoon the sauce over the patties and sprinkle with the parsley. Serve hot, with the noodles on the side.

Instead of spending time carefully scooping out potato skins, go the easy route and steam a big batch of potatoes in the Instant Pot, mash them up skins and all, and then transform them into this hot and cheesy casserole. There's just enough cheese and butter to make these potatoes feel like a treat without going totally overboard in the calorie department. Greek yogurt takes the place of sour cream, adding tanginess and a few extra grams of protein. Look to the recipe note for vegan substitutions.

CHEESY LOADED POTATO CASSEROLE

4 pounds russet potatoes

4 green onions, white and green, thinly sliced, plus 1 green onion, green part only, thinly sliced, for garnish

1 tablespoon unsalted butter

1 cup plain 2 percent Greek yogurt, homemade (page 34) or store-bought

1 cup 2 percent milk

1 cup shredded Cheddar cheese

1 teaspoon fine sea salt

½ teaspoon garlic powder

¼ teaspoon ground black pepper

½ teaspoon sweet paprika

PREP	10 MINUTES
COOK	1 HOUR
PR	QPR
COOL	5 MINUTES
SERVES	8

1 Pour 1 cup water into the Instant Pot and place the wire metal steam rack into the pot. Place the potatoes on the rack in as even a layer as possible.

2 Secure the lid and set the Pressure Release to **Sealing**. Select the **Steam** setting and set the cooking time for 15 minutes at high pressure. (The pot will take about 10 minutes to come up to pressure before the cooking program begins.)

3 While the potatoes are cooking, preheat the oven to 400°F. Lightly grease an 8-inch square baking dish with butter or nonstick cooking spray.

4 When the cooking program ends, perform a quick pressure release by moving the pressure release to **Venting**. Open the pot and, using tongs, transfer the potatoes to a cutting board and let cool for about 5 minutes, until comfortable to handle.

5 Peel the potatoes and transfer them to a large bowl. Chop up the skins and add them and the green onions to the bowl. Using a potato masher, mash the potatoes until fairly smooth. Add the butter, yogurt, milk, ½ cup of the cheese, the salt, garlic powder, and pepper and stir just until combined.

6 Spoon the potatoes into the baking dish. Sprinkle the paprika and the remaining ½ cup cheese on top. Cover the dish with aluminum foil.

Nutrition Information

Per serving: 243 calories, 7 grams fat, 34 grams carbohydrates, 3 grams fiber, 11 grams protein

7 Bake the potatoes for 20 minutes, then uncover and bake for about 15 more minutes, until the casserole is heated through and the cheese on top is bubbling and lightly browned. Remove from the oven and sprinkle with the green onion.

8 Using a serving spoon, scoop the potatoes out onto plates and serve hot.

A perfect holiday dish for vegans, vegetarians, and adventurous omnivores, this brown rice pilaf is laced with garlic and vegetables and topped with lightly browned, toothsome Soy Curls. The Soy Curls soak up a poultry seasoning blend and brown in a skillet while the rice and vegetables cook in the Instant Pot, so the dish comes together quickly. It can also be easily doubled if you're expecting a crowd.

"CHICK'N" AND BROWN RICE PILAF

Spice Blend

- 2 teaspoons poultry seasoning
- 1 teaspoon sweet paprika
- 1 teaspoon onion powder
- 1 teaspoon nutritional yeast
- 1 teaspoon fine sea salt
- ½ teaspoon garlic powder
- ½ teaspoon ground black pepper

Brown Rice Pilaf

- 2 tablespoons vegan buttery spread
- 2 garlic cloves, minced
- 1 yellow onion, diced
- 2 carrots, diced
- 2 celery stalks, diced
- 1 cup medium-grain brown rice
- 1½ cups low-sodium vegetable broth (page 261)

- 4 ounces Butler Soy Curls (see page 13)
- 2 cups boiling water
- Chopped fresh flat-leaf parsley, for serving

PREP	0 MINUTES
COOK	45 MINUTES
SOAK	10 MINUTES
PR	10 MINUTES NPR
SERVES	4

1 To make the spice blend: In a small bowl, stir together the poultry seasoning, paprika, onion powder, nutritional yeast, salt, garlic powder, and pepper. Set the bowl near the Instant Pot.

2 To make the rice pilaf: Select the **Sauté** setting on the Instant Pot and heat 1 tablespoon of the buttery spread and the garlic for 2 minutes, until the garlic is bubbling but not browned. Add the onion, carrots, and celery and sauté for about 4 minutes, until the onion begins to soften. Add half of the spice blend and sauté for 1 more minute. Add the rice and broth and stir to combine, using a wooden spoon or spatula to nudge any browned bits from the bottom of the pot.

3 Secure the lid and set the Pressure Release to **Sealing**. Press the **Cancel** button to reset the cooking program, then select the **Pressure Cook** or **Manual** setting and set the cooking time for 25 minutes at high pressure. (The pot will take about 5 minutes to come up to pressure before the cooking program begins.)

4 While the rice and vegetables are cooking, prepare the Soy Curls: Put the Soy Curls into a medium heatproof bowl, pour in the boiling water, and stir to combine. Let the curls soak for 10 minutes. Drain the curls in a colander, pushing out any excess liquid with the back of a spoon.

5 Heat the remaining 1 tablespoon buttery spread in a skillet over medium heat. Add the Soy Curls and sauté for about 10 minutes, until lightly browned. Remove from the heat.

6 When the cooking program ends, let the pressure release naturally for 10 minutes, then move the Pressure Release to **Venting** to release any remaining steam.

7 Open the pot and spoon the rice and vegetables into serving bowls. Top with the Soy Curls and parsley and serve warm.

Nutrition Information

Per serving: 346 calories, 12 grams fat, 47 grams carbohydrates, 6 grams fiber, 14 grams protein

This simple, nutritious dish of greens and beans makes a good side or main dish. Serve it with a protein for dinner, then spoon the leftovers over rice for lunch the next day. Dark blue-green Lacinato kale, aka Tuscan or dinosaur kale, is a good source of vitamin A and phytonutrients. For a touch of richness, top this dish with a dollop of plain yogurt or Cashew Sour Cream.

BLACK-EYED PEAS AND KALE

8 ounces (1 cup plus 2 tablespoons) dried black-eyed peas

6 cups water

2 teaspoons fine sea salt

3 tablespoons extra-virgin olive oil, plus more for drizzling

4 garlic cloves, minced

1 yellow onion, diced

½ teaspoon red pepper flakes

1 pound Lacinato kale, stemmed and leaves chopped into 1-inch pieces

Lemon wedges, for serving

Plain 2 percent Greek yogurt, homemade (page 34) or store-bought, or Cashew Sour Cream (page 265), for serving

SOAK	10 TO 12 HOURS
PREP	0 MINUTES
COOK	35 MINUTES
PR	10 MINUTES NPR
SERVES	6

1 In a bowl, combine the black-eyed peas, 4 cups of the water, and 1 teaspoon of the salt and stir to dissolve the salt. Let soak for 10 to 12 hours, then drain in a colander.

2 Select the **Sauté** setting on the Instant Pot and heat the oil and garlic for 2 minutes, until the garlic is bubbling but not browned. Add the onion and sauté for about 4 minutes, until the onion has softened. Add the red pepper flakes and the remaining 1 teaspoon salt and sauté for 1 more minute. Stir in the kale and sauté for about 3 minutes, until fully wilted. Stir in the remaining 2 cups water and black-eyed peas, scraping down the sides of the pot to make sure the peas are submerged.

3 Secure the lid and set the Pressure Release to **Sealing**. Press the **Cancel** button to reset the cooking program, then select the **Pressure Cook** or **Manual** setting and set the cooking time for 15 minutes at high pressure. (The pot will take about 10 minutes to come up to pressure before the cooking program begins.)

4 When the cooking program ends, let the pressure release naturally for at least 10 minutes, then move the Pressure Release to **Venting** to release any remaining steam. Open the pot and give the mixture a stir.

5 Ladle onto plates and drizzle with oil. Serve warm, with the lemon wedges on the side.

Nutrition Information

Per serving: 183 calories, 7 grams fat, 29 grams carbohydrates, 10 grams fiber, 10 grams protein

In this healthy, filling Asian-inspired dish, whole-wheat pasta is cooked in the Instant Pot and then tossed in a creamy, spicy peanut sauce. The topping of crisp seared tofu adds not only wonderful texture but also plenty of protein, vitamins, and minerals.

SESAME PEANUT NOODLES WITH SEARED TOFU

2 tablespoons cold-pressed avocado oil

1 tablespoon toasted sesame oil

2 garlic cloves, minced

2 cups water

8 ounces whole-wheat penne or elbow pasta

½ teaspoon fine sea salt

One 14-ounce block extra-firm tofu, drained

2 tablespoons low-sodium soy sauce

2 tablespoons rice vinegar

2 teaspoons agave nectar or brown rice syrup

1½ tablespoons sambal oelek or Sriracha sauce

¼ cup all-natural creamy peanut butter

2 green onions, green part only, thinly sliced, for serving

1 teaspoon toasted sesame seeds, for serving

PREP	0 MINUTES
COOK	20 MINUTES
PR	5 MINUTES NPR
REST	3 MINUTES
SERVES	4

1 Select the **Sauté** setting on the Instant Pot and heat 1 tablespoon of the avocado oil, the sesame oil, and the garlic for 2 minutes, until the garlic is bubbling but not browned. Add the water, pasta, and ¼ teaspoon of the salt to the pot and stir to combine, using a wooden spoon or spatula to nudge the pasta under the water as much as possible.

2 Secure the lid and set the Pressure Release to **Sealing**. Press the **Cancel** button to reset the cooking program, then select the **Pressure Cook** or **Manual** setting and set the cooking time for 6 minutes at high pressure. (The pot will take about 5 minutes to come up to pressure before the cooking program begins.)

3 While the noodles are cooking, cut the tofu into ½-inch-thick slices. Sandwich the slices in a single layer between double layers of paper towels or a folded kitchen towel and press firmly to wick away as much moisture as possible. Cut the slices into ½-inch cubes and sprinkle with the remaining ¼ teaspoon salt.

4 Heat the remaining 1 tablespoon avocado oil in a large nonstick skillet over medium-high heat. Add the tofu in a single layer and sear for 6 minutes total, turning once halfway through cooking, until lightly browned on both sides. Remove from the heat.

5 When the cooking program ends, let the pressure release naturally for 5 minutes, then move the Pressure Release to **Venting** to release any remaining steam. Open the pot and add the soy sauce, vinegar, agave nectar, sambal oelek, and peanut butter and stir to combine, using the spoon or spatula to break up any clumps of noodles. Let rest for 3 minutes, then stir again.

6 Spoon the noodles into serving bowls. Top with the seared tofu, green onions, and sesame seeds and serve warm.

Nutrition Information

Per serving: 510 calories, 25 grams fat, 53 grams carbohydrates, 8 grams fiber, 21 grams protein

A bubbling, bright red soup packed with mushrooms and tofu is a staple in most Korean restaurants. This vegan version is full of savory and complex flavors thanks to *doenjang* (fermented bean paste), *gochujang* (spicy-sweet red pepper paste), *gochugaru* (red pepper flakes), and kimchi.

KOREAN HOT POT WITH TOFU AND MUSHROOMS

1 tablespoon cold-pressed avocado oil

1 tablespoon toasted sesame oil

6 garlic cloves, minced

2 tablespoons gochugaru

1 cup vegan kimchi (such as Eden or Mother in Law's brand), drained and chopped

6 ounces shiitake mushrooms, stemmed and thinly sliced

1½ tablespoons gochujang

2½ tablespoons doenjang

2½ cups water

One 14-ounce package silken tofu, drained

One 7-ounce package enoki mushrooms, trimmed

4 green onions, white and green parts, sliced ¼ inch thick

Cooked brown rice, for serving

PREP	0 MINUTES
COOK	25 MINUTES
PR	10 MINUTES NPR
REST	3 MINUTES
SERVES	4

1 Select the **Sauté** setting on the Instant Pot and heat the avocado and sesame oils for 2 minutes. Add the garlic and gochugaru and sauté for 1 minute, until aromatic. Add the kimchi and shiitake mushrooms and sauté for about 3 minutes, until the mushrooms are beginning to wilt. Add the gochujang and doenjang and stir to combine.

2 Pour in the water and use a wooden spatula to nudge any browned bits from the bottom of the pot. Add the tofu and use the spatula to break it into 1-inch pieces.

3 Secure the lid and set the Pressure Release to **Sealing**. Press the **Cancel** button to reset the cooking program, then select the **Pressure Cook** or **Manual** setting and set the cooking time for 5 minutes at low pressure. (The pot will take about 10 minutes to come up to pressure before the cooking program begins.)

4 When the cooking program ends, let the pressure release naturally for at least 10 minutes, then move the Pressure Release to **Venting** to release any remaining steam. Open the pot and add the enoki mushrooms and green onions on top, then use the spatula to push them down into the hot pot so they are covered with liquid. Press the **Cancel** button to reset the cooking program, then select the **Sauté** setting. Let the hot pot come to a boil (this will take a minute or two), then press the **Cancel** button to turn off the pot. Let rest for about 3 minutes, until the boiling stops and the mushrooms are just cooked through.

5 Ladle the hot pot into serving bowls and serve right away, with bowls of rice on the side.

Note: Do not substitute regular red pepper flakes for the Korean *gochugaru*. Korean red pepper is much less spicy.

Nutrition Information

Per serving: 239 calories, 13 grams fat, 16 grams carbohydrates, 6 grams fiber, 13 grams protein

Broccoli, asparagus, and snap peas are steamed in the Instant Pot, then folded into this green jambalaya. This leaves the vegetables tender-crisp and ensures the smoky, spicy flavor of the dish shines through. Serve it on its own, or top it with pan-seared tofu for added protein.

GARDEN PATCH JAMBALAYA

8 ounces broccoli florets, cut or broken into bite-size pieces

8 ounces asparagus, trimmed and cut into 1-inch lengths

8 ounces sugar snap peas, ends trimmed

2 tablespoons extra-virgin olive oil

2 garlic cloves, minced

1 yellow onion, diced

1 celery stalk, diced

1 green bell pepper, seeded and cut into 1 by ¼-inch strips

1 teaspoon dried oregano

½ teaspoon smoked paprika

½ teaspoon freshly ground black pepper

⅛ teaspoon cayenne pepper

1 teaspoon fine sea salt

2 cups low-sodium vegetable broth (page 261)

1½ cups long-grain brown rice

Hot sauce (such as Crystal or Tabasco), for serving

PREP	0 MINUTES
COOK	55 MINUTES
PR	QPR AND 10 MINUTES NPR
REST	3 MINUTES
SERVES	6

1 Pour 1 cup water into the Instant Pot and place a steamer basket into the pot. Add the broccoli, asparagus, and peas to the steamer basket.

2 Secure the lid and set the Pressure Release to **Sealing**. Select the **Steam** setting and set the cooking time for 0 (zero) minutes at low pressure. (The pot will take about 15 minutes to come up to pressure before the cooking program begins.)

3 When the cooking program ends, perform a quick release by moving the Pressure Release to **Venting**. Open the pot and, wearing heat-resistant mitts, lift out the steamer basket. Lift out the inner pot, pour out the water, and return the inner pot to the housing.

4 Press the **Cancel** button to reset the cooking program, then select the **Sauté** setting and heat the oil and garlic for about 3 minutes, until the garlic is bubbling and golden but not browned. Add the onion, celery, and bell pepper and sauté for about 4 minutes, until the onion begins to soften. Add the oregano, paprika, black pepper, cayenne, and salt and sauté for about 1 more minute. Stir in the broth. Then add the rice and stir, making sure all of the grains are submerged in the liquid.

5 Secure the lid and set the Pressure Release to **Sealing**. Press the **Cancel** button to reset the cooking program, then select the **Pressure Cook** or **Manual** setting and set the cooking time for 25 minutes at low pressure. (The pot will take about 5 minutes to come up to pressure before the cooking program begins.)

6 When the cooking program ends, let the pressure release naturally for 10 minutes, then move the Pressure Release to **Venting** to release any remaining steam. Open the pot and add the steamed vegetables, gently folding them into the rice mixture. Cover the pot and let rest for 3 minutes to allow the vegetables to warm through.

7 Open the pot once more. Spoon the jambalaya into bowls and serve immediately, with the hot sauce on the side.

Nutrition Information

Per serving: 241 calories, 6 grams fat, 42 grams carbohydrates, 6 grams fiber, 7 grams protein

Steamed squash is a great base for a healthy meal. Mash cooked butternut squash with a little butter or olive oil and serve it alongside chicken or pork chops. Top strands of spaghetti squash with marinara sauce (page 126) or arrabbiata sauce (page 70) for a low-calorie side dish, or toss with olive oil, salt, and pepper and pair with Greek Chicken Meatballs (page 155) instead of bread or pasta.

When you steam a whole squash in the Instant Pot, no peeling is required. You will need to cut it into quarters (or halves if it's quite small) and remove the seeds before cooking, but that's as far as the preparation goes.

STEAMED BUTTERNUT OR SPAGHETTI SQUASH

PREP	5 MINUTES
COOK	15 MINUTES
PR	QPR
COOL	5 MINUTES

1 Pour water into the Instant Pot, using 1 cup for a 3- or 6-quart pot or 1½ cups for an 8-quart pot. Place the wire metal steam rack into the pot.

2 Trim off the stem end of the squash, cut the squash into quarters, and scoop out and discard the seeds. Arrange the squash quarters in a single layer on the rack in the pot, nesting them if necessary.

3 Secure the lid and set the Pressure Release to **Sealing**. Select the **Steam** setting and set the cooking time for 7 minutes at high pressure. (The pot will take about 10 minutes to come up to pressure before the cooking program begins.)

4 When the cooking program ends, perform a quick pressure release by moving the Pressure Release to **Venting**. Open the pot and, using tongs, transfer the squash to a plate or cutting board and let cool for about 5 minutes, until cool enough to handle.

5 Use a spoon to scoop the flesh from the skin of the butternut squash, or use a fork to separate the strands of the spaghetti squash. Discard the skin. Use immediately, or let cool to room temperature, transfer to an airtight container, and refrigerate for up to 3 days.

Note: In a 6-quart pot, use a squash no larger than 3½ pounds; in a 3-quart pot, no larger than 1½ pounds; and in an 8-quart pot, no larger than 4½ pounds.

A light take on a classic pasta recipe, this dish functions as more of a side, with lots of nutritious vegetables per serving. If you like, you can add some sliced vegan sausages (page 104) to make it a full meal. If you don't have any vegan Parmesan cheese on hand, you can whip up a batch while the squash is steaming. Sprinkle it on this marinara-topped spaghetti squash for a totally plant-based plate and use the remainder on other Italian dishes.

SPAGHETTI SQUASH MARINARA WITH VEGAN PARMESAN CHEESE

3 tablespoons extra-virgin olive oil

3 garlic cloves, minced

One 28-ounce can whole San Marzano-style tomatoes and their liquid

2 teaspoons Italian seasoning

1 teaspoon fine sea salt

½ teaspoon red pepper flakes (optional)

One 3½-pound steamed spaghetti squash (page 125)

½ cup Vegan Parmesan Cheese, store-bought or homemade (page 265), for serving

Chopped fresh basil, for serving

PREP	10 MINUTES
COOK	30 MINUTES
PR	QPR
SERVES	8

1 Select the **Sauté** setting and heat the oil and garlic for about 2 minutes, until the garlic is bubbling but not browned. Add the tomatoes and their liquid and use a wooden spoon or spatula to crush the tomatoes against the side of the pot. Stir in the Italian seasoning, salt, and red pepper flakes (if using) and cook, stirring occasionally, for about 10 minutes, until the sauce has thickened a bit.

2 Press the **Cancel** button to turn off the pot. The sauce will continue to simmer and thicken for a couple of minutes as the pot cools down, and it will stay warm due to the residual heat.

3 Use a fork to separate the strands of the spaghetti squash and transfer to plates. Discard the skin. Ladle the sauce over the spaghetti squash. Sprinkle each portion with 1 tablespoon of the vegan Parmesan and a little basil and serve right away.

Nutrition Information

Per serving (spaghetti squash, marinara, and Parmesan): 168 calories, 9 grams fat, 19 grams carbohydrates, 4 grams fiber, 4 grams protein

5

Seafood

A handful of chopped tomatoes adds brightness to this pot of perfectly cooked mussels. High in good-for-you fats and in vitamin B_{12}, zinc, iron, and folic acid, mussels are a great addition to a healthy diet and look beautiful in a big serving bowl on the table. This recipe makes enough for a main course for two, accompanied with salad, or for a first course for four.

MUSSELS WITH TOMATOES AND WHITE WINE BROTH

1 tablespoon extra-virgin olive oil

1 tablespoon unsalted butter or extra-virgin olive oil

1 shallot, minced

3 garlic cloves, minced

¾ cup grape or cherry tomatoes, quartered

½ teaspoon dried thyme

¼ teaspoon fine sea salt

½ cup dry white wine

1 cup seafood or fish stock (see Notes)

2 pounds mussels in the shell, scrubbed clean

1 tablespoon chopped fresh flat-leaf parsley

Whole-wheat sourdough bread, toasted, for serving

PREP	0 MINUTES
COOK	20 MINUTES
PR	QPR
SERVES	2

1 Select the **Sauté** setting and heat the oil, butter, shallot, and garlic for about 4 minutes, until the butter is melted, the shallots are softened, and the garlic is bubbling but not browned. Add the cherry tomatoes, thyme, and salt and sauté for about 2 more minutes, until the tomatoes are slightly softened. Add the wine, bring to a simmer, and cook for about 3 minutes, until most of the wine has evaporated. Pour in the stock and bring to a simmer. Add the mussels to the pot, discarding any that do not close to the touch, and stir to coat them in the cooking liquid.

2 Secure the lid and set the pressure release to **Sealing**. Press the **Cancel** button to reset the cooking program, then select the **Pressure Cook** or **Manual** setting and set the cooking time for 2 minutes at low pressure. (The pot will take about 10 minutes to come up to pressure before the cooking program begins.)

3 When the cooking program ends, perform a quick release by moving the Pressure Release to **Venting**. Open the pot. Spoon the mussels into a large, shallow serving bowl, discarding any that failed to open. Pour the cooking liquid over the top.

4 Sprinkle with the parsley and serve right away, with the bread on the side for soaking up the cooking liquid.

Notes: My favorite seafood stock is Better Than Bouillon Lobster Base. For 1 cup, reconstitute 1 teaspoon of the base in 1 cup boiling water.

Most of the fat in this recipe comes from the butter and olive oil in the cooking liquid. If you eat the mussels and just a few spoonfuls of the liquid, you will have consumed far less fat and calories than are reflected in the nutrition data.

Nutrition Information

Per serving: 495 calories, 21 grams fat, 19 grams carbohydrates, 1 gram fiber, 44 grams protein

High in protein and relatively low in calories, shrimp are a good addition to a healthy diet. Here, they are gently poached in the Instant Pot, then layered on toasted rye bread spread with a lemony avocado mash. A generous garnish of fresh dill pairs well with the aromatic rye bread and gives these toasts a little Scandinavian flair. Serve them as a light snack, appetizer, or brunch dish.

SHRIMP AND AVOCADO TOAST

Shrimp

2 cups water

1½ teaspoons fine sea salt

1 pound frozen extra-large shrimp (21/30), thawed, peeled, and deveined

1 tablespoon extra-virgin olive oil

1 tablespoon fresh lemon juice

1 teaspoon chopped fresh dill

½ teaspoon freshly ground black pepper

Avocado Mash

2 avocados, pitted and peeled

2 tablespoons fresh lemon juice

½ teaspoon fine sea salt

8 thin slices rye bread (from thinly sliced dense, square loaf), toasted

Chopped fresh dill, for serving

Freshly ground black pepper, for serving

PREP	5 MINUTES
COOK	15 MINUTES
PR	QPR
SERVES	8

1 To poach the shrimp: Combine the water and salt in the Instant Pot and stir to dissolve the salt. Secure the lid and set the Pressure Release to **Sealing**. Select the **Steam** setting and set the cooking time for 0 (zero) minutes at low pressure. (The pot will take about 10 minutes to come up to pressure before the cooking program begins.)

2 When the cooking program ends, perform a quick release by moving the pressure release to **Venting**. Open the pot and stir in the shrimp, using a wooden spoon to nudge them all down into the water. Cover the pot and leave the shrimp for 5 minutes on the **Keep Warm** setting. The shrimp will gently poach and cook through. Drain the shrimp in a colander and transfer them to a medium bowl. Add the oil, lemon juice, dill, and pepper and stir to combine. Set aside.

3 To make the avocado mash: In a medium bowl, mash the avocados with the lemon juice and salt.

4 To serve, spread the mashed avocado onto the toasted rye bread and spoon the shrimp on top. Top each toast with the dill, a grind of pepper, and a little drizzle of the olive oil–lemon juice marinade from the shrimp.

Note: This method for cooking the shrimp might seem strange: first, you bring water to a boil on the low pressure setting, and then you open the pot and add the shrimp. Bringing the water to a boil heats up the whole pot, and all that heat keeps the water plenty hot for poaching the shrimp, even when the cooking program has ended. The gentle heat results in shrimp that are more tender than shrimp cooked under pressure. After much trial and error, this has turned out to be my favorite method for cooking shrimp.

Nutrition Information

Per serving: 255 calories, 9 grams fat, 30 grams carbohydrates, 9 grams fiber, 15 grams protein

This recipe borrows elements from a handful of different countries' takes on ceviche, a high-protein, low-fat seafood salad-cocktail. A squeeze of ketchup goes into the marinade for an Ecuadorian twist, avocado lends a little Mexican flair, and steamed sweet potato and corn on the side is a Peruvian custom. If fresh corn is not in season, substitute frozen corn.

SHRIMP CEVICHE WITH SWEET POTATOES AND CORN

Shrimp

2 cups water

1½ teaspoons fine sea salt

1 pound extra-large shrimp (21/30), peeled and deveined

1 tablespoon extra-virgin olive oil

1 tablespoon fresh lemon juice

1 teaspoon chopped fresh dill

⅛ teaspoon ground black pepper

Marinade

½ cup fresh lime juice

2 tablespoons ketchup

½ small red onion, thinly sliced

1 tablespoon chopped fresh cilantro

1 jalapeño chile, seeded and minced

1 avocado, diced

One 12-ounce cucumber, diced

1 cup grape tomatoes, quartered

For Serving

2 ears yellow corn, husks and silk removed, halved crosswise, and steamed (page 267)

8 ounces sweet potatoes, steamed (page 229), peeled, and sliced

PREP	5 MINUTES
COOK	15 MINUTES
PR	QPR
COOL	5 MINUTES
SERVES	4

1 To poach the shrimp: Combine the water and salt in the Instant Pot and stir to dissolve the salt. Secure the lid and set the Pressure Release to **Sealing**. Select the **Steam** setting and set the cooking time for 0 (zero) minutes at low pressure. (The pot will take about 10 minutes to come up to pressure before the cooking program begins.)

2 While the water is heating, prepare an ice bath.

3 To make the marinade: In a small bowl, stir together the lime juice, ketchup, onion, cilantro, and jalapeño.

4 When the cooking program ends, perform a quick release by moving the pressure release to **Venting**. Open the pot and stir in the shrimp, using a wooden spoon to nudge them all down into the water. Cover the pot and leave the shrimp for 5 minutes on the **Keep Warm** setting. The shrimp will gently poach and cook through. Transfer the shrimp to the ice bath, let the shrimp cool down for 5 minutes, then drain the shrimp in a colander and transfer to a medium bowl.

5 Add the avocado, cucumber, and tomatoes to the bowl with the shrimp. Pour in the marinade and fold gently to coat the shrimp and vegetables, taking care not to mash the avocado.

6 Spoon the ceviche into bowls and serve right away, with the corn and sweet potatoes on the side.

Note: If you are using smaller shrimp, the cooking time will be a minute or two less. Check the shrimp after 3 minutes to see if they are fully opaque.

Nutrition Information

Per serving: 387 calories, 6 grams fat, 48 grams carbohydrates, 9 grams fiber, 27 grams protein

Here, you quickly sauté the seafood in the Instant Pot, take it out when it's just cooked through, and then use the flavorful, garlicky olive oil as the base for the hearty, whole-wheat penne pasta cooked with spicy tomato sauce. Just before serving, the seafood is mixed with the pasta, so it is never overcooked. I usually have a 1-pound bag of mixed seafood (scallops, calamari, and shrimp) from Trader Joe's in my freezer, so I just pop it in the fridge to thaw a day ahead of making this dish.

CIOPPINO PASTA

2 tablespoons extra-virgin olive oil, plus more for drizzling

3 garlic cloves, thinly sliced

1 pound frozen seafood blend, thawed

1 yellow onion, sliced

2 shallots, sliced

4 celery stalks, sliced

1 teaspoon dried oregano

½ teaspoon red pepper flakes

2 cups seafood or fish stock (see Notes, page 131) or bottled clam juice

8 ounces whole-wheat penne

One 28-ounce can whole San Marzano-style tomatoes and their liquid

2 tablespoons chopped fresh flat-leaf parsley

Freshly ground black pepper, for serving

Lemon wedges, for serving

PREP	0 MINUTES
COOK	25 MINUTES
PR	5 MINUTES NPR
SERVES	4

1 Select the **Sauté** setting on the Instant Pot and heat the oil and garlic for 3 minutes, until the garlic is bubbling but not browned. Add the seafood blend and sauté for 2 to 3 minutes, until just cooked through. Using a slotted spoon, transfer the seafood to a dish and set aside. There will be some liquid left in the pot.

2 Add the onion, shallots, and celery to the pot and sauté for about 4 minutes, until the onion begins to soften. Add the oregano and red pepper flakes and sauté for 1 more minute. Stir in the stock and pasta, using a wooden spoon or spatula to nudge the pasta under the liquid as much as possible. It's fine if a few pieces are sticking up above the liquid. Add the tomatoes and their liquid on top of the pasta, crushing the tomatoes with your hands as you add them to the pot. Do not stir them in.

3 Secure the lid and set the Pressure Release to **Sealing**. Press the **Cancel** button to reset the cooking program, then select the **Pressure Cook** or **Manual** setting and set the cooking time for 6 minutes at high pressure. (The pot will take about 10 minutes to come up to pressure before the cooking program begins.)

4 When the cooking program ends, let the pressure release naturally for 5 minutes, then move the Pressure Release to **Venting** to release any remaining steam. Open the pot and stir in the seafood and parsley.

5 Spoon the pasta into bowls, drizzle with oil, and top with a few grinds of black pepper. Serve right away, with the lemon wedges on the side.

Note: If you like, you can substitute 1 pound bay scallops or peeled, deveined shrimp for the seafood blend.

Nutrition Information

Per serving: 432 calories, 8 grams fat, 62 grams carbohydrates, 10 grams fiber, 28 grams protein

Seafood risotto sounds fancy, but it's actually very easy to make. This is a great dish to serve for a romantic dinner, along with a green salad and a good white wine (a little goes into the risotto, too). You'll look like a gourmet chef, and all you had to do was turn on your Instant Pot. Since the meal will be light, you'll have room left over for dessert. I suggest a wedge of Flourless Chocolate Torte (page 256).

SEAFOOD RISOTTO

2 tablespoons extra-virgin olive oil

3 garlic cloves, minced

3 shallots, minced

¾ teaspoon fine sea salt

1 cup short-grain brown rice

½ cup dry white wine

2 cups seafood stock (see Notes, page 131), fish stock, or low-sodium vegetable broth (page 261)

1 pound frozen seafood blend, thawed

¼ teaspoon freshly ground black pepper

1 tablespoon fresh lemon juice

1 tablespoon chopped fresh flat-leaf parsley, for serving

PREP	0 MINUTES
COOK	50 MINUTES
PR	10 MINUTES NPR
SERVES	4

1 Select the **Sauté** setting on the Instant Pot and heat the oil, garlic, shallots, and salt for 4 minutes, until the shallots have softened. Stir in the rice and sauté for about 3 minutes, until the rice turns opaque and the shallots begin to brown. Pour in the wine and cook for about 3 minutes, until the liquid has evaporated and the rice begins to sizzle. Stir in the stock, then scrape down the sides of the pot to make sure all of the grains are submerged in the stock.

2 Secure the lid and set the Pressure Release to **Sealing**. Press the **Cancel** button to reset the cooking program, then select the **Pressure Cook** or **Manual** setting and set the cooking time for 30 minutes at high pressure. (The pot will take about 5 minutes to come up to pressure before the cooking program begins.)

3 When the cooking program ends, let the pressure release naturally for 10 minutes, then move the Pressure Release to **Venting** to release any remaining steam. Open the pot and stir in the seafood blend and pepper. Press the **Cancel** button to reset the cooking program, then select the **Sauté** setting. Cook the risotto for about 4 more minutes, stirring often, until the seafood is cooked through. Press the **Cancel** button to turn off the pot. Stir in the lemon juice.

4 Spoon the risotto into bowls, sprinkle with the parsley, and serve right away.

Nutrition Information

Per serving: 330 calories, 8 grams fat, 41 grams carbohydrates, 4 grams fiber, 20 grams protein

This creamy and comforting chowder is studded with potatoes, vegetables, and chunks of tender cod. It's made with half-and-half instead of heavy cream to lighten it up, and it's thickened with just enough cornstarch to give it a rich texture. Serve it as the main course for lunch or dinner, or in cups alongside a salad or sandwich.

NEW ENGLAND FISH CHOWDER

1 tablespoon unsalted butter

1 yellow onion, diced

2 celery stalks, diced

2 carrots, diced

½ teaspoon fine sea salt

1½ teaspoons chopped fresh thyme leaves

1 teaspoon Old Bay seasoning

½ cup dry white wine

1½ pounds Yukon gold or other waxy potatoes, cut into ½-inch cubes

3 cups seafood stock (see Notes, page 131), fish stock, or bottled clam juice

2 pounds skinless cod fillets, cut into 1-inch pieces

½ cup half-and-half

2 tablespoons cornstarch

1 tablespoon chopped fresh flat-leaf parsley, for serving

PREP	0 MINUTES
COOK	35 MINUTES
PR	15 MINUTES NPR
SERVES	6

1 Select the **Sauté** setting on the Instant Pot and melt the butter for 2 minutes. Add the onion, celery, carrots, and salt and sauté for 5 minutes, until the onion has softened. Add the thyme, Old Bay, and wine and bring to a simmer for about 5 minutes, until most of the liquid has evaporated. Add the potatoes and stir to combine. Pour in the stock, then add the fish on top. Do not stir it in.

2 Secure the lid and set the Pressure Release to **Sealing**. Press the **Cancel** button to reset the cooking program, then select the **Pressure Cook** or **Manual** setting and set the cooking time for 1 minute at high pressure. (The pot will take about 20 minutes to come up to pressure before the cooking program begins.)

3 When the cooking program ends, let the pressure release naturally for 15 minutes, then move the Pressure Release to **Venting** to release any remaining steam.

4 In a small bowl or measuring cup, stir together the half-and-half and cornstarch until smooth. Open the pot, pour in the half-and-half mixture, and stir to combine. (It's fine if the fish breaks up into smaller pieces as you stir the chowder.)

5 Press the **Cancel** button to reset the cooking program, then select the **Sauté** setting. Let the chowder come up to a simmer and cook for about 1 minute, until slightly thickened. Press the **Cancel** button to turn off the pot.

6 Ladle the chowder into bowls, sprinkle with the parsley, and serve hot.

Nutrition Information

Per serving: 349 calories, 8 grams fat, 50 grams carbohydrates, 5 grams fiber, 25 grams protein

This is a quick and easy take on a Spanish-style *caldereta*, or "stew." Seasoned with fragrant saffron and sweet paprika, it's a one-pot meal of fish, shrimp, and potatoes in a vibrant broth. There are plenty of other vegetables, too, including leeks, bell pepper, and carrots.

COD AND SHRIMP STEW WITH TOMATOES AND SAFFRON

2 tablespoons extra-virgin olive oil

4 garlic cloves, chopped

1 leek, white part only, thinly sliced into rounds and rinsed

1 yellow onion, diced

1 green bell pepper, seeded and diced

1 carrot, diced

½ teaspoon fine sea salt

½ cup dry white wine

1 cup seafood stock (see Notes, page 131), fish stock, or bottled clam juice

¼ teaspoon saffron threads

1 tablespoon sweet paprika

1 bay leaf

2 tablespoons tomato paste

1 pound Yukon gold or red potatoes, cut into 1-inch pieces

1 pound skinless cod fillets, cut into 1-inch pieces

8 ounces peeled and deveined medium shrimp

2 tablespoons chopped fresh flat-leaf parsley, for serving

PREP	0 MINUTES
COOK	20 MINUTES
PR	QPR
REST	5 MINUTES
SERVES	4

1 Select the **Sauté** setting on the Instant Pot and heat the oil and garlic for 3 minutes, until the garlic is bubbling but not browned. Add the leek, onion, bell pepper, carrot, and salt and sauté for about 5 minutes, until the leek and onion have softened.

2 Add the wine and stock, using a wooden spoon or spatula to nudge any browned bits from the bottom of the pot. Add the saffron, paprika, bay leaf, and tomato paste and stir to combine. Add the potatoes in an even layer, using the spoon or spatula to nudge them into the liquid.

3 Secure the lid and set the Pressure Release to **Sealing**. Press the **Cancel** button to reset the cooking program, then select the **Pressure Cook** or **Manual** setting and set the cooking time for 3 minutes at high pressure. (The pot will take about 5 minutes to come up to pressure before the cooking program begins.)

4 When the cooking program ends, perform a quick release by moving the Pressure Release to **Venting**. Open the pot and stir in the cod. Press the **Cancel** button to reset the cooking program, then select the **Sauté** setting. Bring just to a simmer (this will take about 2 minutes), then stir in the shrimp and let come to a simmer again (this will only take about 1 minute). Press the **Cancel** button to turn off the pot and let sit for about 5 minutes, just until the shrimp and cod are cooked through. The simmering will gradually slow down, and the carryover heat will cook everything through even though the pot is turned off. Remove and discard the bay leaf.

5 Ladle the stew into bowls and sprinkle with the parsley. Serve warm.

Note: If the seafood was previously frozen, make sure the seafood is thoroughly thawed. It will cook much more evenly and quickly.

Nutrition Information

Per serving: 435 calories, 12 grams fat, 91 grams carbohydrates, 6 grams fiber, 31 grams protein

Salads are at their best when they're full of textural contrasts, and this San Diego–inspired bowl has crunch to spare. It combines toasted (not fried) tortilla strips, tender, lean white fish, and a colorful, vitamin C–rich mango salsa on a bed of crisp lettuce and cabbage. A scoop of beans and some avocado slices top things off, for a seriously satisfying meal.

FISH TACO SALADS WITH FRESH MANGO SALSA

Fish

1½ pounds skinless snapper fillets

1½ teaspoons chili powder

¾ teaspoon fine sea salt

Tortilla Strips

Two 7-inch corn tortillas, cut into 2 by ¼-inch strips

2 teaspoons fresh lime juice

2 teaspoons extra-virgin olive oil

¼ teaspoon chili powder

⅛ teaspoon fine sea salt

Salsa

1 large mango, peeled, pitted, and diced

1 jalapeño chile, seeded and diced

½ small red onion, diced

1 tablespoon chopped fresh cilantro

2 teaspoons fresh lime juice

¼ teaspoon fine sea salt

Salad

2 cups firmly packed shredded green cabbage

1 head romaine, sliced crosswise into ½-inch-wide ribbons

1 tablespoon extra-virgin olive oil

2 teaspoons lime juice

¼ teaspoon fine sea salt

1 To cook the fish: Pat the fish fillets dry with paper towels, then sprinkle them all over with the chili powder and salt.

2 Pour 1 cup water into the Instant Pot and place the wire metal steam rack into the pot. Arrange the fillets in a single layer on the rack.

3 Secure the lid and set the Pressure Release to **Sealing**. Select the **Pressure Cook** or **Manual** setting and set the cooking time for 3 minutes at low pressure. (The pot will take about 10 minutes to come up to pressure before the cooking program begins.)

4 While the fish is cooking, make the tortilla strips: Line a small sheet pan with parchment paper or aluminum foil. In a bowl, combine the tortilla strips, lime juice, oil, chili powder, and salt and toss until the strips are evenly coated. Spread the strips in a single layer on the prepared pan and toast in a toaster oven (or in a conventional oven at 425°F) for about 8 minutes, until lightly browned and crisp.

5 To make the salsa: In a small bowl, combine the mango, jalapeño, onion, cilantro, lime juice, and salt and stir until evenly mixed.

Nutrition Information

Per serving: 494 calories, 17 grams fat, 44 grams carbohydrates, 14 grams fiber, 44 grams protein

1 large avocado, pitted, peeled, and sliced

1½ cups drained cooked black beans (page 44), or one 15-ounce can black beans, rinsed and drained

Lime wedges, for serving

PREP	0 MINUTES
COOK	15 MINUTES
PR	5 MINUTES NPR
SERVES	4

6 When the cooking program ends, let the pressure release naturally for 5 minutes, then move the Pressure Release to **Venting** to release any remaining steam. Open the pot and, wearing heat-resistant mitts, grasp the handles of the steam rack, lift the fish out of the pot, and transfer it to a plate. Using a fork, flake the fish into bite-size pieces, discarding any errant bones.

7 To make the salad: In a large bowl, combine the cabbage, romaine, oil, lime juice, and salt and toss to coat evenly.

8 Transfer the salad to four bowls. Top with the fish, salsa, avocado, black beans, and tortilla strips. Serve right away, with the lime wedges on the side.

Serve a few salmon patties on a bed of greens or atop a salad bowl, or tuck them into slider buns with a little tartar sauce for an easy appetizer. Crispy on the outside and soft on the inside, these patties are an adult- and kid-friendly way to put seafood into your diet. Salmon fillets are cooked quickly in the Instant Pot, then blended in a food processor with other ingredients into a patty mixture. You can either bake the patties or cook them on the stove top (see Note).

SALMON AND SPINACH PATTIES

Two 8-ounce skin-on or skinless salmon fillets

1 tablespoon fresh lemon juice

¾ teaspoon fine sea salt

½ teaspoon freshly ground black pepper

1 slice sourdough or gluten-free bread, cut into ½-inch cubes

2 cups firmly packed baby spinach

1 large egg

1 shallot, minced

¼ cup chopped fresh flat-leaf parsley

1½ tablespoons extra-virgin olive oil

Lemon wedges, for serving

1 Pour 1 cup water into the Instant Pot and place the wire metal steam rack into the pot. Place the salmon fillets, skin side down if skin on, on the rack and drizzle the lemon juice over them. Sprinkle the fillets with ½ teaspoon of the salt and the pepper.

2 Secure the lid and set the Pressure Release to **Sealing**. Select the **Steam** setting and set the cooking time for 4 minutes at low pressure. (The pot will take about 10 minutes to come up to pressure before the cooking program begins.)

3 While the salmon is cooking, ready the bread and spinach for the patty mixture. In a food processor, combine the bread and spinach and process using 1-second pulses, until the bread and spinach are finely chopped. Leave them in the processor.

4 Preheat the oven to 400°F. Line a sheet pan with a silicone baking mat or parchment paper and grease lightly with olive oil or nonstick cooking spray.

5 When the cooking program ends, let the pressure release naturally for 5 minutes, then move the Pressure Release to **Venting** to release any remaining steam. Open the pot and, wearing heat-resistant mitts, grasp the handles of the steam rack, lift the salmon out of the pot, and transfer it to a plate.

6 Peel away the salmon skin, if any, then, using a fork, flake the fish, removing any errant bones. Let the salmon cool for 5 minutes, until no longer piping hot, then add it to the food processor along with the egg, shallot, and parsley. Process using about six 1-second pulses, just until a cohesive mixture forms, stopping to scrape down the sides as needed.

Nutrition Information

Per patty: 125 calories, 6 grams fat, 4 grams carbohydrates, 0 grams fiber, 13 grams protein

PREP	10 MINUTES
COOK	25 MINUTES
PR	5 MINUTES NPR
COOL	5 MINUTES
MAKES	10 PATTIES

7 Using your hands, shape the mixture into ten patties, using ¼ cup of the mixture for each patty and making the patties about ½ inch thick. As the patties are shaped, place them on the prepared pan. Drizzle patties evenly with the oil.

8 Bake the patties for about 10 minutes, until lightly golden on the bottom and cooked through. Remove from the oven and immediately sprinkle with the remaining ¼ teaspoon salt.

9 Serve the patties warm, with the lemon wedges on the side.

Note: If you like, you can cook the patties in a skillet on the stove top instead of in the oven. Instead of drizzling the olive oil over the patties, heat the oil in a nonstick skillet over medium heat, then add the patties and cook, turning once, for 3 to 4 minutes on each side, until browned on both sides and cooked through.

Here, homemade basil oil shakes up a classic vinaigrette for spooning over Instant Pot–poached salmon. Fish always comes out moist and flaky when cooked this way, and the vinaigrette dresses up the simply prepared fillets without masking their flavor. To complete the healthy menu, serve the salmon with steamed vegetables and whole-grain couscous or brown rice.

POACHED SALMON WITH BASIL VINAIGRETTE

Salmon

1 cup water

½ cup dry white wine

4 lemon slices, each ½ inch thick

1 shallot, thinly sliced

6 fresh flat-leaf parsley sprigs

1 teaspoon fine sea salt

Two 8-ounce skin-on salmon fillets

½ teaspoon freshly ground black pepper

Basil Vinaigrette

2 tablespoons Basil Oil (page 264)

1 tablespoon white wine vinegar or champagne vinegar

1 garlic clove, pressed or grated

¼ teaspoon fine sea salt

PREP	5 MINUTES
COOK	15 MINUTES
PR	10 MINUTES NPR
SERVES	4

1 To cook the salmon: Combine the water, wine, lemon slices, shallot, parsley, and salt in the Instant Pot and stir to dissolve the salt. Place the salmon fillets, skin side down, into the pot and sprinkle the pepper over the fillets and the cooking liquid.

2 Secure the lid and set the Pressure Release to **Sealing**. Select the **Pressure Cook** or **Manual** setting and set the cooking time for 2 minutes at low pressure. (The pot will take about 10 minutes to come up to pressure before the cooking program begins.)

3 While the fish is cooking, make the vinaigrette: In a jam jar or other tightly lidded container, combine the oil, vinegar, garlic, and salt. Cover and shake vigorously to combine.

4 When the cooking program ends, let the pressure release naturally for 10 minutes, then move the Pressure Release to **Venting** to release any remaining steam. Open the pot and, using a fish spatula or other thin spatula, halve the salmon fillets and transfer to serving plates.

5 Give the vinaigrette another shake to recombine. Serve the salmon warm, with the vinaigrette spooned over the top.

Nutrition Information

Per serving: 273 calories, 16 grams fat, 0 grams carbohydrates, 0 grams fiber, 29 grams protein

This rich, coconutty curry is full of tender chunks of lean, high-protein tilapia and vitamin-rich vegetables. It's cooked entirely on the Instant Pot's Sauté setting, so it takes only 20 minutes to make. Green curry paste is easy to find in the Asian foods section of most grocery stores, but I like to seek out Mae Ploy or Aroy-D brand, both of which are carried in Asian markets and online. The flavors of these pastes are much more intense than those carried in most regular grocery stores.

THAI GREEN CURRY TILAPIA

1 tablespoon coconut oil

1 yellow onion, cut into 1-inch pieces

One 14-ounce can coconut milk, shaken well before opening

3 tablespoons green curry paste

½ cup water

2 large carrots, sliced ¼-inch thick on the diagonal

8 ounces green beans, trimmed and cut into 1-inch pieces

1 red bell pepper, seeded and cut into 1-inch pieces

1½ pounds skinless tilapia fillets, cut into 2-inch pieces

½ cup firmly packed fresh Thai basil leaves, for serving

1 lime, cut into wedges, for serving

Cooked brown jasmine rice or cauliflower rice, for serving

PREP	0 MINUTES
COOK	20 MINUTES
PR	N/A
SERVES	6

1 Select the **Sauté** setting on the Instant Pot and heat the coconut oil for 2 minutes. Add the onion and sauté for about 4 minutes, until the onion has softened, is translucent, and is beginning to brown just a bit. Add ½ cup of the coconut milk and the curry paste and sauté for about 1 more minute, until bubbling and fragrant. Pour in the water and use a wooden spoon or spatula to nudge any browned bits from the bottom of the pot.

2 Stir in the carrots and green beans and the remainder of the coconut milk. Bring the curry to a simmer (this will take about 3 minutes), then let cook, uncovered, for about 4 minutes, until the carrots and green beans are about half-cooked. Stir in the bell pepper and tilapia, bring to a simmer once more, and cook for about 5 minutes, just until the fish is cooked through and the carrots and green beans are fork-tender. Press the **Cancel** button to turn off the pot.

3 Ladle the curry into bowls and sprinkle the basil leaves on top. Serve piping hot, with the lime wedges and rice on the side.

Nutrition Information

Per serving: 350 calories, 20 grams fat, 16 grams carbohydrates, 5 grams fiber, 26 grams protein

6

Poultry

Chicken wings turn out extra juicy and tender when they're first steamed in the Instant Pot, then coated with a sweet and spicy sauce and broiled. There's just enough sauce to flavor the chicken without making the dish overly high in added calories. Serve these wings as a great first course for an Asian-inspired meal (think Thai or Vietnamese) or a decadent afternoon snack.

SWEET AND SPICY CHICKEN WINGS

2 pounds chicken wing drumettes and flats

1 teaspoon fine sea salt

1 teaspoon freshly ground black pepper

1 teaspoon garlic powder

2 tablespoons sambal oelek

1½ tablespoons tamari or low-sodium soy sauce

3 tablespoons honey

1 green onion, white and green parts, thinly sliced, for serving

PREP	5 MINUTES
COOK	30 MINUTES
PR	QPR
SERVES	6

1 Pour 1 cup water into the Instant Pot and place the wire metal steam rack into the pot.

2 Sprinkle the chicken wings all over with the salt, pepper, and garlic powder. Using tongs, arrange the wings on the rack in as even a layer as possible.

3 Secure the lid and set the Pressure Release to **Sealing**. Select the **Pressure Cook** or **Manual** setting and set the time for 10 minutes at high pressure. (The pot will take about 10 minutes to come up to pressure before the cooking program begins.)

4 While the chicken wings are cooking, preheat the broiler and line a sheet pan with aluminum foil. In a small bowl, stir together the sambal oelek, tamari, and honey.

5 When the cooking program ends, perform a quick pressure release by moving the Pressure Release to **Venting**. Open the pot and, wearing heat-resistant mitts, grasp the handles of the steam rack, lift out the wings, and transfer them to a dish. Lift out the inner pot and discard the cooking liquid.

6 Return the wings to the inner pot. Pour the sambal oelek mixture over the wings and stir to coat them evenly. Using tongs, transfer the wings to the prepared pan and pour any remaining sauce over the wings.

7 Broil the wings for about 5 minutes, until browned and charred in spots. Remove the pan from the broiler, flip each wing, and then broil the wings for 4 more minutes, until bubbling and charred on the second side. Transfer the wings to a serving plate.

8 Serve the wings warm with the green onions sprinkled on top.

Nutrition Information

Per serving: 225 calories, 14 grams fat, 10 grams carbohydrates, 0 grams fiber, 16 grams protein

The multipurpose sauce in this recipe is used as both a topping for the chicken and a dressing for the slaw. Eat the tenders and slaw on their own as a low-carb meal, or serve Crispy Sriracha Potatoes (page 232) or JoJo Potatoes (page 235) alongside.

HONEY MUSTARD CHICKEN TENDERS AND SLAW

Chicken

2 pounds chicken tenders

½ teaspoon fine sea salt

½ teaspoon ground black pepper

½ teaspoon sweet paprika

Mustard Sauce

¼ cup water

1 teaspoon cornstarch or arrowroot starch

3 tablespoons yellow mustard

2 tablespoons honey

1 tablespoon raw cider vinegar

1 tablespoon cold-pressed avocado oil

¼ teaspoon dried dill

¼teaspoon fine sea salt

Pinch of cayenne pepper

Slaw

¼ head red cabbage, shredded

¼ head green cabbage, shredded

2 carrots, shredded

¼ cup mayonnaise (regular or vegan)

¼ teaspoon ground black pepper

1 tablespoon chopped fresh dill or flat-leaf parsley, for serving

PREP	5 MINUTES
COOK	25 MINUTES
PR	QPR
SERVES	6

1 To make the chicken: Pour 1 cup water into the Instant Pot. Arrange the chicken strips in a single layer in the pot. Sprinkle with the salt, pepper, and paprika.

2 Secure the lid and set the Pressure Release to **Sealing**. Select the **Steam** setting and set the cooking time for 10 minutes at high pressure. (The pot will take about 10 minutes to come up to pressure before the cooking program begins.)

3 While the chicken is cooking, make the mustard sauce: In a small saucepan, combine the water, cornstarch, mustard, honey, vinegar, oil, dried dill, salt, and cayenne over medium heat. Cook, whisking continuously, for about 3 minutes, until bubbling, thickened, and emulsified. Remove from the heat.

4 To make the slaw: Combine the red and green cabbages, carrots, mayonnaise, pepper, and 2 tablespoons of the mustard sauce and toss to coat evenly.

5 When the cooking program ends, perform a quick pressure release by moving the Pressure Release to **Venting**. Open the pot and, using tongs, transfer the chicken to a dish. Wearing heat-resistant mitts, lift out the inner pot and discard the cooking liquid or save it to use in place of chicken broth in another recipe. Return the chicken to the now-empty pot, add the remaining mustard sauce, and toss to coat evenly.

6 Transfer the chicken to plates and garnish with the fresh dill. Serve warm, with the slaw on the side.

Nutrition Information

Per serving: 302 calories, 12 grams fat, 13 grams carbohydrates, 2 grams fiber, 36 grams protein

A healthier alternative to chips and buffalo dip, these lettuce cups are full of spicy chicken and crunchy vegetables and are topped with a homemade dairy-free ranch dressing. They make a great fork-free appetizer for any occasion, from watching football on the couch to a birthday party or shower. If you are not trying to stay dairy-free, you can substitute store-bought ranch dressing.

BUFFALO CHICKEN LETTUCE CUPS

1¼ pounds boneless, skinless chicken breasts

1 cup low-sodium chicken bone broth (page 260), or 1 cup water plus ½ teaspoon fine sea salt

Buffalo Sauce

1 tablespoon water

1 teaspoon cornstarch or arrowroot starch

¼ cup hot sauce (preferably Frank's RedHot), plus more if needed

1 tablespoon honey

1 teaspoon Worcestershire sauce

Ranch Dressing

½ cup raw whole cashews, soaked in water to cover for 2 hours and drained

6 tablespoons water

3 tablespoons fresh lemon juice

½ teaspoon garlic powder

¼ teaspoon freshly ground black pepper

¼ teaspoon fine sea salt

1 teaspoon dried chives

½ teaspoon dried dill

1 Arrange the chicken breasts in a single layer in the Instant Pot and pour in the broth.

2 Secure the lid and set the Pressure Release to **Sealing**. Select the **Pressure Cook** or **Manual** setting and set the cooking time for 15 minutes at high pressure. (The pot will take about 10 minutes to come up to pressure before the cooking program begins.)

3 While the chicken is cooking, make the buffalo sauce: In a small bowl, stir together the water, cornstarch, hot sauce, honey, and Worcestershire, mixing well.

4 To make the ranch dressing: In a widemouthed 1-pint jar, combine the cashews, water, lemon juice, garlic powder, pepper, salt, chives, and dill. Using an immersion blender, blend for about 2 minutes, until smooth. The dressing can be stored, tightly capped, in the refrigerator for up to 1 week.

5 When the cooking program ends, perform a quick pressure release by moving the Pressure Release to **Venting,** or let the pressure release naturally (this will take about 15 minutes). Open the pot and, using tongs, transfer the chicken to a cutting board or dish. Wearing heat-resistant mitts, lift out the inner pot and discard the cooking liquid or save it to use in place of chicken broth in another recipe. Return the inner pot to the housing. Using two forks, finely shred the chicken.

Nutrition Information

Per serving (2 lettuce cups): 220 calories, 10 grams fat, 10 grams carbohydrates, 2 grams fiber, 25 grams protein

1 tablespoon cold-pressed avocado oil

2 garlic cloves, minced

1 head butter or romaine lettuce, leaves separated (12 leaves)

2 carrots, shredded

2 celery stalks, thinly sliced

PREP	10 MINUTES
COOK	30 MINUTES
PR	QPR OR NPR
MAKES	12 LETTUCE CUPS; SERVES 6

6 Press the **Cancel** button to reset the cooking program, then select the **Sauté** setting. Add the oil and garlic to the pot and sauté for 2 minutes, until the garlic is bubbling but not browned. Stir the buffalo sauce to recombine, then pour it into the pot and cook, stirring continuously, for about 1 minute, until thickened. Press the **Cancel** button to turn off the pot. Add the shredded chicken and toss to coat it evenly. Taste and adjust the seasoning with more hot sauce if needed.

7 Spoon the warm chicken into the lettuce cups. Top each cup with some carrots and celery and 2 teaspoons of the ranch dressing and serve.

For this refreshing salad, crisp vegetables, shredded chicken, and a variety of antipasto platter staples are tossed in a zesty Italian vinaigrette. It's gluten-free and dairy-free, and it makes a nice summer dinner or workday lunch. Serve crusty bread or garlic bread alongside the salad for a heartier meal.

ANTIPASTO CHICKEN CHOPPED SALAD

1 cup water
1 teaspoon fine sea salt
3 garlic cloves
2 bay leaves
1½ pounds boneless, skinless chicken breasts

Italian Vinaigrette

¼ cup extra-virgin olive oil
2 tablespoons red wine vinegar
½ teaspoon agave nectar
½ teaspoon dried oregano
¼ teaspoon fine sea salt
¼ teaspoon ground black pepper
1 small garlic clove, crushed

1 cup frozen peas
½ cup finely diced red onion
½ cup sliced black olives
⅓ cup sliced pepperoncini
¼ cup drained oil-packed sun-dried tomatoes, cut into thin strips
1 bell pepper, seeded and diced
1 cup grape tomatoes, halved
2 tablespoons chopped fresh basil
1 head romaine lettuce, chopped
½ head iceberg lettuce, chopped
Ground black pepper, for serving

PREP	5 MINUTES
COOK	25 MINUTES
PR	QPR
REST	5 MINUTES
SERVES	6

1 Combine the water, salt, garlic, and bay leaves in the Instant Pot and stir to dissolve the salt. Add the chicken breasts in an even layer.

2 Secure the lid and set the Pressure Release to **Sealing**. Select the **Pressure Cook** or **Manual** setting and set the cooking time for 15 minutes at high pressure. (The pot will take about 10 minutes to come up to pressure before the cooking program begins.)

3 While the chicken is cooking, make the vinaigrette: In a jam jar or other tightly lidded container, combine the oil, vinegar, agave nectar, oregano, salt, pepper, and garlic. Cover and shake vigorously to combine.

4 When the cooking program ends, perform a quick pressure release by moving the Pressure Release to **Venting**. Open the pot and, using tongs, transfer the chicken to a cutting board or dish. Discard the cooking liquid or save it to use in place of chicken broth in another recipe.

5 Using two forks, shred the chicken into bite-size pieces. Transfer the still-hot chicken to a large salad bowl, add the peas, and stir to combine. Let rest for 5 minutes to allow the peas to thaw and the chicken to cool.

6 Add the vinaigrette, onion, olives, pepperoncini, sun-dried tomatoes, bell pepper, grape tomatoes, basil, and both lettuces and toss until everything is evenly coated with the vinaigrette. Transfer the salad to plates, top each serving with a few grinds of black pepper, and serve right away.

Nutrition Information

Per serving: 280 calories, 15 grams fat, 12 grams carbohydrates, 5 grams fiber, 27 grams protein

A Middle Eastern spice blend, *za'atar* adds punch to this chicken salad. The blend varies from country to country and region to region, but it is typically made up of thyme, oregano, sumac, salt, and sesame seeds. Look for it in Middle Eastern markets and in the spice section of natural foods stores. Serve the shredded chicken and dressing with salad vegetables as suggested, or use the tahini dressing as a spread and pile the chicken into pitas or onto whole-grain sandwich bread for a handheld, diet-friendly Mediterranean meal.

ZA'ATAR-SPICED CHICKEN SALAD WITH TAHINI DRESSING

Chicken

1 cup water

¾ teaspoon fine sea salt

2 garlic cloves, smashed

1 bay leaf

1½ pounds boneless, skinless chicken breasts

1½ tablespoons za'atar, plus more for serving

1½ tablespoons extra-virgin olive oil

1 tablespoon fresh lemon juice

Salad

3 hearts romaine lettuce, chopped

3 Persian cucumbers, sliced

1 large carrot, cut lengthwise into ribbons with a vegetable peeler

1½ cups grape tomatoes, sliced

12 tablespoons tahini dressing (page 262)

2 whole-wheat pitas, cut into wedges and toasted, for serving

PREP	5 MINUTES
COOK	20 MINUTES
PR	QPR
SERVES	6

1 To poach the chicken: Combine the water, salt, garlic, and bay leaf in the Instant Pot and stir to dissolve the salt. Add the chicken breasts in an even layer.

2 Secure the lid and set the Pressure Release to **Sealing**. Select the **Pressure Cook** or **Manual** setting and set the cooking time for 10 minutes at high pressure. (The pot will take about 10 minutes to come up to pressure before the cooking program begins.)

3 When the cooking program ends, perform a quick pressure release by moving the Pressure Release to **Venting**. Open the pot and, using tongs, transfer the chicken to a cutting board or dish. Discard the cooking liquid or save it to use in place of chicken broth in another recipe.

4 Using two forks, shred the chicken into bite-size pieces. Transfer the chicken to a medium bowl, add the za'atar, oil, and lemon juice, and stir to combine.

5 To make the salad: Divide the lettuce, cucumbers, carrot, and tomatoes evenly among six serving bowls. Pile the chicken on top of the vegetables, then drizzle each bowl with 2 tablespoons of the dressing and sprinkle with the za'atar. Serve right away, with the pita wedges on the side.

Note: I sometimes make this salad using leftover chicken meat from Whole Chicken in a Hurry (page 167).

Nutrition Information

Per serving: 333 calories, 16 grams fat, 22 grams carbohydrates, 7 grams fiber, 30 grams protein

Here, retro porcupine meatballs get a fresh, healthy makeover with Greek flavors and a cucumber yogurt sauce. They're made with dark-meat chicken in place of beef, and they have tons of flavor from generous amounts of garlic and fresh herbs and from a white wine–tomato sauce. Serve them with steamed vegetables for an easy meal. Because there's rice is in the meatballs, you can skip cooking up a starchy side.

GREEK CHICKEN MEATBALLS

1 red onion, chopped

4 garlic cloves, minced

1 pound 93 percent lean ground dark-meat chicken or ground turkey

½ cup Minute brand quick-cooking brown rice

¼ cup chopped fresh flat-leaf parsley, plus more for serving

2 tablespoons chopped fresh mint, plus more for serving

1 teaspoon dried oregano

¾ teaspoon fine sea salt

½ teaspoon freshly ground black pepper

2 tablespoons extra-virgin olive oil

One 15-ounce can tomato sauce

½ cup dry white wine

¼ cup water

½ cup tzatziki (page 264), for serving

PREP	10 MINUTES
COOK	45 MINUTES
PR	QPR OR NPR
SERVES	4

1 In a medium bowl, combine half of the onion, half of the garlic, the chicken, rice, parsley, mint, oregano, salt, and pepper. Mix with your hands until the rice is evenly distributed throughout the meat; don't worry about overmixing. Shape the mixture into 12 uniform meatballs, each slightly larger than a golf ball.

2 Select the **Sauté** setting on the Instant Pot and heat the oil and the remaining half of the garlic for 2 minutes, until the garlic is bubbling but not browned. Add the remaining half of the onion and sauté for about 2 minutes, until the onion begins to soften. Stir in the tomato sauce, wine, and water and bring to a simmer. Arrange the meatballs in a single layer in the pot and spoon a little sauce over each one.

3 Secure the lid and set the Pressure Release to **Sealing**. Press the **Cancel** button to reset the cooking program, then select the **Pressure Cook** or **Manual** setting and set the cooking time for 30 minutes at high pressure. (The pot will take about 10 minutes to come up to pressure before the cooking program begins.)

4 When the cooking program ends, you can either perform a quick pressure release by moving the Pressure Release to **Venting** or let the pressure release naturally (this will take about 20 minutes) and leave the pot on the **Keep Warm** setting for up to 10 hours.

5 Garnish with the parsley and mint. Serve the meatballs warm with the sauce and tzatziki spooned on top.

Nutrition Information

Per serving (sauce, meatballs, and tzatziki): 371 calories, 17 grams fat, 25 grams carbohydrates, 3 grams fiber, 25 grams protein

It can be hard to find dairy-free pesto pasta recipes. This one fits the bill without sacrificing flavor. No Parmesan is needed in the herby, garlicky pesto sauce, which I have spiked with a little lemon juice to brighten it even more. Tender chunks of chicken add protein and make for a filling one-pot dish.

DAIRY-FREE PESTO CHICKEN PENNE

Pasta and Chicken

1 tablespoon extra-virgin olive oil

2 garlic cloves, minced

1 pound chicken tenders, cut into 1-inch pieces

1 teaspoon Italian seasoning

¼ teaspoon fine sea salt

¼ teaspoon freshly ground black pepper

8 ounces lentil or chickpea penne pasta

2 cups low-sodium chicken bone broth (page 260)

Pesto

1½ cups firmly packed fresh basil leaves

1 cup firmly packed fresh flat-leaf parsley leaves

¼ cup pine nuts, toasted

1 garlic clove, minced

½ teaspoon fine sea salt

¼ teaspoon ground black pepper

2 tablespoons extra-virgin olive oil

2 tablespoons fresh lemon juice

1 cup frozen peas

3 cups firmly packed baby spinach

Vegan Parmesan Cheese (page 265), for serving

PREP	0 MINUTES
COOK	20 MINUTES
PR	5 MINUTES NPR
REST	3 MINUTES
SERVES	6

1 To make the pasta and chicken: Select the **Sauté** setting on the Instant Pot and heat the olive oil and garlic for 2 minutes, until the garlic is bubbling but not browned. Add the chicken, Italian seasoning, salt, and pepper and sauté for about 5 minutes, until the chicken is mostly cooked through. Add the penne in an even layer on top of the chicken, trying to get the pasta to lie as flat as possible. Pour the broth over the penne, using a wooden spoon to nudge down any pasta that is sticking out of the liquid.

2 Secure the lid and set the Pressure Release to **Sealing**. Press the **Cancel** button to reset the cooking program, then select the **Pressure Cook** or **Manual** setting and set the cooking time for 5 minutes at high pressure. (The pot will take about 5 minutes to come up to pressure before the cooking program begins.)

3 While the chicken and pasta are cooking, make the pesto: In a food processor, combine the basil, parsley, pine nuts, garlic, salt, pepper, oil, and lemon juice. Process using about ten 1-second pulses, until a fairly coarse texture forms, stopping to scrape down the sides as needed.

4 When the cooking program ends, let the pressure release naturally for 5 minutes, then move the Pressure Release to **Venting** to release any remaining steam. Open the pot and stir in the peas, spinach, and pesto. (It may look like there is a lot of extra liquid in the pot, but it will absorbed and mix with the pesto to make a creamy sauce.) Let stand for about 2 minutes, stir again, then let sit for 1 more minute, to allow the spinach to wilt and the peas to warm through.

5 Spoon the penne into bowls, sprinkle with vegan Parmesan, and serve right away.

Note: You can also use whole-wheat penne pasta in this recipe. Increase the cooking time to 6 minutes.

Nutrition Information

Per serving: 332 calories, 12 grams fat, 30 grams carbohydrates, 4 grams fiber, 28 grams protein

Many Central Asian cultures lay claim to making the best version of *plov*, a rice pilaf cooked with meat and vegetables. It's commonly prepared with lamb as the protein, but this cumin-spiced version is lightened up with chicken and chickpeas. Serve it as a one-pot meal or accompany it with lightly dressed salad greens.

CHICKEN, CHICKPEA, AND CARROT PLOV

- 2 tablespoons extra-virgin olive oil
- 1 teaspoon cumin seeds
- 3 garlic cloves, minced
- 1 yellow onion, thinly sliced
- 8 ounces carrots, julienned
- 1 teaspoon fine sea salt
- ½ teaspoon freshly ground black pepper
- 1½ pounds boneless, skinless chicken thighs, cut into 1-inch pieces
- 1 cup long-grain brown rice
- 1 cup drained, cooked chickpeas (page 44), or two-thirds 15-ounce can chickpeas, rinsed and drained
- 1¼ cups low-sodium chicken bone broth (page 260)

PREP	0 MINUTES
COOK	45 MINUTES
PR	10 MINUTES NPR
REST	5 MINUTES
SERVES	6

1 Select the **Sauté** setting on the Instant Pot and heat the oil, cumin seeds, and garlic for 3 minutes, until the seeds are bubbling and aromatic and the garlic is bubbling but not browned. Add the onion, carrots, salt, and pepper and sauté for about 5 minutes, until the onion has softened. Add the chicken and stir to combine.

2 Using a wooden spoon or spatula, nudge the mixture into as even a layer as possible. Sprinkle the rice in an even layer in the pot, then sprinkle the chickpeas evenly over the rice. Pour in the broth. Do not stir. You want the rice to remain on top of the chicken rather than end up on the bottom of the pot.

3 Secure the lid and set the Pressure Release to **Sealing**. Press the **Cancel** button to reset the cooking program, then select the **Pressure Cook** or **Manual** setting and set the cooking time for 25 minutes at high pressure. (The pot will take about 10 minutes to come up to pressure before the cooking program begins.)

4 When the cooking program ends, let the pressure release naturally for at least 10 minutes, then move the Pressure Release to **Venting** to release any remaining steam. Open the pot and stir to combine. Let rest for about 5 minutes, to allow the cooking liquid to be absorbed. Stir once more.

5 Spoon the plov into bowls and serve warm.

Nutrition Information

Per serving: 353 calories, 13 grams fat, 37 grams carbohydrates, 6 grams fiber, 27 grams protein

This easy, Asian-inspired dish of shredded chicken cloaked in a creamy, spicy peanut sauce is both tasty and versatile. Mix it with prepared shirataki noodles or spiralized vegetable noodles, spoon it into lettuce cups, or serve it on a bed of steamed bok choy.

SPICY SESAME PEANUT CHICKEN

1¼ pounds boneless, skinless chicken breasts

1 cup low-sodium chicken bone broth (page 260), or 1 cup water plus ½ teaspoon fine sea salt

Sesame Peanut Sauce

¼ cup water

2 tablespoons low-sodium soy sauce or tamari

2 tablespoons rice vinegar

1 teaspoon cornstarch

1 tablespoon cold-pressed avocado oil

1 tablespoon toasted sesame oil

2 garlic cloves, minced

2 teaspoons agave nectar or honey

1½ tablespoons sambal oelek or Sriracha sauce

¼ cup all-natural creamy peanut butter

Toasted sesame seeds or chopped roasted peanuts, for serving

Chopped green onion, white and green parts, for serving

PREP	0 MINUTES
COOK	25 MINUTES
PR	QPR OR NPR
SERVES	5

1 Arrange the chicken breasts in a single layer in the Instant Pot and pour in the broth.

2 Secure the lid and set the Pressure Release to **Sealing**. Select the **Pressure Cook** or **Manual** setting and set the cooking time for 15 minutes at high pressure. (The pot will take about 10 minutes to come up to pressure before the cooking program begins.)

3 When the cooking program ends, perform a quick pressure release by moving the Pressure Release to **Venting**, or let the pressure release naturally (this will take about 20 minutes). Open the pot and, using tongs, transfer the chicken to a cutting board or dish. Wearing heat-resistant mitts, lift out the inner pot and discard the cooking liquid or save it to use in place of chicken broth in another recipe. Return the inner pot to the housing. Using two forks, finely shred the chicken.

4 To make the sesame peanut sauce: In a small bowl, stir together the water, soy sauce, vinegar, and cornstarch, mixing well. Press the **Cancel** button to reset the cooking program, then select the low **Sauté** setting. Add the avocado oil, sesame oil, and garlic to the pot and heat for about 2 minutes, until the garlic is bubbling but not browned. Stir in the soy sauce mixture, agave nectar, sambal oelek, and peanut butter and cook, stirring continuously, for about 1 minute, until thickened. Press the **Cancel** button to turn off the pot. Add the chicken and toss to coat evenly with the sauce.

5 Spoon the chicken onto plates, sprinkle with seasame seeds and green onions, and serve warm.

Notes: If you want a saucier dish, add a splash of the cooking liquid and stir to combine.

To make a lower-calorie version of the peanut sauce, replace the peanut butter with an equal amount of reconstituted peanut powder (such as PB2 or PBfit brand, see page 13), prepared according to the package instructions.

Nutrition Information

Per serving: 263 calories, 15 grams fat, 7 grams carbohydrates, 1 gram fiber, 29 grams protein

The rice gets doubled in volume from a secret, nutritious ingredient: shredded cabbage. Adding shredded vegetables gives the impression of a bigger serving of grains while cutting down on calorie-loaded carbs. To make the recipe dairy-free, substitute Cashew Sour Cream (page 265) for the crema.

SALSA CHICKEN AND SUPERCHARGED RICE

2 pounds boneless, skinless chicken breasts

2 teaspoons chili powder

1 cup salsa picante, homemade (page 262) or store-bought

1 cup Minute brand quick-cooking brown rice

1 cup low-sodium chicken bone broth (page 260)

2 cups firmly packed finely shredded green cabbage

½ cup chopped fresh cilantro

2 green onions, white and green parts, sliced

1 jalapeño chile, seeded and minced

1 tablespoon fresh lime juice

Yogurt Crema

½ cup plain 2 percent Greek yogurt, homemade (page 34) or store-bought

1 tablespoon fresh lime juice

½ teaspoon finely grated lime zest

¼ teaspoon fine sea salt

Hot sauce (such as Cholula or Tapatío), for serving

PREP	10 MINUTES
COOK	40 MINUTES
PR	10 MINUTES NPR
SERVES	6

1 Arrange the chicken in an even single layer in the Instant Pot. Sprinkle the chili powder evenly over the chicken, then pour the salsa on top. Do not stir.

2 In a 1½-quart stainless-steel bowl, combine the rice and broth.

3 Place a tall steam rack into the pot, making sure all of its legs are resting firmly on the bottom. Place the bowl of rice on the rack. (The bowl should not touch the lid once the pot is closed.)

4 Secure the lid and set the Pressure Release to **Sealing**. Select the **Pressure Cook** or **Manual** setting and set the cooking time for 15 minutes at high pressure. (The pot will take about 15 minutes to come up to pressure before the cooking program begins.)

5 While the chicken and rice are cooking, make the yogurt crema: In a small bowl, stir together the yogurt, lime juice and zest, and salt.

6 When the cooking program ends, let the pressure release naturally for 10 minutes, then move the Pressure Release to **Venting** to release any remaining steam. Open the pot and, wearing heat-resistant mitts, remove the bowl and then the rack from the pot. Using tongs, transfer the chicken to a cutting board or dish. Press the **Cancel** button to reset the cooking program, then select the **Sauté** setting. Let the salsa mixture cook for 6 to 8 minutes, stirring occasionally, until slightly thickened.

7 While the salsa mixture cooks, add the cabbage, cilantro, green onions, jalapeño, and lime juice to the rice. Using a fork, gently incorporate the ingredients into the rice, fluffing the grains as you mix.

8 Press the **Cancel** button to turn off the pot. Using two forks, shred the chicken into bite-size pieces. Return the chicken to the pot and stir to combine with the salsa mixture.

9 Divide the rice among six serving bowls and spoon the chicken over the rice. Serve right away, with the crema and hot sauce at the table.

Nutrition Information

Per serving: 240 calories, 5 grams fat, 19 grams carbohydrates, 3 grams fiber, 33 grams protein

Smothered chicken doesn't have to be high in calories to be delicious. This recipe has just one tablespoon of oil, and the chicken skin is removed to reduce the fat, yet the all-important gravy is still rich and satisfying. Serve the chicken over Cauliflower Carrot Mash (page 214) for a super-comforting meal.

SOUTHERN SMOTHERED CHICKEN

2 pounds bone-in chicken thighs and/or drumsticks, skinned

¼ cup whole-wheat pastry flour or gluten-free flour blend

1½ teaspoons fine sea salt

1 teaspoon paprika

½ teaspoon freshly ground black pepper

1 tablespoon cold-pressed avocado oil

1 large yellow onion, sliced

2 garlic cloves, minced

1½ teaspoons poultry seasoning

1 cup low-sodium chicken bone broth (page 260)

½ cup buttermilk

1 teaspoon Dijon mustard

Chopped fresh flat-leaf parsley, for serving

PREP	5 MINUTES
COOK	45 MINUTES
PR	QPR
SERVES	4

1 Pat the chicken dry with paper towels. Combine the flour, salt, paprika, and pepper in a 1-gallon ziplock plastic bag, seal it closed, and shake to combine. Add the chicken to the bag, reseal, and shake to coat it with the seasoned flour. Transfer the chicken pieces to a plate in a single layer, shaking off any excess flour. The coating should be very light.

2 Select the **Sauté** setting on the Instant Pot and heat the oil for about 2 minutes, until shimmering. Using tongs, add the chicken in a single layer and sear for about 4 minutes, until browned on the first side. Flip the pieces and sear for about 3 more minutes, until browned on the second side. Return the chicken to the plate.

3 Add the onion and garlic to the pot and sauté for about 2 minutes, until the onion is slightly softened. Stir in the poultry seasoning and broth, using a wooden spoon or spatula to nudge any browned bits from the bottom of the pot. Return the chicken to the pot in a single layer.

4 Secure the lid and set the Pressure Release to **Sealing**. Press the **Cancel** button to reset the cooking program, then select the **Manual** or **Pressure Cook** setting and set the cooking time for 15 minutes at high pressure. (The pot will take about 10 minutes to come up to pressure before the cooking program begins.)

5 When the cooking program ends, perform a quick pressure release by moving the Pressure Release to **Venting**. Open the pot and, using tongs, transfer the chicken to a serving dish.

6 Press the **Cancel** button to reset the cooking program, then select the **Sauté** setting. Add the buttermilk and mustard to the pot and stir to combine. Simmer the sauce, stirring occasionally, for about 8 minutes, until slightly reduced. Press the **Cancel** button to turn off the pot. Wearing heat-resistant mitts, lift out the inner pot. Using an immersion blender, blend the onion into the sauce, tilting the pot so the blender head is fully submerged.

7 Ladle the sauce over the chicken, sprinkle with the parsley and serve.

Nutrition Information

Per serving: 219 calories, 9 grams fat, 11 grams carbohydrates, 2 grams fiber, 25 grams protein

When you're eating healthy, you don't have to sacrifice silky sauces. Here, just a small amount of cheese gives this sauce its creaminess—no actual cream is used. Mushrooms, spinach, and sun-dried tomatoes add Tuscan flavor (and lots of vegetable servings, too). Serve the chicken over spiralized vegetable noodles, rice, whole-grain pasta, farro, or polenta.

CHICKEN CUTLETS IN TUSCAN CREAM SAUCE

- **1½ pounds boneless, skinless chicken breasts, cut in half lengthwise**
- **¾ teaspoon fine sea salt**
- **¼ teaspoon freshly ground black pepper**
- **1½ tablespoons extra-virgin olive oil**
- **3 garlic cloves, minced**
- **1 yellow onion, diced**
- **8 ounces cremini mushrooms, sliced**
- **1 teaspoon Italian seasoning**
- **½ cup dry white wine**
- **⅓ cup drained oil-packed sun-dried tomato halves, diced**
- **One 6-ounce bag baby spinach**
- **2 tablespoons chopped fresh basil**
- **Two ¾-ounce wedges Laughing Cow light Swiss cheese, or 3 tablespoons cream cheese, at room temperature**
- **¼ cup grated Pecorino Romano cheese**
- **1 teaspoon cornstarch**
- **1 tablespoon water**

PREP	5 MINUTES
COOK	25 MINUTES
PR	5 MINUTES NPR
SERVES	6

1 Pat the chicken breasts dry with paper towels. Sprinkle them all over with ½ teaspoon of the salt and the pepper.

2 Select the **Sauté** setting on the Instant Pot and heat the oil for 2 minutes. Using tongs, add the chicken in a single layer and sear for about 2 minutes, until lightly browned. Flip the chicken and sear for 2 more minutes, until lightly browned on the second side, then transfer to a plate. Add the garlic, onion, mushrooms, and the remaining ¼ teaspoon salt and sauté for about 4 minutes, until the onion begins to soften and the mushrooms begin to wilt and give up their liquid. Add the Italian seasoning, wine, and tomatoes and stir to combine, using a wooden spoon to nudge any browned bits from the bottom of the pot. Let the wine come to a simmer, then add the chicken breasts in a single layer on top.

3 Secure the lid and set the Pressure Release to **Sealing**. Press the **Cancel** button to reset the cooking program, then select the **Pressure Cook** or **Manual** setting and set the cooking time for 5 minutes at high pressure. (The pot will take about 5 minutes to come up to pressure before the cooking program begins.)

4 Let the pressure release naturally for at least 5 minutes, then move the Pressure Release to **Venting** to release any remaining steam. Open the pot and, using tongs, transfer the chicken to a serving plate.

5 Press the **Cancel** button to reset the cooking program and select the **Sauté** setting. Add the spinach and basil and stir until wilted, about 1 minute. Add the Laughing Cow and Pecorino Romano cheeses and stir for 1 minute, until melted. In a small bowl, stir together the cornstarch and water, add to the pot, and stir for about 1 more minute, until the sauce is slightly thickened. Press the **Cancel** button to turn off the pot. Wearing heat-resistant mitts, lift out the inner pot.

6 Spoon the sauce and vegetables over the chicken and serve right away.

Nutrition Information

Per serving: 223 calories, 9 grams fat, 9 grams carbohydrates, 2 grams fiber, 27 grams protein

Goulash is hearty and satisfying, the perfect cold-weather food. This version combines potatoes, carrots, mushrooms, and chicken in a paprika-tinged sauce. If you like, you can leave out the potatoes and serve the goulash over whole-grain noodles.

CHICKEN AND MUSHROOM GOULASH

1½ pounds boneless, skinless chicken thighs, cut into 1-inch cubes

1 teaspoon fine sea salt

½ teaspoon freshly ground black pepper

1 tablespoon cold-pressed avocado oil

1 yellow onion, sliced

8 ounces cremini or button mushrooms, halved if small or quartered if large

2 garlic cloves, minced

3 tablespoons sweet paprika

1 cup low-sodium chicken bone broth (page 260)

1 teaspoon finely grated lemon zest

1 tablespoon fresh lemon juice

1 bay leaf

2 tablespoons tomato paste

1 pound Yukon Gold or other waxy potatoes, cut into ¾-inch cubes

4 carrots, cut into ½-inch-thick rounds

¾ cup plain 2 percent Greek yogurt, homemade (page 34) or store-bought, or Cashew Sour Cream (page 265), for serving

2 tablespoons chopped fresh flat-leaf parsley, for serving

PREP	0 MINUTES
COOK	40 MINUTES
PR	10 MINUTES NPR AND QPR
SERVES	6

1 Sprinkle the chicken all over with the salt and pepper.

2 Select the **Sauté** setting on the Instant Pot and heat the oil for 1 minute. Add the onion and mushrooms and sauté for about 5 minutes, until the onion has softened and the mushrooms are beginning to wilt and brown just a bit. Add the garlic and paprika and sauté for 1 more minute. Stir in the chicken, broth, lemon zest and juice, and bay leaf, using a wooden spoon or spatula to nudge any browned bits from the bottom of the pot. Add the tomato paste in a dollop on top. Do not stir it in.

3 Secure the lid and set the Pressure Release to **Sealing**. Press the **Cancel** button to reset the cooking program, then select the **Pressure Cook** or **Manual** setting and set the cooking time for 10 minutes at high pressure. (The pot will take about 10 minutes to come up to pressure before the cooking program begins.)

4 When the cooking program ends, let the pressure release naturally for at least 10 minutes, then move the Pressure Release to **Venting** to release any remaining steam. Open the pot and remove and discard the bay leaf. Add the potatoes and carrots in an even layer on top of the stew. Do not stir them in.

5 Secure the lid and set the Pressure Release to **Sealing** once again. Press the **Cancel** button to reset the cooking program, then select the **Pressure Cook** or **Manual** setting and set the cooking time for 3 minutes at high pressure. (The pot will take about 10 minutes to come up to pressure before the cooking program begins.)

6 When the cooking program ends, perform a quick pressure release by moving the Pressure Release to **Venting**. Open the pot and stir the goulash to mix in the potatoes and carrots.

7 Spoon the goulash into bowls and top each bowl with a dollop of yogurt and a sprinkling of parsley. Serve right away.

Nutrition Information

Per serving: 268 calories, 8 grams fat, 31 grams carbohydrates, 6 grams fiber, 27 grams protein

Season a chicken all over, pop it into the Instant Pot, and you'll have dinner ready in about 40 minutes flat. Make a salad or microwave some frozen vegetables while the chicken is cooking for a super low-carb meal.

WHOLE CHICKEN IN A HURRY

2 teaspoons poultry seasoning, or 1 teaspoon each dried thyme and dried oregano

1½ teaspoons fine sea salt

1 teaspoon sweet paprika

½ teaspoon freshly ground black pepper

1 tablespoon extra-virgin olive oil

One 4-pound whole chicken

PREP	5 MINUTES
COOK	40 MINUTES
PR	QPR
REST	10 TO 15 MINUTES
SERVES	4

1 Pour 1 cup water into the Instant Pot.

2 In a small bowl, stir together the poultry seasoning, salt, paprika, pepper, and oil.

3 Pat the chicken dry with paper towels. Using a pastry brush or your hands, spread half of the spice-oil mixture all over the backside of the chicken, then flip the bird over and spread the remaining spice-oil mixture over the breast side. Place a long-handled silicone steam rack on a plate. Place the chicken, breast side down, on the rack. Holding the handles of the steam rack, lower the chicken into the pot.

4 Secure the lid and set the Pressure Release to **Sealing**. Select the **Pressure Cook** or **Manual** setting and set the cooking time for 25 minutes at high pressure. (The pot will take about 15 minutes to come up to pressure before the cooking program begins.)

5 When the cooking program ends, perform a quick pressure release by moving the Pressure Release to **Venting**. Open the pot and, wearing heat-resistant mitts, grasp the handles of the steam rack and lift the chicken out of the pot. Transfer the chicken to a cutting board.

6 Let the chicken rest for 10 to 15 minutes. Carve the chicken, arrange on a platter, and serve.

Notes: The leftover drippings will be quite salty, but you can (and should) use them along with the carcass for a delicious chicken bone broth (page 260).

Use any leftover chicken meat for chicken sandwiches or salads the next day, such as Za'atar-Spiced Chicken Salad with Tahini Dressing (page 153).

Nutrition Information

Per serving: 398 calories, 25 grams fat, 1 gram carbohydrate, 0 grams fiber, 44 grams protein

These tender, yogurt-marinated chicken thighs are an easy weeknight dinner. The tandoori spice blend is so flavorful that you won't miss the chicken skin at all. You can pop the chicken thighs into their marinade in the morning, and they'll take less than a half hour to cook at dinnertime. While the chicken cooks, toss together a salad or warm up some vegetables for a balanced meal.

TANDOORI-SPICED CHICKEN THIGHS

½ cup plain 2 percent Greek yogurt, homemade (page 34) or store-bought

1 teaspoon fine sea salt

2 teaspoons sweet paprika

1 teaspoon ground cumin

1 teaspoon ground coriander

1 teaspoon ground cinnamon

½ teaspoon ground ginger

½ teaspoon ground turmeric

½ teaspoon garlic powder

¼ teaspoon cayenne pepper

⅛ teaspoon ground nutmeg

2 pounds boneless, skinless chicken thighs

1 tablespoon cold-pressed avocado oil

2 garlic cloves, minced

½-inch knob fresh ginger, peeled and minced

½ cup water

1 tablespoon chopped fresh cilantro, for serving

Cooked rice or cauliflower rice or naan, for serving

Lime wedges, for serving

MARINATE	1 HOUR TO OVERNIGHT
COOK	30 MINUTES
PR	QPR OR NPR
SERVES	6

1 In a large bowl, stir together the yogurt, salt, paprika, cumin, coriander, cinnamon, ginger, turmeric, garlic powder, cayenne, and nutmeg. Add the chicken and toss to coat evenly with the yogurt. Cover the bowl and marinate the chicken in the refrigerator for at least 1 hour or up to overnight.

2 Select the **Sauté** setting on the Instant Pot and heat the oil, garlic, and ginger for 3 minutes, until the garlic and ginger are bubbling and aromatic but not browned. Stir in the chicken thighs and their marinade and the water. Use a wooden spoon or spatula to nudge the chicken thighs into a single layer in the pot.

3 Secure the lid and set the Pressure Release to **Sealing**. Press the **Cancel** button to reset the cooking program. Select the **Pressure Cook** or **Manual** setting and set the cooking time for 15 minutes at high pressure. (The pot will take about 10 minutes to come up to pressure before the cooking program begins.)

4 When the cooking program ends, perform a quick pressure release by moving the Pressure Release to **Venting**, or let the pressure release naturally (this will take about 20 minutes). Open the pot and use a slotted spoon to transfer the chicken thighs to a serving dish.

5 Sprinkle the chicken with the cilantro and serve right away, with the rice and lime wedges on the side.

Nutrition Information

Per serving: 219 calories, 9 grams fat, 2 grams carbohydrates, 1 gram fiber, 32 grams protein

Rice and lean turkey yield delicious meatballs, especially when they're cooked in a tomato sauce that's seasoned with some of the primary spices that traditionally go into paella: oregano, smoked paprika, and saffron. Because there's rice in the meatballs, all you need to complete your menu is a big green salad.

PAELLA TURKEY MEATBALLS

1 large yellow onion, chopped

2 garlic cloves, minced

1 pound 93 percent lean ground turkey

½ cup Minute brand quick-cooking brown rice

¾ teaspoon fine sea salt

½ teaspoon freshly ground black pepper

1 tablespoon extra-virgin olive oil

One 15-ounce can tomato sauce

1 cup frozen peas

1 teaspoon dried oregano

½ teaspoon smoked paprika

¼ teaspoon cayenne pepper

¼ teaspoon saffron threads

¾ cup water

PREP	10 MINUTES
COOK	45 MINUTES
PR	QPR OR NPR
SERVES	4

1 In a medium bowl, combine half of the onion, half of the garlic, the ground turkey, rice, salt, and black pepper. Mix with your hands until the rice is evenly distributed throughout the meat; don't worry about overmixing. Shape the mixture into 12 uniform meatballs, each slightly larger than a golf ball.

2 Select the **Sauté** setting on the Instant Pot and heat the oil and the remaining garlic for 2 minutes, until the garlic is bubbling but not browned. Add the remaining onion and sauté for 2 more minutes, until the onion begins to soften. Stir in the tomato sauce, peas, oregano, paprika, cayenne, saffron, and water, and bring to a simmer. Arrange the meatballs in a single layer in the pot and spoon a little sauce over each one.

3 Secure the lid and set the Pressure Release to **Sealing**. Press the **Cancel** button to reset the cooking program, then select the **Pressure Cook** or **Manual** setting and set the cooking time for 30 minutes at high pressure. (The pot will take about 10 minutes to come up to pressure before the cooking program begins.)

4 When the cooking program ends, you can either perform a quick pressure release by moving the Pressure Release to **Venting** or let the pressure release naturally (this will take about 25 minutes) and leave the pot on the **Keep Warm** setting for up to 10 hours.

5 Serve the meatballs warm with the sauce spooned on top.

Nutrition Information

Per serving: 371 calories, 13 grams fat, 37 grams carbohydrates, 6 grams fiber, 28 grams protein

Mexican *tortas* meet sloppy joes in these delightfully messy sandwiches. They're lightened up with ground turkey, and they get a smoky, spicy kick from chipotle chile. Feel free to substitute a teaspoon of smoked paprika for the chipotle if you want to tone down the heat.

CHIPOTLE TURKEY SLOPPY JOES

1 tablespoon extra-virgin olive oil

1 pound 93 percent lean ground turkey

1 yellow onion, diced

2 carrots, diced

1 green bell pepper, seeded and diced

2 garlic cloves, chopped

1 canned chipotle chile in adobo sauce, minced

2 tablespoons hot sauce (such as Cholula or Tapatío)

2 tablespoons fresh lime juice

2 tablespoons agave nectar, or 3 tablespoons dark brown sugar

¼ cup tomato paste

4 whole-wheat hamburger buns, for serving

¼ cup thinly sliced red onion, for serving

1 small avocado, pitted, peeled, and sliced, for serving

PREP	0 MINUTES
COOK	30 MINUTES
PR	QPR OR NPR
SERVES	4

1 Select the **Sauté** setting on the Instant Pot and heat the oil for 2 minutes. Add the turkey and sauté, breaking it up with a wooden spoon as it cooks, for about 5 minutes, until no traces of pink remain. Add the yellow onion, carrots, bell pepper, and garlic and sauté for about 5 more minutes, until the vegetables soften. Stir in the chipotle, hot sauce, lime juice, and agave nectar. Add the tomato paste in a dollop on top. Do not stir it in.

2 Secure the lid and set the Pressure Release to **Sealing**. Press the **Cancel** button to reset the cooking program, then select the **Pressure Cook** or **Manual** setting and set the cooking time for 10 minutes at high pressure. (The pot will take about 5 minutes to come up to pressure before the cooking program begins.)

3 When the cooking program ends, you can either perform a quick pressure release by moving the Pressure Release to **Venting** or let the pressure release naturally (this will take about 20 minutes) and leave the pot on the **Keep Warm** setting for up to 10 hours. Open the pot and stir the tomato paste into the sloppy joe mixture.

4 Ladle the sloppy joe mixture onto the bun bottoms and top with the red onion and avocado. Close with the bun tops and serve hot.

Note: For smaller appetites, use 100-calorie whole-wheat sandwich thins instead of hamburger buns and stretch the recipe to six servings.

Nutrition Information

Per serving: 490 calories, 19 grams fat, 57 grams carbohydrates, 10 grams fiber, 33 grams protein

7

Pork, Lamb, and Beef

Here is a speedy dinner that looks like it was ordered in a fancy restaurant. The rich, mushroom-studded, lick-your-plate-good sauce is dairy-free. If you don't have Marsala on hand, a dry red wine will work in its place. For a nearly carb-free option, serve the chops with noodles or rice.

PORK CHOPS MARSALA

2 pounds boneless pork chops, ½inch thick (6 chops)

¼ cup whole-wheat pastry flour or gluten-free flour blend

1½ teaspoons fine sea salt

¾ teaspoon ground black pepper

¾ teaspoon smoked paprika

1 tablespoon extra-virgin olive oil

3 ounces pancetta, cubed

4 garlic cloves, minced

8 ounces cremini or button mushrooms, sliced

½ cup low-sodium chicken bone broth (page 260)

½ cup dry Marsala

½ teaspoon dried thyme

½ teaspoon dried oregano

1 tablespoon tomato paste

1 tablespoon fresh lemon juice

1 tablespoon chopped fresh flat-leaf parsley

Cooked brown rice, cauliflower rice, zucchini noodles, or shirataki noodles, for serving

1 Line a large plate with paper towels. Pat the pork chops dry with additional paper towels.

2 Combine the flour, salt, pepper, and paprika in a 1-gallon ziplock plastic bag, seal it closed, and shake to combine. Add the pork chops to the bag, reseal, and shake to coat them with the seasoned flour. Transfer the chops to the prepared plate, shaking off any excess flour and placing them in a single layer. The coating should be light, and there should still be a couple of tablespoons of seasoned flour left in the bag.

3 Select the **Sauté** setting on the Instant Pot and heat the oil for 1 minute. Add the pancetta and garlic and sauté for about 3 minutes, until the garlic is bubbling but not browned and the pancetta is beginning to render a bit of fat. Add the mushrooms and cook for about 2 more minutes, just until they start to soften. Stir in the broth and Marsala, using a wooden spoon or spatula to nudge any browned bits from the bottom of the pot. Stir in the thyme, oregano, tomato paste, and lemon juice and bring to a simmer. Simmer for about 2 minutes, just until the Marsala no longer smells of raw alcohol. Add the pork chops, arranging them in as even a layer as possible. Quickly spoon some of the cooking liquid over each chop.

4 Secure the lid and set the Pressure Release to **Sealing**. Press the **Cancel** button to reset the cooking program, then select the **Pressure Cook** or **Manual** setting and set the cooking time for 15 minutes at high pressure. (The pot will take about 10 minutes to come up to pressure before the cooking program begins.)

5 When the cooking program ends, let the pressure release naturally for at least 15 minutes, then move the Pressure Release to **Venting** to release any remaining steam. Open the pot and, using a slotted spoon or spatula, transfer the pork chops to a serving dish.

Nutrition Information

Per serving: 312 calories, 14 grams fat, 5 grams carbohydrates, 1 gram fiber, 37 grams protein

PREP	5 MINUTES
COOK	40 MINUTES
PR	15 MINUTES NPR
SERVES	6

6 Press the **Cancel** button to reset the cooking program, then select the **Sauté** setting. Simmer the sauce, stirring occasionally, for 6 to 8 minutes, until reduced and thickened. Wearing heat-resistant mitts, lift out the inner pot and pour the sauce over the chops. Press the **Cancel** button to turn off the pot.

7 Sprinkle the pork chops with the parsley and serve hot, with the rice on the side.

The spicing in this recipe recalls the flavors of *pinchos morunos*, Spanish-style, North African–inspired pork skewers. But instead of threading pork onto skewers, whole pork chops are marinated in a fragrant spice rub, then seared and cooked under pressure in the Instant Pot. I like to serve these chops with a side salad and rice.

PORK CHOPS WITH CUMIN AND CORIANDER

1 tablespoon ground cumin

1 tablespoon ground coriander

2 teaspoons sweet paprika

1 teaspoon ground turmeric

1 teaspoon garlic powder

1 teaspoon dried oregano

1 teaspoon fine sea salt

½ teaspoon freshly ground black pepper

2 tablespoons fresh lemon juice

3 tablespoons extra-virgin olive oil

2 pounds boneless pork chops, ½ inch thick (6 chops)

1 cup water

1 tablespoon chopped fresh flat-leaf parsley, for serving

Lemon wedges, for serving

PREP	10 MINUTES
MARINATE	1 HOUR TO OVERNIGHT
COOK	25 MINUTES
PR	10 MINUTES NPR
SERVES	6

1 In a small bowl, combine the cumin, coriander, paprika, turmeric, garlic powder, oregano, salt, pepper, lemon juice, and 1 tablespoon of the oil and stir together until a very thick paste forms. Using your hands, spread the paste all over the pork chops, then place them into a large zip-lock plastic bag or airtight container. Let the pork chops marinate for at least 1 hour on the counter or up to overnight in the refrigerator.

2 Select the **Sauté** setting on the Instant Pot and heat 1 tablespoon of the oil for about 2 minutes, until shimmering. Swirl the oil to make sure it coats the center of the pot. Using tongs, add half of the pork chops in a single layer and sear for about 2 minutes, until lightly browned on the first side. Flip the chops and sear for about 2 more minutes, until lightly browned on the second side. Transfer the chops to a plate. Repeat with the remaining pork chops.

3 Pour the water into the pot and, using a wooden spoon or spatula, nudge any browned bits from the bottom of the pot. (Take your time doing this, as the spices will have stuck to the bottom of the pot.) Place the wire metal steam rack into the pot. Using tongs, transfer the pork chops to the pot, placing them on the rack in two layers.

4 Secure the lid and set the Pressure Release to **Sealing**. Press the **Cancel** button to reset the cooking program, then select the **Pressure Cook** or **Manual** setting and set the cooking time for 10 minutes at high pressure. (The pot will take about 5 minutes to come up to pressure before the cooking program begins.)

5 When the cooking program ends, let the pressure release naturally for at least 10 minutes, then move the Pressure Release to **Venting** to release any remaining steam. Open the pot and, using tongs, transfer the pork chops to a serving dish.

6 Sprinkle the chops with the parsley, drizzle with the remaining 1 tablespoon oil, and serve right away, with the lemon wedges on the side.

Nutrition Information

Per serving: 260 calories, 15 grams fat, 4 grams carbohydrates, 1 gram fiber, 29 grams protein

Pork goes well with fruit, especially cherries. In this recipe, the sweet-tart flavor of the cherries also pairs perfectly with the balsamic vinegar, sweetening the sauce just enough so that no added sugar is needed. Make sure you're using pork loin and not pork *tenderloin* for this recipe. The tenderloin is leaner and more delicate, so it's better suited to stir-frying or high-heat roasting.

PORK WITH BALSAMIC AND CHERRIES

2½ pounds boneless pork loin, cut into 1½-inch cubes

1 teaspoon fine sea salt

1 teaspoon freshly ground black pepper

1 tablespoon cold-pressed avocado oil

1 yellow onion, sliced

¾ teaspoon dried rosemary, crushed

⅓ cup aged balsamic vinegar

¼ cup plus 1 tablespoon water

1 tablespoon Dijon mustard

1 tablespoon cornstarch

1 pound frozen pitted cherries, thawed

PREP	0 MINUTES
COOK	35 MINUTES
PR	10 MINUTES NPR
SERVES	6

1 Season the pork all over with the salt and pepper.

2 Select the high **Sauté** setting on the Instant Pot and heat the oil for about 2 minutes, until shimmering. Add the pork in as even a layer as possible and let it sear for about 4 minutes, until it begins to turn opaque and brown just a bit. Give it a stir, then let cook for about 4 more minutes, until mostly opaque (it's fine if some pieces are still pink). Transfer the pork to a dish.

3 Add the onion to the pot and sauté for about 2 minutes, until it begins to soften. Add the rosemary, vinegar, ¼ cup of the water, and the mustard and stir to combine, using a wooden spoon or spatula to nudge any browned bits from the bottom of the pot. Work quickly so that not too much liquid evaporates. Add the pork and stir to coat with the liquid.

4 Press the **Cancel** button to reset the cooking program, then select the **Pressure Cook** or **Manual** setting and set the cooking time for 15 minutes at high pressure. (The pot will take about 10 minutes to come up to pressure before the cooking program begins.)

5 When the cooking program ends, let the pressure release naturally for at least 10 minutes, then move the Pressure Release to **Venting** to release any remaining steam. Open the pot and, using a slotted spoon, transfer the pork to a serving dish. Cover with aluminum foil to keep warm.

6 In a small bowl, stir together the cornstarch and the remaining 1 tablespoon water. Add the cornstarch mixture and the cherries to the pot and stir to combine. Press the **Cancel** button to reset the cooking program, then select the **Sauté** setting. Let the sauce mixture come to a simmer for about 1 minute, until thickened.

7 Uncover the pork, ladle the sauce over the top, and serve right away.

Nutrition Information

Per serving: 328 calories, 10 grams fat, 21 grams carbohydrates, 2 grams fiber, 38 grams protein

Pork shoulder becomes infused with a Greek spice blend and lots of lemon juice as it braises to a fall-apart texture in the Instant Pot. The trick is to cut meat into 2-inch cubes before cooking, which take far less time to cook than a whole shoulder roast. Much of the fat renders out of the pork as it cooks, and you'll use a small amount of it to crisp the shredded pork in a skillet, so no extra oil is needed. The cucumber-packed yogurt sauce, whole-grain flatbread, and crisp vegetables make these wraps a hearty yet healthy meal.

CRISPY PULLED PORK GYROS

½ cup water

¼ cup fresh lemon juice

1½ teaspoons fine sea salt

1 teaspoon dried oregano

1 teaspoon dried thyme

1 teaspoon dried rosemary

1 teaspoon ground cumin

1 teaspoon garlic powder

1 teaspoon freshly ground black pepper

One 3-pound boneless pork shoulder roast, cut into 2-inch cubes

8 whole-wheat pitas, split and warmed

1 head romaine lettuce, shredded

1 small red onion, thinly sliced

1 cup cherry or grape tomatoes, quartered

2 Persian cucumbers, thinly sliced

1 cup tzatziki (page 264), for serving

PREP	0 MINUTES
COOK	1 HOUR
PR	20 MINUTES NPR
SERVES	8

1 Combine the water, lemon juice, salt, oregano, thyme, rosemary, cumin, garlic powder, and pepper in the Instant Pot and stir to combine. Add the pork and stir to coat evenly.

2 Secure the lid and set the Pressure Release to **Sealing**. Select the **Meat/Stew** setting and set the cooking time for 35 minutes at high pressure. (The pot will take about 15 minutes to come up to pressure before the cooking program begins.)

3 Let the pressure release naturally for at least 20 minutes, then move the Pressure Release to **Venting** to release any remaining steam. Open the pot and, using tongs, transfer the pork to a cutting board or plate. Using two forks, shred the meat into bite-size pieces.

4 Using a ladle or spoon, skim off a tablespoon of fat from the cooking liquid and add it to a large, heavy skillet (it's fine if you get a little bit of the cooking liquid; it will evaporate off as the meat cooks). Heat the skillet over medium-high heat, then add the pork to the skillet, spreading it in an even layer. Cook, stirring occasionally, for 8 to 10 minutes, until the pork is crisp and browned. (Alternatively, spread the pork in an even layer on a sheet pan and broil until crisp, about 5 minutes.)

5 Serve the pork right away in the pitas along with the lettuce, onion, tomatoes, cucumber, and tzatziki.

Nutrition Information

Per serving: 400 calories, 18 grams fat, 35 grams carbohydrates, 6 grams fiber, 28 grams protein

Bologneseis usually a simmer-all-day affair, but not when you use the Instant Pot. This recipe takes just a half hour to make and results in a meaty, hearty sauce. Serve it over whole-grain pasta, spiralized vegetable noodles, shirataki fettuccine noodles (the tofu variety of shirataki is my favorite), or steamed spaghetti squash (page 125).

GROUND PORK BOLOGNESE

2 slices center-cut bacon, diced

1 pound 80 percent lean ground pork

4 garlic cloves, minced

1 large yellow onion, diced

2 large carrots, diced

2 celery stalks, diced

1 teaspoon fine sea salt

2 teaspoons Italian seasoning

½ teaspoon dried sage

½ cup dry white wine

One 28-ounce can whole San Marzano-style tomatoes and their liquid

2 tablespoons tomato paste

Hot cooked noodles of choice

3 tablespoons chopped fresh flat-leaf parsley, for serving

6 tablespoons grated Parmesan cheese, for serving (optional)

PREP	0 MINUTES
COOK	30 MINUTES
PR	QPR OR NPR
SERVES	8

1 Select the **Sauté** setting on the Instant Pot, add the bacon, and sauté for about 2 minutes, until it begins to sizzle. Add the pork and sauté, breaking it up with a wooden spoon as it cooks, for about 5 minutes, until no traces of pink remain. Add the garlic, onion, carrots, celery, and salt and sauté for about 5 more minutes, until the onion has softened and is translucent.

2 Stir in the Italian seasoning, sage, and wine. Add the tomatoes and their liquid, crushing the tomatoes with your hands as you add them to the pot. Add the tomato paste on top in a dollop. Do not stir in the tomatoes and tomato paste.

3 Secure the lid and set the Pressure Release to **Sealing**. Press the **Cancel** button to reset the cooking program, then select the **Manual** or **Pressure Cook** setting and set the cooking time for 10 minutes at high pressure. (It will take about 10 minutes for the pot to come up to pressure before the cooking program begins.)

4 When the cooking program ends, perform a quick pressure release by moving the Pressure Release to **Venting**, or let the pressure release naturally (this will take about 20 minutes). Open the pot and stir the Bolognese, mixing in the tomato paste and using the spoon or spatula to crush any larger pieces of the tomatoes against the side of the pot.

5 Ladle the Bolognese over the noodles. Serve hot, sprinkled with the parsley and Parmesan.

Notes: For a sauce with less fat and fewer calories, substitute ground turkey or lean ground beef for the pork.

If you prefer a thicker sauce, reduce the sauce on the **Sauté** setting for 10 minutes after pressure cooking. To avoid spattering, do not stir the sauce while it simmers, and leave it to cool down for 5 minutes after turning off the pot.

Nutrition information

Per serving: 208 calories, 12 grams fat, 11 grams carbohydrates, 3 grams fiber, 12 grams protein

Ribs are almost always a crowd-pleaser, but they can be time-consuming to prepare. Here, they are seasoned, steamed in the Instant Pot, and then finished in the oven with a sweet and tangy mustard glaze. They cook for less than an hour and come out just as tender as if you had barbecued or baked them for hours. Serve them with steamed corn and coleslaw for a balanced meal.

HONEY DIJON BABY BACK RIBS

One 3-pound rack baby back ribs
1 teaspoon fine sea salt
1 teaspoon ground black pepper

Honey Dijon Sauce

¼ cup water
1 teaspoon cornstarch or arrowroot starch
3 tablespoons Dijon mustard
2 tablespoons honey
1 tablespoon raw cider vinegar
1 tablespoon cold-pressed avocado oil
¼ teaspoon dried thyme
¼ teaspoon fine sea salt
¼ teaspoon freshly ground black pepper
⅛ teaspoon cayenne pepper

PREP	5 MINUTES
COOK	55 MINUTES
PR	QPR
SERVES	4

1 Pat the ribs dry with paper towels, then cut them into three- or four-rib sections. Season the ribs all over with the salt and pepper.

2 Pour 1 cup water into the Instant Pot and place the wire metal steam rack into the pot. Stack the ribs on the rack.

3 Secure the lid and set the Pressure Release to **Sealing**. Select the **Steam** setting and set the cooking time for 20 minutes at high pressure. (The pot will take about 15 minutes to come up to pressure before the cooking program begins.)

4 While the ribs are steaming, preheat the oven to 375°F and line a sheet pan with a silicone baking mat or aluminum foil.

5 To make the sauce: In a small saucepan, combine the water, cornstarch, mustard, honey, vinegar, oil, thyme, salt, black pepper, and cayenne. Cook over medium heat, whisking continuously, for about 3 minutes, until thickened and emulsified. Remove from heat.

6 When the cooking program ends, perform a quick release by moving the Pressure Release to **Venting**. Open the pot and, using tongs, transfer the ribs to the prepared pan.

7 Brush the ribs on both sides with the sauce mixture, then turn the ribs bone side down. Bake for 20 minutes, until the sauce is bubbling and sticky. Remove from the oven and serve warm.

Note: For barbecued ribs, substitute ¾ cup of your favorite barbecue sauce for the honey Dijon sauce. I like Stubb's brand Original and Spicy versions, as they tend to have the lowest amount of sugar of any of the barbecue sauces I can find at most grocery stores.

Nutrition Information

Per serving: 289 calories, 18 grams fat, 11 grams carbohydrates, 0 grams fiber, 22 grams protein

Faster, healthier, and easier to make than the typical pot of *fabada asturiana*, this saffron-scented pot of pork and beans is hearty and rich. Tender chunks of pork shoulder take on a smoky flavor from center-cut bacon, which is leaner than other cuts, and from a spoonful of smoked paprika.

SPANISH-STYLE PORK AND WHITE BEANS

8 ounces (1 cup plus 2 tablespoons) Great Northern beans

4 cups water

1½ teaspoons fine sea salt

3 slices center-cut bacon

1 yellow onion, diced

3 garlic cloves, chopped

2½ cups low-sodium chicken bone broth (page 260)

1 tablespoon tomato paste

1 teaspoon smoked paprika

⅛ teaspoon saffron threads (optional)

¼ teaspoon freshly ground black pepper

1 bay leaf

2 pounds boneless pork shoulder or country ribs, cut into 1-inch cubes

SOAK	12 HOURS
PREP	0 MINUTES
COOK	45 MINUTES
PR	30 MINUTES NPR
SERVES	8

1 In a bowl, combine the beans, water, and 1 teaspoon of the salt and stir to dissolve the salt. Leave to soak for 12 hours, then drain in a colander.

2 Select the **Sauté** setting on the Instant Pot, wait for 2 minutes for the pot to heat up, and then add the bacon. Sauté for about 4 minutes, until some of the bacon fat has rendered out and there is browning on the bottom of the pot. Add the onion, garlic, and the remaining ½ teaspoon salt and sauté for about 3 minutes, until the onion begins to soften.

3 Add ½ cup of the broth, the tomato paste, paprika, saffron, and pepper and stir to combine. Cook for about 3 minutes, until the broth has mostly evaporated. Pour in the remaining 2 cups broth and use a wooden spoon or spatula to nudge any browned bits from the bottom of the pot. Stir in the soaked beans and bay leaf. Add the pork in an even layer on top of the beans, using the spoon or spatula to nudge the pork under the cooking liquid. It's fine if the pieces of pork are sticking up a bit out of the liquid.

4 Secure the lid and set the Pressure Release to **Sealing**. Press the **Cancel** button to reset the cooking program, then select the **Pressure Cook** or **Manual** setting and set the cooking time for 15 minutes at high pressure. (The pot will take about 15 minutes to come up to pressure before the cooking program begins.)

5 When the cooking program ends, let the pressure release naturally (this will take about 30 minutes). Open the pot and stir the pork and beans.

6 Spoon the pork and beans into bowls and serve hot.

Nutrition Information

Per serving: 368 calories, 20 grams fat, 21 grams carbohydrates, 8 grams fiber, 25 grams protein

Black bean garlic sauce is basically umami in a jar, adding a big dose of savory flavor to this tender braised pork. Look for it near the hoisin and soy sauces in Chinese grocery stores and the Asian foods section of most grocery stores. Serve the pork with steamed vegetables and brown rice for an easy, well-balanced dinner.

BRAISED PORK SHOULDER WITH CHINESE BLACK BEAN SAUCE

2 teaspoons cold-pressed avocado oil

1-inch piece fresh ginger, peeled and minced

3 garlic cloves, minced

½ cup plus 1 tablespoon water

3 tablespoons black bean garlic sauce

2 tablespoons tamari or low-sodium soy sauce

2 tablespoons Chinese rice wine (Shaoxing brand) or dry sherry

2 pounds boneless pork shoulder, cut into 2-inch cubes

1 tablespoon cornstarch

1 green onion, white and green parts, thinly sliced, for serving

PREP	0 MINUTES
COOK	45 MINUTES
PR	10 MINUTES NPR
SERVES	6

1 Select the **Sauté** setting on the Instant Pot and heat the oil, ginger, and garlic for 3 minutes, until the garlic is bubbling and beginning to brown. Add ½ cup of the water, the black bean sauce, tamari, and rice wine and stir to combine. Add the pork pieces, stirring to coat them in the cooking liquid.

2 Secure the lid in the **Sealing** position. Press the **Cancel** button to reset the cooking program, then select the **Meat/Stew**, **Pressure Cook**, or **Manual** setting and set the cooking time for 30 minutes at high pressure. (The pot will take about 10 minutes to come up to pressure before the cooking program begins.)

3 When the cooking program ends, let the pressure release naturally for at least 10 minutes, then move the Pressure Release to **Venting** to release any remaining steam. Open the pot and, using tongs, transfer the pork to a serving plate.

4 In a small bowl, stir together the cornstarch and the remaining 1 tablespoon water. Add the cornstarch mixture to the cooking liquid in the pot and stir to combine. Press the **Cancel** button to reset the cooking program, then select the **Sauté** setting. Let the mixture come to a simmer and cook for 1 minute, until thickened. Press the **Cancel** button to turn off the pot.

5 Spoon the thickened sauce over the pork. Sprinkle the green onion over the pork and serve right away.

Note: You can make this recipe with 2 pounds boneless pork chops in place of the boneless pork shoulder. For ¾-inch-thick chops, lower the pressure cooking time to 15 minutes. For 1-inch-thick chops, lower the pressure cooking time to 20 minutes.

Nutrition Information

Per serving: 355 calories, 26 grams fat, 3 grams carbohydrates, 1 gram fiber, 26 grams protein

Tangy flavors of capers and lemon mellow and flavor the sauce as this lean yet tender pork loin braises. It takes about an hour to cook, and you can make it in the morning, leave it in the pot on the Keep Warm setting all day long, and then cook the potatoes and artichokes right before dinnertime. A convenient dinner that looks and tastes this gourmet is a true weeknight win.

PORK LOIN WITH LEMON, CAPERS, AND ARTICHOKES

One 2-pound boneless pork loin roast

1 teaspoon fine sea salt

¾ teaspoon freshly ground black pepper

1 tablespoon cold-pressed avocado oil

1 yellow onion, thinly sliced

2 garlic cloves, minced

¾ cup low-sodium chicken bone broth (page 260)

2 tablespoons fresh lemon juice

1 tablespoon Dijon mustard

2 tablespoons capers

1 teaspoon dried thyme

One 12-ounce bag frozen artichoke hearts

1 pound creamer potatoes or other small potatoes, halved if larger than 1¼ inches in diameter

2 tablespoons chopped fresh flat-leaf parsley, for serving

1 Pat the pork roast dry with paper towels. Season the pork all over with the salt and pepper.

2 Select the high **Sauté** setting on the Instant Pot and heat the oil for about 2 minutes, until shimmering. Using tongs, lower the pork roast, fat side down, into the pot and sear for 6 minutes, until browned on the first side. Flip the roast and sear for 5 more minutes, until browned on the second side. Transfer the roast to a plate.

3 Add the onion and garlic to the pot and sauté for about 3 minutes, until the onion is beginning to soften. Stir in the broth, lemon juice, mustard, capers, and thyme, using a wooden spoon or spatula to nudge any browned bits from the bottom of the pot. Return the roast, fat side up, to the pot, then spoon some of the cooking liquid over the top.

4 Secure the lid and set the Pressure Release to **Sealing**. Press the **Cancel** button to reset the cooking program, then select the **Meat/ Stew** setting and set the cooking time for 40 minutes at high pressure. (The pot will take about 5 minutes to come up to pressure before the cooking program begins.)

5 When the cooking program ends, perform a quick pressure release by moving the Pressure Release to **Venting**, or let the pressure release naturally (this will take about 25 minutes). Open the pot and, using tongs, transfer the roast to a cutting board. Tent the roast with aluminum foil to keep it warm.

Nutrition Information

Per serving: 318 calories, 8 grams fat, 22 grams carbohydrates, 3 grams fiber, 41 grams protein

PREP	5 MINUTES
COOK	1 HOUR 15 MINUTES
PR	QPR OR NPR
SERVES	6

6 Add the artichoke hearts and potatoes to the Instant Pot. Secure the lid and set the Pressure Release to **Sealing**. Press the **Cancel** button to reset the cooking program, then select the **Pressure Cook** or **Manual** setting for 5 minutes at high pressure. (It will take about 10 minutes for the pot to come up to pressure before the cooking program begins.)

7 When the cooking program ends, perform a quick pressure release by moving the Pressure Release to **Venting**. Open the pot and, using a slotted spoon, transfer the vegetables to a serving dish.

8 Carve the pork loin into ½-inch-thick slices. Serve with the potatoes and artichokes, sprinkled with the parsley, and with some of the cooking liquid spooned over the pork and vegetables.

Note: This recipe works with a larger or smaller pork roast, too, up to a maximum of 4 pounds. The cooking time will be 20 minutes per pound.

This traditional, satisfying Irish stew is made with lean, high protein lamb stew meat and flavored with Guinness beer and thyme. Serve it on St. Patrick's Day or any time you're in the mood for a hearty meal. You can cook the stew up to the first pressure release ahead of time, then add the vegetables and pressure cook for a couple more minutes right before dinnertime. Serve the stew on its own or over sautéed cabbage for added nutrition.

IRISH LAMB STEW

1½ pounds lamb stew meat, cut into 1-inch cubes

1 teaspoon fine sea salt

1 teaspoon freshly ground black pepper

1 tablespoon cold-pressed avocado oil

1 yellow onion, diced

3 garlic cloves, chopped

1 cup Guinness imperial stout

2 teaspoons Worcestershire sauce

2 teaspoons Dijon mustard

1 tablespoon chopped fresh thyme, or 1 teaspoon dried thyme

1 bay leaf

2 tablespoons tomato paste

12 ounces carrots, cut into ½-inch-thick rounds

1½ pounds Yukon gold or other waxy potatoes, cut into ¾-inch dice

1 tablespoon cornstarch

1 tablespoon water

PREP	0 MINUTES
COOK	45 MINUTES
PR	10 MINUTES NPR AND QPR
REST	5 MINUTES
SERVES	6

1 Season the lamb all over with the salt and pepper. Select the **Sauté** setting on the Instant Pot and heat the oil for 2 minutes. Add the onion and garlic and sauté for about 5 minutes, until the onion softens and begins to brown. Add the stout, Worcestershire, mustard, thyme, and bay leaf and stir to combine, using a wooden spoon or spatula to nudge any browned bits from the bottom of the pot. Add the lamb and stir to combine with the cooking liquid. Add the tomato paste in a dollop on top of the lamb. Do not stir it in.

2 Secure the lid and set the Pressure Release to **Sealing**. Press the **Cancel** button to reset the cooking program, then select the **Meat/Stew** setting and set the cooking time for 20 minutes at high pressure. (The pot will take about 5 minutes to come up to pressure before the cooking program begins.)

3 When the cooking program ends, let the pressure release naturally for at least 10 minutes, then move the Pressure Release to **Venting** to release any remaining steam. Open the pot, remove and discard the bay leaf, and stir in the carrots and potatoes.

4 Secure the lid once again and set the Pressure Release to **Sealing**. Press the **Cancel** button to reset the cooking program, then select the **Pressure Cook** or **Manual** setting and set the cooking time for 3 minutes at high pressure. (The pot will take about 10 minutes to come up to pressure before the cooking program begins.)

5 When the cooking program ends, perform a quick pressure release by moving the Pressure Release to **Venting**.

6 In a small bowl, stir together the cornstarch and water. Open the pot and quickly stir the cornstarch mixture into the stew. Re-cover and let rest for about 5 minutes to thicken the cooking liquid.

7 Ladle the stew into bowls and serve piping hot.

Nutrition Information

Per serving: 330 calories, 9 grams fat, 33 grams carbohydrates, 4 grams fiber, 26 grams protein

The one thing that prevents me from making cabbage rolls more often is rolling them. This recipe comes together so much faster than the traditional dish, and it tastes exactly like it, just without all of the prep work! Just chop up the cabbage and make a casserole-style dish in the Instant Pot, saving yourself a whole lot of time. And it packs a protein punch with a minimum of fat.

CABBAGE ROLL CASSEROLE

- 2 tablespoons cold-pressed avocado oil
- 1 large yellow onion, diced
- 1 pound 96 percent extra-lean ground beef
- ½ teaspoon fine sea salt
- ½ teaspoon freshly ground black pepper
- 1 cup Minute brand quick-cooking brown rice
- One 15-ounce can tomato sauce
- 1 cup water
- 2 carrots, grated
- ½ small head green cabbage, chopped
- ¾ cup plain 2 percent Greek yogurt, homemade (page 34) or store-bought, or Cashew Sour Cream (page 265), for serving
- ¼ cup chopped fresh flat leaf parsley, for serving

PREP	0 MINUTES
COOK	40 MINUTES
PR	10 MINUTES NPR
SERVES	6

1 Select the **Sauté** setting on the Instant Pot and heat the oil for 2 minutes. Add the onion and sauté for about 4 minutes, until it softens and is translucent. Add the beef, salt, and pepper and sauté, breaking the meat up with a wooden spoon as it cooks, for about 5 minutes, until no traces of pink remain. Add the rice, tomato sauce, and water and stir to mix thoroughly. Sprinkle the carrots on top of the meat-and-rice mixture in an even layer. Repeat with the cabbage. Do not stir them in.

2 Secure the lid and set the Pressure Release to **Sealing**. Press the **Cancel** button to reset the cooking program, then select the **Pressure Cook** or **Manual** setting and set the cooking time for 15 minutes at high pressure. (The pot will take about 10 minutes to come up to pressure before the cooking program begins.)

3 When the cooking program ends, let the pressure release naturally for at least 10 minutes, then move the Pressure Release to **Venting** to release any remaining steam. Open the pot and stir the casserole to combine all of the ingredients evenly.

4 Spoon the casserole into bowls and top each serving with a dollop of yogurt and a sprinkle of parsley. Serve warm.

Note: You can substitute 93 percent lean ground turkey for the ground beef in this recipe.

Nutrition Information

Per serving: 271 calories, 9 grams fat, 29 grams carbohydrates, 5 grams fiber, 20 grams protein

Using extra-lean ground beef helps to cut down on the saturated fat and calories in this salad, so you can eat these crunchy corn tostadas without guilt. Beans and fresh vegetables contribute lots of fiber and vitamins to this one-dish meal that's filling, nutritious, and full of flavor. You'll also notice there's no cheese. A few slices of avocado add all of the buttery richness this dairy-free recipe needs.

GROUND BEEF TOSTADA SALADS

1 tablespoon cold-pressed avocado oil

2 garlic cloves, minced

1 large yellow onion, diced

2 pounds 96 percent extra-lean ground beef

3 tablespoons chili powder

2 teaspoons ground cumin

2 teaspoons dried oregano

½ cup water

1 teaspoon fine sea salt

3 cups drained cooked black beans or pinto beans (page 44), warmed, or two 15-ounce cans black beans or pinto beans, rinsed, drained, and warmed

Twelve 7-inch corn tostada shells, for serving

2 heads romaine lettuce, shredded, for serving

1½ cups cherry or grape tomatoes, halved, for serving

1 large avocado, pitted, peeled, and sliced, for serving

¼ cup chopped fresh cilantro, for serving

Hot sauce (such as Cholula or Tapatío), for serving

PREP	0 MINUTES
COOK	25 MINUTES
PR	QPR OR NPR
SERVES	6

1 Select the high **Sauté** setting on the Instant Pot and heat the oil and garlic for 2 minutes, until the garlic is bubbling but not browned. Add half of the onion and sauté for about 3 minutes, until the onion has softened and is just beginning to brown. Add the beef and sauté, using a wooden spoon to break up the meat as it cooks, for about 3 more minutes. Stir in the chili powder, cumin, oregano, water, and salt. It's fine if some pink remains; the beef does not have to be fully cooked at this point.

2 Secure the lid and set the Pressure Release to **Sealing**. Press the **Cancel** button to reset the cooking program, then select the **Pressure Cook** or **Manual** setting and set the cooking time for 10 minutes at high pressure. (The pot will take about 5 minutes to come up to pressure before the cooking program begins.)

3 When the cooking program ends, you can either perform a quick pressure release by moving the Pressure Release to **Venting** or let the pressure release naturally (this will take about 25 minutes) and leave the pot on the **Keep Warm** setting for up to 10 hours. Open the pot and give the meat a stir.

4 Place the tostada shells on plates. Using a slotted spoon, spoon the meat and beans onto the shells. Top with the lettuce, tomatoes, the remaining half of the onion, the avocado, and cilantro. Serve right away, with the hot sauce on the side.

Nutrition Information

Per serving: 537 calories, 20 grams fat, 46 grams carbohydrates, 13 grams fiber, 41 grams protein

Italian spices and sun-dried tomatoes flavor this meat loaf. A pound of spinach is mixed with the beef, so you're well on your way to creating a balanced, healthy meal. Serve the meat loaf with Cauliflower Carrot Mash (page 214) for a kid-friendly dinner with vegetables in both dishes.

FLORENTINE BEEF MEAT LOAF

- **1 pound 96 percent extra-lean ground beef**
- **1 pound frozen chopped spinach, thawed and squeezed of excess water**
- **1 small yellow onion, finely chopped**
- **¾ cup dried whole-wheat bread crumbs**
- **¼ cup oil-packed sun-dried tomatoes, drained and minced**
- **1 large egg**
- **2 teaspoons Italian seasoning**
- **1 teaspoon garlic powder**
- **1 teaspoon fine sea salt**
- **½ teaspoon red pepper flakes (optional)**
- **¼ cup no-sugar-added ketchup**

PREP	10 MINUTES
COOK	55 MINUTES
PR	QPR OR NPR
SERVES	4

1 Pour 1 cup water into the Instant Pot.

2 Lightly grease a 7 by 3-inch round cake pan with olive oil or nonstick cooking spray. In a large bowl, combine the beef, spinach, onion, bread crumbs, tomatoes, egg, Italian seasoning, garlic powder, salt, and red pepper flakes (if using). Mix well with your hands until all of the ingredients are evenly distributed. Transfer the meat mixture to the prepared pan, shaping it into an even layer.

3 Cover the pan tightly with aluminum foil and place it on a long-handled silicone steam rack. Then, holding the handles of the steam rack, lower it into the Instant Pot. (If you don't have the long-handled rack, use the wire metal steam rack and a homemade sling as described on page 10.)

4 Secure the lid and set the Pressure Release to **Sealing**. Select the **Pressure Cook** or **Manual** setting and set the cooking time for 40 minutes at high pressure. (It will take about 10 minutes for the pot to come up to pressure before the cooking program begins.) Preheat the broiler of a toaster oven (or conventional oven) 5 to 10 minutes before the meat loaf is ready.

5 When the cooking program ends, perform a quick release by moving the Pressure Release to **Venting**, or let the pressure release naturally (this will take about 15 minutes). Open the pot and, wearing heat-resistant mitts, grasp the handles of the steam rack and lift the pan out of the pot. Uncover the pan, taking care not to get burned by the steam, and spread the ketchup evenly over the top of the meat loaf.

6 Broil the meat loaf for a few minutes, just until the ketchup is warmed through and forms a glaze. Cut into slices and serve.

Nutrition Information

Per serving: 358 calories, 9 grams fat, 23 grams carbohydrates, 3 grams fiber, 41 grams protein

Tender tips of sirloin beef in a mushroom gravy are a classic comfort food. This version is lighter than most, as it calls for only a tablespoon of oil. Serve the gravy as is or look to the recipe Note for the optional step of quickly thickening the gravy with a little cornstarch. Beef tips go great with egg noodles. Look for the cholesterol-free whole-grain version from No Yolks brand.

BEEF TIPS WITH ONION AND MUSHROOM GRAVY

- 2 pounds beef sirloin tips
- 1 teaspoon fine sea salt
- ½ teaspoon freshly ground black pepper
- 1 tablespoon cold-pressed avocado oil
- 3 garlic cloves, minced
- 1 large onion, sliced
- 8 ounces cremini mushrooms, sliced
- ½ teaspoon dried thyme
- 1 tablespoon Worcestershire sauce
- 1 tablespoon Dijon mustard
- ½ cup low-sodium roasted beef bone broth (page 260)
- 1 tablespoon tomato paste

PREP	0 MINUTES
COOK	40 MINUTES
PR	10 MINUTES NPR
SERVES	6

1 Season the beef all over with the salt and pepper.

2 Select the **Sauté** setting on the Instant Pot and heat the oil and garlic for 3 minutes, until the garlic is bubbling but not browned. Add the onion and mushrooms and sauté for about 5 minutes, until the onions have softened and the mushrooms are wilted and beginning to give up their liquid. Add the beef and sauté for 3 more minutes, until it is mostly opaque on the surface; it does not have to be cooked all the way through. Stir in the thyme, Worcestershire, mustard, and broth. Add the tomato paste in a dollop on top. Do not stir it in.

3 Secure the lid and set the Pressure Release to **Sealing**. Press the **Cancel** button to reset the cooking program, then select the **Meat/Stew** program and set the cooking time for 20 minutes at high pressure. (The pot will take about 10 minutes to come up to pressure before the cooking program begins.)

4 When the cooking program ends, let the pressure release for at least 10 minutes, then move the Pressure Release to **Venting** to release any remaining steam. Open the pot and stir to incorporate the tomato paste.

5 Spoon the beef tips onto plates and serve hot, with the gravy spooned over the top.

Note: If you prefer a thicker gravy, you can thicken it after it has finished pressure cooking. Stir together 1 tablespoon cornstarch and 1 tablespoon water, then pour the mixture into the cooked beef tips and cook on the **Sauté** setting for about 2 minutes, until thickened.

Nutrition Information

Per serving: 269 calories, 12 grams fat, 7 grams carbohydrates, 1 gram fiber, 33 grams protein

On some nights, the absolute best thing for the dinner table is a big, comforting casserole. In this cottage pie sweet potatoes, a healthier choice than the traditional Irish potatoes, lend a pretty orange color and extra vitamin C, and they cook right on top of the filling in the Instant Pot.

SWEET POTATO COTTAGE PIE

- 1 tablespoon cold-pressed avocado oil
- 2 garlic cloves, minced
- 1 yellow onion, diced
- 2 pounds 96 percent extra-lean ground beef
- ½ cup low-sodium roasted beef bone broth (page 260)
- 1 teaspoon dried thyme
- 1 teaspoon dried sage
- 1 teaspoon freshly ground black pepper
- 1½ teaspoons fine sea salt
- 2 tablespoons Worcestershire sauce
- One 16-ounce bag frozen mixed vegetables (peas, green beans, carrots, and corn), thawed
- 3 tablespoons tomato paste
- 2 pounds sweet potatoes, peeled and cut into 1-inch-thick wedges
- ¼ cup unsweetened nondairy milk
- 1 cup shredded Cheddar cheese (optional)
- ¼ cup sliced green onions, white and green parts, for serving

PREP	0 MINUTES
COOK	35 MINUTES
PR	QPR
SERVES	6

1 Select the **Sauté** setting on the Instant Pot and heat the oil and garlic for 2 minutes, until the garlic is bubbling but not browned. Add the onion and sauté for about 3 minutes, until it begins to soften. Add the beef and sauté, breaking it up with a wooden spoon as it cooks, for about 7 minutes, until cooked through and no traces of pink remain. Add the broth, thyme, sage, pepper, ¾ teaspoon of the salt, the Worcestershire, and mixed vegetables and stir to mix well. Add the tomato paste in a dollop on top of the meat mixture. Do not stir it in.

2 Place a tall steam rack into the pot, making sure all of its legs are resting firmly on the bottom. Place the sweet potato rounds on the rack.

3 Secure the lid and set the Pressure Release to **Sealing**. Press the **Cancel** button to reset the cooking program, then select the **Pressure Cook** or **Manual** setting and set the cooking time for 4 minutes at high pressure. (The pot will take about 15 minutes to come up to pressure before the cooking program begins.)

4 When the cooking program ends, perform a quick pressure release by moving the Pressure Release to **Venting**. Open the pot and, using tongs, gently transfer the sweet potatoes to a bowl. Add the milk and the remaining ¾ teaspoon salt to the potatoes and, using a potato masher, mash until smooth.

5 Wearing heat-resistant mitts, remove the rack from the pot. Stir ½ cup of the mashed sweet potatoes into the beef mixture in the pot. Transfer the beef mixture to a broiler-safe 9 by 13-inch baking dish, dollop the remaining mashed potatoes on top, and spread them out with a fork, creating a surface texture. If using the cheese, sprinkle it evenly over the surface.

6 Broil the cheese-topped cottage pie for about 3 minutes, until the cheese is bubbling and browned. If you have not used the cheese, broil the pie for about 5 minutes, until the potatoes are lightly browned.

7 Spoon the cottage pie onto plates, sprinkle with the green onions, and serve right away.

Nutrition Information

Per serving: 269 calories, 9 grams fat, 12 grams carbohydrates, 2 grams fiber, 34 grams protein

Of course, despite the name, this pot roast isn't actually cooked all day on a barbecue grill or in a smoker. It becomes fall-apart tender in an Instant Pot in less than two hours' time—even more tender than a cooked-all-day piece of meat. A little smoked paprika lends that smoky barbecue aroma, and your favorite barbecue sauce coats every bite of the high-protein shredded beef.

SHREDDED BBQ POT ROAST

One 2½-pound boneless chuck roast

1 teaspoon fine sea salt

¾ teaspoon freshly ground black pepper

¾ teaspoon garlic powder

¾ teaspoon smoked paprika

1 tablespoon cold-pressed avocado oil

1 yellow onion, sliced

½ cup water (see Notes)

½ cup barbecue sauce of choice (I like Stubb's Original or Spicy)

1 Pat the chuck roast dry with paper towels. Season the roast all over with the salt, pepper, garlic powder, and paprika.

2 Select the high **Sauté** setting on the Instant Pot and heat the oil for 2 minutes, until shimmering. Using tongs, lower the roast into the pot and sear for about 5 minutes, until browned on the first side. Flip the roast and sear for 4 more minutes, until browned on the second side. Transfer to a plate.

3 Add the onion to the pot and sauté for about 3 minutes, until it begins to soften. Pour in the water and, using a wooden spoon or spatula, nudge any browned bits from the bottom of the pot. Work quickly so that not too much water evaporates. Return the roast to the pot.

4 Secure the lid and set the Pressure Release to **Sealing**. Press the **Cancel** button to reset the cooking program, then select the **Meat/ Stew** setting and set the cooking time for 1 hour 15 minutes at high pressure. (The pot will take about 5 minutes to come up to pressure before the cooking program begins.)

5 When the cooking program ends, let the pressure release naturally (this will take about 20 minutes). Open the pot and, using tongs, carefully transfer the roast to a cutting board. It may fall apart a bit as you remove it from the pot.

6 Wearing heat-resistant mitts, lift out the inner pot. Pour the cooking liquid into a fat separator (see Notes) with a strainer on top to catch the onions. Pour the liquid back into the inner pot and discard the fat. Stir the onions back into the cooking liquid along with the barbecue sauce. Press the **Cancel** button to reset the cooking program, then select the **Sauté** program. Bring the sauce to a simmer and simmer for about 10 minutes, stirring occasionally, until thickened. Press the **Cancel** button to turn off the pot.

Nutrition Information

Per serving: 263 calories, 8 grams fat, 7 grams carbohydrates, 1 gram fiber, 40 grams protein

PREP	0 MINUTES
COOK	1 HOUR 45 MINUTES
PR	20 MINUTES NPR
SERVES	6

7 While the sauce is simmering, snip off any twine tying the roast together, then use two forks to pull the meat apart. Chop the longer shreds if needed. Once you've turned off the pot, return the shredded meat to the cooking liquid and stir to combine.

8 Serve the pot roast right away, or select the **Keep Warm** setting and leave for up to 10 hours before serving, then serve warm.

Notes: If you're using an 8-quart Instant Pot, add an extra ½ cup water (1 cup total).

If you do not have a fat separator, pour the cooking liquid through a fine-mesh strainer into a measuring pitcher and reserve the onions. Using a large spoon, skim off the and discard the fat from the strained liquid, then return the defatted liquid and the onions to the inner pot and simmer as directed.

You can cook a larger pot roast using the same method (up to 4 pounds in the 6-quart Instant Pot). Keep the amount of water the same and increase the barbecue sauce to taste. For each additional 8 ounces meat, increase the cooking time by 10 minutes.

This version of chili mac is amazingly easy to make: the noodles, beef, and other ingredients all cook in the same pot, and it takes about a half hour from start to finish. The dish gets a flavor boost from the unusual cinnamon-spiked spice blend that makes Cincinnati chili so special. Serve it in the classic style, with shredded cheese and diced onions on top. If you're craving traditional chili mac, look to the recipe Notes for that variation, as well as for a tip on using gluten-free noodles.

CINCINNATI CHILI MAC

Spice Blend

1 tablespoon sweet paprika

2 teaspoons ground cumin

1½ teaspoons ground cinnamon

1 teaspoon ground coriander

1 teaspoon natural cocoa powder

1 teaspoon mustard powder

½ teaspoon ground ginger

¼ teaspoon ground cloves

¼ teaspoon cayenne pepper

2 teaspoons cold-pressed avocado oil

2 garlic cloves, minced

1 yellow onion, diced, plus ¾ cup chopped, for serving

1 pound 96 percent extra-lean ground beef

2 cups low-sodium roasted beef bone broth (page 260)

8 ounces whole-wheat elbow pasta

One 14½-ounce can petite diced tomatoes and their liquid

1½ cups drained cooked kidney beans (page 44), or one 15-ounce can kidney beans, rinsed and drained

¾ cup shredded Cheddar cheese or vegan cheese shreds, for serving

Yellow mustard, for serving

Tabasco sauce, for serving

1 To make the spice blend: In a small bowl, stir together the paprika, cumin, cinnamon, coriander, cocoa powder, mustard powder, ginger, cloves, and cayenne.

2 Select the **Sauté** setting on the Instant Pot and heat the oil and garlic for 2 minutes, until the garlic is bubbling but not browned. Add the diced onion and sauté for about 2 minutes, until it begins to soften. Add the beef and sauté for 3 minutes, using a wooden spoon to break up the meat as it cooks. Stir in the spice blend and sauté for about 2 more minutes, until the beef is mostly cooked through and the spices are aromatic.

3 Pour in the broth, using a wooden spoon or spatula to nudge any browned bits from the bottom of the pot. Add the pasta in an even layer, using the spoon to nudge the noodles under the liquid as much as possible. It's fine if a few pieces are sticking up out of the water. Pour the tomatoes and their liquid and the kidney beans evenly over the ground beef and pasta mixture. Do not stir them in.

4 Secure the lid and set the Pressure Release to **Sealing**. Press the **Cancel** button to reset the cooking program, then select the **Pressure Cook** or **Manual** setting and set the cooking time for 6 minutes at high pressure. (The pot will take about 10 minutes to come up to pressure before the cooking program begins.)

5 When the cooking program ends, let the pressure release naturally for 5 minutes, then move the Pressure Release to **Venting** to release any remaining steam. Open the pot and stir the chili mac to combine. Let sit for 5 minutes, then stir once more.

Nutrition Information

Per serving: 374 calories, 10 grams fat, 44 grams carbohydrates, 13 grams fiber, 30 grams protein

PREP	5 MINUTES
COOK	25 MINUTES
PR	5 MINUTES NPR
REST	5 MINUTES
SERVES	6

6 Ladle the chili mac into bowls and top each serving with 2 tablespoons of the cheese and 2 tablespoons of the chopped onion. Serve hot, with the mustard and the Tabasco at the table.

Notes: For a traditional chili mac flavor, substitute 3 tablespoons chili powder for the spice blend.

For a gluten-free chili mac, substitute 8 ounces chickpea-based pasta for the whole-wheat pasta. Reduce the cooking time to 4 minutes with a quick pressure release. Although many Instant Pot pasta recipes don't work well with gluten-free noodles, this one is an exception.

Make the sauce for this lasagna in the Instant Pot earlier in the day and let it hang out on the Keep Warm setting, then boil the noodles (or don't if you're using a no-boil variety), preheat the oven, and assemble your lasagna just before dinnertime. I love making this lasagna on the weekend: it's the perfect balance of effort and time for a lazy Sunday. The meat sauce includes a whole pound of spinach for some extra nutrients and fiber, and lean beef keeps things from getting too rich or greasy.

BEEF AND SPINACH LASAGNA

Meat Sauce

- 1 tablespoon extra-virgin olive oil
- 3 garlic cloves, minced
- 1 pound 96 percent extra-lean ground beef
- ½ cup water
- 2 teaspoons Italian seasoning
- 1 teaspoon fine sea salt
- One 28-ounce can whole San Marzano-style tomatoes and their liquid
- ¼ cup tomato paste
- One 16-ounce bag frozen spinach, thawed and squeezed of excess liquid

- 8 ounces whole-grain lasagna noodles (see Note), regular or no-boil noodles

Ricotta Mixture

- 2 large eggs
- 2 cups part-skim ricotta cheese
- 1 cup grated Parmesan or Pecorino Romano cheese
- 2 teaspoons Italian seasoning

- 2 cups shredded mozzarella cheese

1 If you are using regular lasagna noodles, put a large pot of water on the stove and bring to a boil for boiling the noodles.

2 To make the meat sauce: Select the **Sauté** setting on the Instant Pot and heat the oil and garlic for 3 minutes, until the garlic is bubbling and golden but not browned. Add the beef and sauté, breaking it up with a wooden spoon as it cooks, for about 5 minutes, until no traces of pink remain. Stir in the water, Italian seasoning and salt. Add the tomatoes in a layer on top of the beef, crushing them with your hands as you add them to the pot. Add the tomato paste in a dollop on top. Do not stir in the tomatoes or tomato paste.

3 Secure the lid and set the Pressure Release to **Sealing**. Press the **Cancel** button to reset the cooking program, then select the **Pressure Cook** or **Manual** setting and set the cooking time for 20 minutes at high pressure. (The pot will take about 10 minutes to come up to pressure before the cooking program begins.)

4 While the meat sauce is cooking, boil the lasagna noodles according to the package instructions (skip this step if using no-boil noodles). Lay the noodles out flat in a single layer on a sheet pan lined with plastic wrap. When you fill up the sheet pan, add another layer of plastic wrap and arrange the remaining noodles on top. Cover with plastic wrap so the noodles don't dry out.

5 To make the ricotta mixture: In a medium bowl, lightly whisk the eggs until blended. Stir in the ricotta, Parmesan, and Italian seasoning, mixing well.

Nutrition Information

Per serving: 488 calories, 20 grams fat, 39 grams carbohydrates, 5 grams fiber, 38 grams protein

PREP	15 MINUTES
COOK	1 HOUR 35 MINUTES
PR	15 MINUTES NPR
REST	15 MINUTES
SERVES	8

6 When the cooking program ends, let the pressure release naturally for at least 15 minutes, then move the Pressure Release to **Venting** to release any remaining steam. At this point, you can continue with the recipe right away or leave the sauce on the **Keep Warm** setting for up to 10 hours.

7 Open the pot and stir the spinach into the sauce. Press the **Cancel** button to reset the cooking program, then select the **Sauté** setting. Let the sauce simmer for about 10 minutes, until it has thickened up a bit. Press the **Cancel** button to turn off the pot.

8 While the sauce is simmering, preheat the oven to 375°F.

9 Ladle 1 cup of the meat sauce into a broiler-safe 9 by 13-inch baking dish and spread it in an even layer. Arrange a layer of lasagna noodles on top of the sauce. Spoon 1 cup of the ricotta mixture onto the noodles and spread it evenly, taking care not to move the noodles around under the cheese. Ladle 1½ cups of the meat sauce evenly over the ricotta, then sprinkle ⅔ cup of the mozzarella evenly over the meat sauce. Repeat the layers of noodles, ricotta, sauce, and mozzarella once more, using the same amounts, then add a third layer of noodles, ricotta, and sauce. Reserve the remaining ⅔ cup mozzarella.

10 Cover the baking dish tightly with aluminum foil. Bake for 45 minutes, until heated through and bubbling. Remove the aluminum foil, sprinkle the remaining mozzarella on top, and broil for about 3 minutes, just until the cheese is bubbly and browned on top. Remove the lasagna from the oven and let rest for 15 minutes before serving.

11 Cut the lasagna into squares and serve warm.

Note: The organic brown rice lasagna noodles made by Tinkyada are my go-to choice for gluten-free, whole-grain lasagna noodles. For the best texture, always rinse them in cold water after cooking. This step will also cool the noodles down, making them easier to handle with your bare hands as you transfer them to the sheet pan.

This is a weeknight-friendly take on *nihari*, a popular Indian and Pakistani stew (it's also commonly made with lamb). A yogurt marinade, a fragrant spice blend, and 25 minutes of cooking under pressure give you restaurant flavor in short order. Serve it with a green salad and some rice, cauliflower rice, or naan.

INDIAN-STYLE BEEF CURRY

Marinated Beef

½ cup plain 2 percent Greek yogurt, homemade (page 34) or store-bought

1-inch piece fresh ginger, peeled and grated

3 garlic cloves, grated

1 teaspoon fine sea salt

¼ teaspoon cayenne pepper

2 pounds beef stew meat

Spice Blend

1 tablespoon sweet paprika

1½ teaspoons ground cinnamon

1½ teaspoons ground coriander

1 teaspoon ground cumin

1 teaspoon ground ginger

1 teaspoon ground cardamom

½ teaspoon freshly ground black pepper

½ teaspoon ground nutmeg

½ teaspoon ground cloves

1 To marinate the beef: Combine the yogurt, fresh ginger, garlic, salt, and cayenne in a medium bowl and stir to combine. Stir in the beef, coating evenly. Cover the bowl and marinate in the refrigerator for at least 1 hour or up to overnight.

2 To make the spice blend: In a small bowl, stir together the paprika, cinnamon, coriander, ground cumin, ground ginger, cardamom, black pepper, nutmeg, and cloves.

3 Select the **Sauté** setting on the Instant Pot and heat the oil, cumin seeds, and fennel seeds for 3 minutes, until the seeds are bubbling and aromatic. Add the onions and sauté for about 10 minutes, until softened and just beginning to caramelize. Add the spice blend and stir for 1 minute, until fragrant.

4 Add the beef and marinade and sauté, scraping the bottom of the pot as you stir, for about 5 minutes, until the beef is opaque on the exterior; the beef does not need to be cooked through. Add the water and bay leaves and stir to combine, using a wooden spoon or spatula to nudge any remaining browned bits from the bottom of the pot.

5 Secure the lid and set the Pressure Release to **Sealing**. Press the **Cancel** button to reset the cooking program. Select the **Pressure Cook** or **Manual** setting and set the cooking time for 20 minutes. (The pot will take about 10 minutes to come up to pressure before the cooking program begins.)

6 While the beef is cooking, toast the flour. Heat a small skillet over medium heat. Add the flour and cook, stirring continuously, for about 4 minutes, until light brown and toasty. Remove from the heat and transfer to a small heatproof bowl.

Nutrition Information

Per serving: 322 calories, 15 grams fat, 12 grams carbohydrates, 3 grams fiber, 36 grams protein

- 3 tablespoons cold-pressed avocado oil
- 1 teaspoon cumin seeds
- 1 teaspoon fennel seeds
- 2 yellow onions, thinly sliced
- ¾ cup water
- 2 bay leaves
- 2 tablespoons all-purpose flour or gluten-free flour blend
- 3 tablespoons chopped fresh cilantro, for serving
- ½-inch piece ginger, julienned, for serving
- Cooked brown rice, cauliflower rice, or whole-wheat naan, for serving

PREP	10 MINUTES
MARINATE	1 HOUR TO OVERNIGHT
COOK	55 MINUTES
PR	15 MINUTES NPR
SERVES	6

7 When the cooking program ends, let the pressure release naturally for at least 15 minutes, then move the Pressure Release to **Venting** to release any remaining steam. Open the pot and remove and discard the bay leaves.

8 Ladle a small amount of the cooking liquid into the bowl with the toasted flour and stir to combine, then add the mixture to the pot. Press **Cancel** to reset the cooking program, then select the **Sauté** setting. Let the mixture come to a simmer for 1 minute, until thickened. Press the **Cancel** button to turn off the pot. Sprinkle the cilantro and julienned ginger over the curry.

9 Ladle the curry into bowls. Serve hot, with the rice on the side.

Note: You can substitute 4 tablespoons *nihari masala*, the spice mixture traditionally used for the stew, in place of the spice blend. It is available in Indian grocery stores and online. If you go this route, omit the salt, cumin seeds, and fennel seeds.

8

Vegetables and Side Dishes

No outdoor grilling is required to get charred flavor and impressive grill marks on your artichokes. A cast-iron grill pan will do the job very well, which means you can make this dish any time fresh artichokes are in the market. Serve them with a simple, light dip made from Greek yogurt and curry powder. It's much lower in fat than traditional aioli, and it's good with other vegetables and with crudités, too. To make things even simpler, forgo the dip and just squeeze fresh lemon juice over the artichokes when they're hot off the grill pan.

PAN-GRILLED ARTICHOKES WITH CURRY DIP

Curry Dip

½ cup plain 2 percent Greek yogurt, homemade (page 34) or store-bought

1 tablespoon fresh lemon juice

1 teaspoon honey

½ teaspoon curry powder

¼ teaspoon fine sea salt

¼ teaspoon freshly ground black pepper

Artichokes

4 medium globe artichokes (see Note)

2 tablespoons extra-virgin olive oil

¼ teaspoon fine sea salt

¼ teaspoon freshly ground black pepper

Chopped fresh flat-leaf parsley for sprinkling

1 To make the curry dip: In a small bowl, stir together the yogurt, lemon juice, honey, curry powder, salt, and pepper.

2 To prepare and cook the artichokes: Pull off any damaged leaves from an artichoke, then, holding the artichoke firmly on its side on a cutting board, use a serrated bread knife or a very sharp chef's knife to cut off the top one-third of the leaves. Next, cut off the stem flush with the bottom of the artichoke. Using kitchen shears, trim off any thorny tips that remain on the leaves. Repeat with the remaining artichokes.

3 Pour 1 cup water into the Instant Pot and place the wire metal steam rack into the pot. Arrange the artichokes in a single layer on the rack. Secure the lid and set the Pressure Release to **Sealing**. Select the **Steam** setting and set the cooking time for 10 minutes at high pressure. (The pot will take about 10 minutes to come up to pressure before the cooking program begins.)

4 When the cooking program ends, let the pressure release naturally for 5 minutes, then move the Pressure Release to **Venting** to release any remaining steam. Open the pot and test an artichoke for doneness by trying to pull out an inner leaf. If it releases easily, the artichokes are ready.

5 If the leaf is difficult to free, the artichokes need to be cooked longer. Secure the lid again and set the Pressure Release to **Sealing**. Press the **Cancel** button to reset the cooking program, then select the **Steam** setting and cook for 1 more minute at high pressure. Perform a quick pressure release by moving the Pressure Release to **Venting** and again test for doneness. If necessary, cook for 1 minute longer, using the same process.

Nutrition Information

Per serving: 152 calories, 7 grams fat, 18 grams carbohydrates, 11 grams fiber, 7 grams protein

PREP	10 MINUTES
COOK	30 MINUTES
PR	5 MINUTES NPR
SERVES	4

6 Using tongs, transfer the artichokes to the cutting board, allowing any excess liquid to drain back into the pot. Wearing heat-resistant mitts, slice each artichoke in half from top to bottom. Using a paring knife or teaspoon, scoop out and discard the fuzzy chokes and small, flimsy inner leaves.

7 Warm a grill pan over medium heat for about 4 minutes, until hot. Brush the cut sides of the artichoke halves with the oil, then sprinkle all over with the salt and pepper. Place the halves, cut sides down, on the hot pan and cook for about 4 minutes, until nice charred grill marks have developed. Transfer the artichokes to a serving plate.

8 Sprinkle the artichokes with the parsley and serve warm, with the curry dip on the side.

Note: You can steam artichokes of any size in the Instant Pot. The 6-quart models will accommodate four medium (3-inch-diameter) or large (4-inch-diameter) artichokes or two jumbo ($4\frac{1}{2}$- to 5-inch-diameter) artichokes. Set the cooking time for 10 minutes for medium artichokes, 12 minutes for large artichokes, or 15 minutes for jumbo artichokes.

The next time you cook a pot of chickpeas or white beans, save the cooking water and simmer it in a saucepan on the stove top until it's reduced by half. In culinary circles, this liquid gold is known as aquafaba, which translates as "bean water" in Italian. You can use it as an egg substitute in many recipes, including as the base of the garlicky aioli here, which is perfect for dipping tender spears of asparagus. A pinch of xanthan gum thickens the aioli to a more traditional texture, but you can leave it out and still have a very good dipping sauce.

ASPARAGUS WITH VEGAN AIOLI

2 pounds asparagus spears, trimmed and peeled

Vegan Aioli

¼ cup aquafaba (see Note, page 47)

1 tablespoon drained cooked chickpeas or white beans, home cooked (page 44) or canned

1 tablespoon fresh lemon juice

½ teaspoon fine sea salt

¼ teaspoon freshly ground black pepper

⅛ teaspoon xanthan gum (optional)

½ cup cold-pressed avocado oil

1 large garlic clove, chopped

PREP	0 MINUTES
COOK	15 MINUTES
PR	QPR
SERVES	8

1 Pour 1 cup water into the Instant Pot and place the wire metal steam rack into the pot. Arrange the asparagus on the rack.

2 Secure the lid and set the Pressure Release to **Sealing**. Select the **Steam** setting and set the cooking time for 0 (zero) minutes at low pressure. (The pot will take about 15 minutes to come up to pressure before the cooking program begins.)

3 While the asparagus is steaming, make the vegan aioli: In a wide-mouthed 1-pint jar, combine the aquafaba, chickpeas, lemon juice, salt, pepper, xanthan gum (if using), oil, and garlic. Plunge an immersion blender into the mixture, then blend for about 1 minute, until thick and smooth. Leftover aioli can be stored in an airtight container in the refrigerator for up to 5 days.

4 When the cooking program ends, perform a quick release by moving the Pressure Release to **Venting**. Open the pot and, wearing heat-resistant mitts, grasp the handles of the steam rack and lift out the rack. Transfer the asparagus to a serving plate.

5 Serve the asparagus right away, with the aioli on the side.

Nutrition Information

Per serving: 155 calories, 14 grams fat, 5 grams carbohydrates, 2 grams fiber, 3 grams protein

A sweet and tangy glaze makes these carrots appeal to adults and kids alike. They're steamed to a soft, tender texture, so if you like your carrots a little firmer, cook the carrots for only 1 minute. Either way, they'll be done in about 15 minutes, and using baby carrots means there's no prep work to be done.

BABY CARROTS WITH HONEY LEMON BUTTER

1 pound baby carrots
1 tablespoon unsalted butter
2 teaspoons honey
1 teaspoon fresh lemon juice
⅛ teaspoon fine sea salt

PREP	0 MINUTES
COOK	15 MINUTES
PR	QPR
SERVES	4

1 Pour 1 cup water into the Instant Pot and place a steamer basket into the pot. Add the carrots to the steamer basket.

2 Secure the lid and set the Pressure Release to **Sealing**. Select the **Steam** setting and set the cooking time for 2 minutes at high pressure. (The pot will take about 10 minutes to come up to pressure before the cooking program begins.)

3 When the cooking program ends, perform a quick pressure release by moving the Pressure Release to **Venting**. Open the pot and, wearing heat-resistant mitts, lift out the inner pot. Lift out the steamer basket and set aside with the carrots aside. Discard the water and return the inner pot to the housing.

4 Press the **Cancel** button to reset the cooking program, then select the **Sauté** setting and add the butter, honey, lemon juice, and salt. When the butter has melted, stir in the carrots and then toss to coat them with the butter mixture. Sauté for 1 to 2 minutes, until the carrots are lightly coated and no liquid remains in the pot. Press the **Cancel** button to turn off the pot.

5 Transfer the carrots to a serving bowl. Serve warm.

Note: To make this recipe vegan, substitute vegan buttery spread and agave nectar or pure maple syrup for the butter and honey.

Nutrition Information

Per serving: 76 calories, 3 grams fat, 12 grams carbohydrates, 3 grams fiber, 1 gram protein

When you're craving a little crunch (and something more exciting than plain steamed broccoli), toast a couple of garlic cloves in olive oil and then toss in the florets. The combination becomes an instantly flavorful side dish, and all you need to crisp the garlic is a tablespoon of oil.

BROCCOLI WITH CRISPY GARLIC CHIPS

1 pound broccoli, cut into bite-size florets

1 tablespoon extra-virgin olive oil

2 garlic cloves, thinly sliced

⅛ teaspoon fine sea salt

PREP	0 MINUTES
COOK	10 MINUTES
PR	QPR
SERVES	4

1 Pour 1 cup water into the Instant Pot and place a steamer basket into the pot. Add the broccoli to the steamer basket.

2 Secure the lid and set the Pressure Release to **Sealing**. Select the **Steam** setting and set the cooking time for 0 (zero) minutes at low pressure. (The pot will take about 10 minutes to come up to pressure before the cooking program begins.)

3 While the broccoli is steaming, warm the oil and garlic in a large skillet over medium-low heat for about 1 minute, until the garlic is bubbling but not browned. Turn off the heat. The garlic will continue to cook from the carryover heat and become a toasty light brown.

4 When the cooking program ends, perform a quick pressure release by moving the Pressure Release to **Venting**. Open the pot and, wearing heat-resistant mitts, lift out the steamer basket and pour the broccoli into the skillet with the garlic. Add the salt and toss to combine.

5 Transfer the broccoli to a serving plate and serve warm.

Nutrition Information

Per serving: 72 calories, 3 grams fat, 6 grams carbohydrates, 3 grams fiber, 1 gram protein

These days, multiple brands make everything bagel seasoning (aka everything but the bagel seasoning). My favorites are from Pereg and Trader Joe's. The heady blend gives new life to steamed vegetables, with toasty sesame and poppy seeds, garlic, onion, and salt, all in one little shaker. Carrots, green beans, and broccoli are delicious prepared this way, too.

EVERYTHING BRUSSELS SPROUTS

1 pound small brussels sprouts, trimmed and halved lengthwise if large

1 tablespoon unsalted butter or vegan buttery spread

2 teaspoons everything bagel seasoning mix (see Note)

PREP	0 MINUTES
COOK	15 MINUTES
PR	QPR
SERVES	4

1 Pour 1 cup water into the Instant Pot and place a steamer basket into the pot. Add the brussels sprouts to the steamer basket.

2 Secure the lid and set the Pressure Release to **Sealing**. Select the **Steam** setting and set the cooking time for 1 minute at high pressure. (The pot will take about 10 minutes to come up to pressure before the cooking program begins.)

3 When the cooking program ends, perform a quick pressure release by moving the Pressure Release to **Venting**. Open the pot and, wearing heat-resistant mitts, lift out the steamer basket. Lift out the inner pot, discard the water, and return the pot to the housing.

4 Press the **Cancel** button to reset the cooking program, then select the **Sauté** setting and heat the butter for about 2 minutes, until it has melted and begins to foam and become aromatic. Add the brussels sprouts and sauté for 1 minute, stirring to coat with the butter. Press the **Cancel** button to turn off the pot.

5 Transfer the brussels sprouts to a serving dish. Sprinkle with the seasoning blend and serve right away.

Note: If you can't find this seasoning blend, mix up the following: 1½ teaspoons toasted sesame seeds, 1½ teaspoons poppy seeds, 1 teaspoon dried minced onion, 1 teaspoon dried minced garlic, ½ teaspoon flaky sea salt. This amount is enough for three batches of brussels sprouts. Store the seasoning in an airtight container in the pantry for up to 3 months.

Nutrition Information

Per serving: 77 calories, 3 grams fat, 11 grams carbohydrates, 4 grams fiber, 4 grams protein

This mash of cauliflower and carrots is inspired by a sweet potato–based version dished up by Jurassic Cart, my favorite food cart in Portland, Oregon. Serve it as is alongside any main dish, or "load it up" like they do at the cart with some green onions, avocado, and Sriracha sauce on top. It's a lighter alternative to mashed potatoes, and the sweetness from the carrots makes the cauliflower much tastier than if it were served on its own.

CAULIFLOWER CARROT MASH

½ head cauliflower, cut into 2-inch florets

1 pound carrots, halved lengthwise and then crosswise

¼ cup coconut milk

1 teaspoon fine sea salt

1 green onion, white and green parts, thinly sliced, for serving

1 small avocado, pitted, peeled, and sliced, for serving

1 tablespoon Sriracha sauce, for serving

PREP	5 MINUTES
COOK	20 MINUTES
PR	QPR
SERVES	6

1 Pour 1 cup water into the Instant Pot and place a steamer basket into the pot Add the cauliflower and carrots to the steamer basket.

2 Secure the lid and set the pressure release to **Sealing**. Select the **Pressure Cook** or **Manual** setting and set the cooking time for 4 minutes at low pressure. (It will take about 15 minutes for the pot to come up to pressure before the cooking program begins.)

3 When the cooking program ends, perform a quick pressure release by moving the Pressure Release to **Venting**.

4 Wearing heat-resistant mitts, lift the steamer basket out of the pot and transfer the cauliflower and carrots to a large bowl. Add the coconut milk and salt, then use an immersion blender to puree the vegetables until smooth.

5 Spoon the mash into bowls or onto plates, top with the green onion, avocado, and Sriracha sauce, and serve warm.

Nutrition Information

Per serving (mash only, no toppings): 65 calories, 2 grams fat, 11 grams carbohydrates, 4 grams fiber, 2 grams protein

Steamed cauliflower is tossed with butter, chives, parsley, and dill. This fragrant mix of fresh herbs really perks up the cauliflower, making it the perfect side dish for springtime. Serve it alongside pork chops or any other main dish.

CAULIFLOWER FLORETS WITH HERBED BUTTER

1 head cauliflower, cut into bite-size florets

1 tablespoon unsalted butter or vegan buttery spread

1 tablespoon chopped fresh dill

1 tablespoon chopped fresh flat-leaf parsley or cilantro

1 tablespoon chopped chives or green onion, white and green parts

½ teaspoon fine sea salt

¼ teaspoon freshly ground black pepper

PREP	0 MINUTES
COOK	10 MINUTES
PR	QPR
SERVES	6

1 Pour 1 cup water into the Instant Pot and place a steamer basket into the pot. Add the cauliflower to the steamer basket.

2 Secure the lid and set the Pressure Release to **Sealing**. Select the **Steam** setting and set the cooking time for 0 (zero) minutes at low pressure. (The pot will take about 10 minutes to come up to pressure before the cooking program begins.)

3 When the cooking program ends, perform a quick pressure release by moving the Pressure Release to **Venting**. Open the pot and, wearing heat-resistant mitts, lift out the steamer basket. Lift out the inner pot and discard the water before quickly returning the cauliflower to the inner pot. Add the butter, dill, parsley, chives, salt, and pepper, and toss to melt the butter and coat the cauliflower.

4 Transfer the cauliflower to a serving bowl and serve warm.

Nutrition Information

Per serving: 60 calories, 2 grams fat, 8 grams carbohydrates, 4 grams fiber, 3 grams protein

If you have never tried celery root, aka celeriac, a gnarled-looking bulb-type root vegetable with a mild celery flavor, this German-style salad is a great starter dish. It calls for steaming the celery root in the Instant Pot and then marinating it with onions in a champagne vinegar–mustard vinaigrette. This dish is good the day you make it and even better the next day, after the celery root has had a chance to soak up some of the dressing. It goes well on any menu on which you'd serve potato salad, adding a lighter touch than what it is replacing.

CELERY ROOT SALAD

1 medium-size celery root, peeled and quartered lengthwise

Champagne Vinaigrette

¼ cup champagne vinegar or white wine vinegar

3 tablespoons cold-pressed avocado oil

2 teaspoons Dijon mustard

½ teaspoon fine sea salt

1 small yellow onion, thinly sliced

1 tablespoon chopped fresh chives, for serving

PREP	0 MINUTES
COOK	25 MINUTES
PR	QPR
COOL	10 MINUTES
CHILL	2 HOURS TO OVERNIGHT
SERVES	4

1 Pour 1 cup water into the Instant Pot and place a steamer basket into the pot. Add the celery root to the steamer basket.

2 Secure the lid and set the Pressure Release to **Sealing**. Select the **Steam** setting and set the cooking time for 15 minutes at high pressure. (The pot will take about 10 minutes to come up to pressure before the cooking program begins.)

3 While the celery root is steaming, make the vinaigrette: In a jam jar or other tightly lidded container, combine the vinegar, oil, mustard, and salt. Cover and shake vigorously to combine.

4 When the cooking program ends, perform a quick pressure release by moving the Pressure Release to **Venting**. Open the pot and, using tongs, transfer the celery root to a cutting board. Let cool for 10 minutes, then cut it into ⅛-inch-thick slices.

5 Combine the celery root and onion in a medium bowl. Shake the vinaigrette once more, then pour it over the vegetables and toss to coat evenly. Cover and chill the salad for at least 2 hours or up to overnight.

6 Spoon the salad onto plates, sprinkle with the chives, and serve right away.

Note: This salad is good with beets in place of the celery root, too. Steam them according to the chart on page 267.

Nutrition Information

Per serving: 137 calories, 12 grams fat, 7 grams carbohydrates, 8 grams fiber, 3 grams protein

Green beans or romano beans, their flatter, wider cousins, work equally well in this recipe. Both types become tender and soft after cooking for a little longer than I'd usually cook green beans. That's because I want them to have the silky texture of the long-braised beans common in Italian cuisine. Of course, if you prefer your beans with more bite, you can shorten the cooking time by 2 to 3 minutes. I like to serve these beans as a side dish with rotisserie chicken for a super-easy weeknight meal, or as a holiday side that's lighter than the traditional green bean casserole.

ITALIAN BRAISED GREEN BEANS AND TOMATOES

2 tablespoons extra-virgin olive oil

2 garlic cloves, thinly sliced

1 yellow onion, diced

½ teaspoon fine sea salt

¼ teaspoon freshly ground black pepper

¼ teaspoon red pepper flakes (optional)

¼ teaspoon dried thyme

⅓ cup water

1 pound green beans, trimmed

One 14½-ounce can petite diced tomatoes and their liquid

PREP	0 MINUTES
COOK	25 MINUTES
PR	QPR
SERVES	4

1 Select the **Sauté** setting and heat the oil and garlic for 2 minutes, until the garlic is bubbling but not browned. Add the onion and sauté for about 3 minutes, until it begins to soften. Add the salt, black pepper, red pepper flakes, and thyme and sauté for 1 more minute.

2 Pour in the water and use a wooden spoon or spatula to nudge any browned bits from the bottom of the pot. Add the green beans and stir to coat with the cooking liquid. Pour the tomatoes evenly on top. Do not stir them in.

3 Secure the lid and set the Pressure Release to **Sealing**. Press the **Cancel** button to reset the cooking program, then select the **Pressure Cook** or **Manual** setting and set the cooking time for 7 minutes at high pressure. (The pot will take about 10 minutes to come up to pressure before the cooking program begins.)

4 When the cooking program ends, perform a quick release by moving the Pressure Release to **Venting**. Open the pot and stir lightly to combine, being careful not to break up the beans.

5 Using a slotted spoon, gently transfer the beans to a serving bowl, then spoon the tomatoes and onions over the top. Serve right away.

Nutrition Information

Per serving: 146 calories, 7 grams fat, 19 grams carbohydrates, 6 grams fiber, 4 grams protein

A fresh herbal South American condiment, chimichurri is traditionally used on grilled meat, but it's also fantastic on corn for a summery side dish. You can make a double batch of the chimichurri if you like, as it will keep for a week in the fridge. Use it on other steamed vegetables or stir it into soups, such as Greek Lentil Soup (page 84) or Sweet Potato Soup (page 88), to brighten their flavors.

CHIMICHURRI CORN ON THE COB

4 ears corn, husks and silk removed and halved crosswise

Chimichurri

¼ cup red wine vinegar

¼ cup minced red onion

¼ cup chopped fresh flat-leaf parsley

1 garlic clove, pressed or grated

½ teaspoon dried oregano

¼ teaspoon fine sea salt

¼ teaspoon freshly ground black pepper

¼ teaspoon red pepper flakes

2 tablespoons extra-virgin olive oil

PREP	0 MINUTES
COOK	15 MINUTES
PR	QPR
SERVES	4

1 Pour 1 cup water into the Instant Pot and place a steamer basket into the pot. Add the corn to the steamer basket.

2 Secure the lid and set the Pressure Release to **Sealing**. Select the **Steam** setting and set the cooking time for 3 minutes at high pressure. (The pot will take about 10 minutes to come up to pressure before the cooking program begins.)

3 While the corn is steaming, make the chimichurri: In a small bowl, stir together the vinegar, onion, parsley, garlic, oregano, salt, black pepper, and red pepper flakes. Let sit for 5 minutes to allow the flavors to meld and the oregano to hydrate in the vinegar, then stir in the oil.

4 When the cooking program ends, perform a quick pressure release by moving the Pressure Release to **Venting**. Open the pot and, wearing heat-resistant mitts, lift the steamer basket out of the pot. Transfer the corn to a serving platter.

5 While the corn is still hot, spoon the chimichurri on top. Serve warm.

Nutrition Information

Per serving: 158 calories, 8 grams fat, 19 grams carbohydrates, 2 grams fiber, 3 grams protein

Yogurt made in the Instant Pot is the base for this dip that's full of fresh herbs and crunchy vegetables. A little bit of extra-virgin olive oil adds just enough richness to make it irresistible. Scoop it up with crudités or crackers for an appetizer or afternoon snack.

CRUNCHY VEGETABLE DIP

1½ cups plain 2 percent yogurt, homemade (page 34) or store-bought

1 Persian cucumber, finely chopped

1 carrot, finely chopped

1 celery stalk, finely chopped

1 small red bell pepper, seeded and finely chopped

2 green onions, white and green parts, finely chopped

1 tablespoon chopped fresh dill

1 tablespoon chopped fresh flat-leaf parsley

¼ teaspoon garlic powder

¼ teaspoon freshly ground black pepper

½ teaspoon fine sea salt

1 tablespoon extra-virgin olive oil

PREP	5 MINUTES
COOK	0 MINUTES
PR	N/A
CHILL	1 HOUR TO OVERNIGHT
MAKES	ABOUT 2½ CUPS

1 In a medium bowl, combine all of the ingredients and stir to mix well. Cover and chill in the refrigerator for at least 1 hour or up to overnight to allow the flavors to meld.

2 When ready to serve, stir the dip again, then serve chilled. Leftover dip will keep in an airtight container in the refrigerator for up to 3 days.

Nutrition Information

Per ½ cup serving: 87 calories, 4 grams fat, 10 grams carbohydrates, 2 grams fiber, 4 grams protein

A few slices of bacon add richness and just a touch of smoky flavor to this pot of beets. Countless recipes instruct you to save the beet greens for another use, but here you cook them right in the same pot as the beets. The sliced beets and chopped greens meld together to become a tender, braised pot of vegetable goodness. Look to the recipe Note for a vegan variation.

BACON-BRAISED BEETS AND GREENS

2 bunches medium beets and their greens

3 slices center-cut bacon, cut into ½-inch pieces

2 garlic cloves, minced

1 large red onion, diced

½ teaspoon fine sea salt

¾ cup water

¼ teaspoon freshly ground black pepper

PREP	20 MINUTES
COOK	30 MINUTES
PR	QPR
SERVES	6

1 Cut the beets from the beet greens. Rinse any grit off of the greens, dry them between towels or in a salad spinner, and then cut them into ½-inch-wide ribbons. Peel the beets and slice them into ⅓-inch-thick wedges.

2 Select the **Sauté** setting on the Instant Pot, wait 2 minutes for the pot to heat up, and add the bacon. Sauté for about 4 minutes, until some of the bacon fat has rendered out and there is browning on the bottom of the pot. Add the garlic, onion, and salt and sauté for about 3 minutes, until the onion begins to soften. Add the water and pepper and use a wooden spoon or spatula to nudge any browned bits from the bottom of the pot. Add the beet greens and sauté for 1 minute, until they are starting to wilt. Stir in the beets.

3 Secure the lid and set the Pressure Release to **Sealing**. Press the **Cancel** button to reset the cooking program, then select the **Pressure Cook** or **Manual** setting and set the cooking time for 10 minutes at high pressure. (The pot will take about 10 minutes to come up to pressure before the cooking program begins.)

4 When the cooking program ends, perform a quick pressure release by moving the Pressure Release to **Venting**. Open the pot and stir the beets and greens.

5 Transfer the beets and greens to a serving bowl and serve warm.

Note: To make this dish vegan, omit the bacon and start the recipe by heating 1 tablespoon extra-virgin olive oil for 2 minutes, then add the garlic, onion, and salt and continue with the recipe. For more flavor, substitute low-sodium vegetable broth (page 261) for the water.

Nutrition Information

Per serving: 67 calories, 1 gram fat, 13 grams carbohydrates, 3 grams fiber, 3 grams protein

Yes, you can make a creamy, delicious bowl of spinach that's dairy-free, gluten-free, and rich. This one starts with a bag of spinach straight out of the freezer, and it's easy enough that you'll want to make it all the time. It's a great side dish to bring for a holiday potluck.

VEGAN CREAMED SPINACH

1 teaspoon extra-virgin olive oil

2 garlic cloves, chopped

1 large yellow onion, diced

One 16-ounce bag frozen spinach

½ cup low-sodium vegetable broth (page 261) or chicken bone broth (page 260)

½ cup raw whole cashews, soaked in water to cover for 2 hours and drained

2 tablespoons fresh lemon juice

3 tablespoons water

1 teaspoon nutritional yeast

¼ teaspoon fine sea salt

¼ teaspoon freshly ground black pepper

⅛ teaspoon ground nutmeg

PREP	0 MINUTES
COOK	15 MINUTES
PR	QPR
SERVES	6

1 Select the **Sauté** setting on the Instant Pot and heat the oil and garlic for 2 minutes, until the garlic is bubbling but not browned. Add the onion and sauté for 3 minutes, until it begins to soften. Stir in the spinach and broth.

2 Secure the lid and set the Pressure Release to **Sealing**. Press the **Cancel** button to reset the cooking program, then select the **Pressure Cook** or **Manual** setting and set the cooking time for 1 minute at high pressure. (The pot will take about 10 minutes to come up to pressure before the cooking program begins.)

3 While the spinach is cooking, combine the cashews, lemon juice, water, nutritional yeast, and salt in a widemouthed 1-pint Mason jar. Lower an immersion blender into the jar and blend the mixture for about 2 minutes, until very smooth.

4 When the cooking program ends, perform a quick pressure release by moving the Pressure Release to **Venting**. Open the pot and stir in the cashew mixture, pepper, and nutmeg.

5 Spoon the spinach into bowls or onto plates and serve warm.

Note: The spinach is used straight from the freezer and thaws in the Instant Pot. Make sure to use the loosely packed bagged spinach rather than the kind that comes in a solid block.

Nutrition Information

Per serving: 101 calories, 6 grams fat, 10 grams carbohydrates, 2 grams fiber, 3 grams protein

This colorful salad takes its inspiration from giardiniera, a pickled-vegetable relish found on both Italian and Italian American tables. Add the sport peppers and pepper flakes for a Chicago-style "hot" salad or leave them out for a milder side dish. Like its relish cousin, this salad is a good addition to nearly any Italian or Italian American meal.

GIARDINIERA SALAD

1 cup water

2 carrots, sliced ¼ inch thick

2 celery stalks, sliced ¼ inch thick

1 pound cauliflower florets, cut into bite-size pieces

1 red bell pepper, seeded and cut into strips ¼ inch wide

2 dill pickles, thinly sliced, or ½ cup dill pickle chips (page 264)

4 sport peppers, banana peppers, or pepperoncini, thinly sliced (optional)

¼ teaspoon red pepper flakes (optional)

2 tablespoons red wine vinegar

1½ tablespoons extra-virgin olive oil

¼ teaspoon fine sea salt

PREP	0 MINUTES
COOK	15 MINUTES
COOL	15 MINUTES
CHILL	2 HOURS
PR	QPR
SERVES	6

1 Pour the water into the Instant Pot and place a steamer basket into the pot. Add the carrots, celery, cauliflower, and bell pepper to the steamer basket, putting the pepper on top.

2 Secure the lid and set the Pressure Release to **Sealing**. Select the **Steam** setting and set the cooking time for 0 minutes at low pressure. (The pot will take about 15 minutes to come up to pressure before the cooking program begins.)

3 When the cooking program ends, perform a quick release by moving the Pressure Release to **Venting**. Open the pot and, wearing heat-resistant mitts, lift out the steamer basket and transfer the vegetables to a large bowl. Add the pickles, sport peppers (if using), red pepper flakes (if using), vinegar, oil, and salt and stir gently to combine.

4 Let the salad cool until it is no longer piping hot (about 15 minutes), stirring occasionally, then cover and chill for at least 2 hours before serving.

5 Spoon the salad into bowls and serve chilled. Any leftover salad will keep in an airtight container in the refrigerator for up to 3 days.

Nutrition Information

Per serving: 72 calories, 4 grams fat, 8 grams carbohydrates, 3 grams fiber, 2 grams protein

I first fell in love with this type of vegetable side dish in my catering days during college. We'd serve up bowls of all kinds of steamed vegetables tossed in olive oil and fresh herbs—so simple and so good for you. Cutting the zucchini into batons makes them look especially inviting to eat. Try carrots this way, too.

ZUCCHINI WITH OLIVE OIL AND PARSLEY

1½ pounds zucchini, quartered lengthwise and cut into 2-inch lengths

1 tablespoon extra-virgin olive oil

1 tablespoon chopped fresh flat-leaf parsley

¼ teaspoon fine sea salt

⅛ teaspoon freshly ground black pepper

PREP	5 MINUTES
COOK	15 MINUTES
PR	QPR
SERVES	6

1 Pour 1 cup water into the Instant Pot and place a steamer basket into the pot. Add the zucchini to the steamer basket.

2 Secure the lid and set the Pressure Release to **Sealing**. Select the **Steam** setting and set the cooking time for 2 minutes at low pressure. (The pot will take about 10 minutes to come up to pressure before the cooking program begins.)

3 When the cooking program ends, perform a quick pressure release by moving the Pressure Release to **Venting**. Open the pot and, wearing heat-resistant mitts, lift out the steamer basket. Lift out the inner pot and discard the water. Quickly return the zucchini to the still-hot inner pot, add the oil, parsley, salt, and pepper, and toss to coat the zucchini.

4 Transfer the zucchini to a serving bowl and serve warm.

Note: The cook time of 2 minutes at low pressure results in soft but not over-cooked zucchini. If you prefer your zucchini firmer to the bite, reduce the cooking time to 1 or even 0 (zero) minutes.

Nutrition Information

Per serving: 44 calories, 3 grams fat, 4 grams carbohydrates, 1 gram fiber, 3 grams protein

Potatoes vary in size, so the cooking times for whole potatoes are given in ranges. If you are unsure of the weight of your potatoes, cook them for the minimum amount of time, then test for doneness. If they are not yet fork-tender, steam them for a few more minutes.

You can steam potatoes whole, quartered, sliced, or cubed. The 6-quart Instant Pot can hold a maximum of 4 pounds potatoes, but I find that I get the most even and consistent results when steaming 3 pounds or less.

The following timetable applies to all kinds of potatoes, including starchy russets, waxy creamers, and sweet potatoes. Cook whole potatoes on the wire metal steam rack and quartered, cubed, or sliced potatoes in a steamer basket.

STEAMED POTATOES (REGULAR AND SWEET)

1 Pour 1 cup water into the Instant Pot. If cooking whole potatoes, place the wire metal steam rack into the pot; if cooking prepared potatoes, place a steamer basket into the pot. Add the potatoes to the pot.

2 Secure the lid and set the Pressure Release to **Sealing**. Select the **Steam** setting, then refer to the time chart for setting the cooking time; use high pressure. (Depending on the quantity of potatoes, the pot will take 10 to 15 minutes to come up to pressure before the cooking program begins.)

3 When the cooking program ends, perform a quick release by moving the Pressure Release to **Venting**. Open the pot and use tongs to remove whole potatoes or wear heat-resistant mitts to lift out the steamer basket.

4 Serve immediately or let cool to room temperature, transfer to an airtight container, and refrigerate for up to 3 days.

Whole Potatoes	Cooking Time (in minutes, at high pressure)
Baby (1 to 2 ounces each)	5
Small (3 to 4 ounces each)	8 to 10
Medium (6 to 8 ounces each)	10 to 12
Large (about 10 ounces each)	12 to 15
Extra Large (12 to 14 ounces each)	20 to 25
Jumbo (16 to 18 ounces each)	28 to 30
Prepared Potatoes	**Cooking Time (in minutes, at high pressure)**
Quartered (medium size)	5
Sliced (½ to ¾ inch thick)	3 to 4
Cubed (1 inch)	3

This is my version of *vinegret*, a substantial Russian salad made from cooked beets, carrots, and potatoes. Traditionally, the vegetables are chopped very small, but I like them in larger pieces for a more rustic presentation. A simple white wine vinegar dressing keeps the flavors light and bright. When I want something fast and easy, I'll make this salad and pair it with any protein (think a can of tuna or sardines) for lunch.

BEET, CARROT, AND POTATO SALAD

1 pound beets, peeled and cut into ⅓-inch-thick wedges

1 pound carrots, cut into ½-inch-thick rounds

12 ounces Yukon Gold potatoes, cut into ¾-inch cubes

1 cup frozen peas

½ cup dill pickle chips (page 264) or sauerkraut

½ small yellow onion, thinly sliced

1 tablespoon cold-pressed avocado oil

1 tablespoon white wine vinegar

2 tablespoons chopped fresh dill, for serving

PREP	2 MINUTES
COOK	20 MINUTES
PR	QPR
COOL	15 MINUTES
SERVES	6

1 Pour 1 cup water into the Instant Pot and place a steamer basket into the pot. Add the beets, carrots, and potatoes to the basket, putting the potatoes on top.

2 Secure the lid and set the Pressure Release to **Sealing**. Select the **Steam** setting and set the cooking time for 3 minutes at high pressure. (The pot will take about 15 minutes to come up to pressure before the cooking program begins.)

3 When the cooking program ends, perform a quick release by moving the Pressure Release to **Venting**. Open the pot and, wearing heat-resistant mitts, lift out the steamer basket and transfer the vegetables to a large bowl. Add the peas and stir gently to combine. Let sit for 15 minutes to allow the peas to thaw and the rest of the vegetables to cool to room temperature.

4 Add the pickles, onion, oil, and vinegar to the cooled vegetables and stir to combine. The salad can served at room temperature or chilled. To serve chilled, cover and refrigerate for at least 2 hours so the pickles have time to season the rest of the vegetables and the flavors have time to meld.

5 To serve, spoon the salad into bowls and sprinkle with the dill. Leftover salad will keep in an airtight container in the refrigerator for up to 3 days.

Nutrition Information

Per serving: 150 calories, 3 grams fat, 28 grams carbohydrates, 5 grams fiber, 5 grams protein

Steaming these potatoes in the Instant Pot and then roasting them in the oven results in soft, pillowy interiors and crispy, crusty exteriors. The coating of Sriracha and butter makes them irresistible. Cook this recipe any time you want a simple side dish that packs lots of flavor and a spicy heat.

CRISPY SRIRACHA POTATOES

2 pounds Yukon Gold potatoes, cut into 1½-inch pieces

1½ tablespoons unsalted butter or vegan buttery spread

1½ tablespoons Sriracha sauce

½ teaspoon flaky sea salt

1 tablespoon chopped fresh cilantro or flat-leaf parsley

PREP	5 MINUTES
COOK	35 MINUTES
PR	QPR
SERVES	6

1 Preheat the oven to 425°F. Line a sheet pan with parchment paper, a silicone baking mat, or aluminum foil.

2 Pour 1 cup water into the Instant Pot and place a steamer basket into the pot. Add the potatoes to the steamer basket.

3 Secure the lid and set the Pressure Release to **Sealing**. Select the **Steam** setting and set the cooking time for 3 minutes at high pressure. (The pot will take about 10 minutes to come up to pressure before the cooking program begins.)

4 When the cooking program ends, perform a quick pressure release by moving the Pressure Release to **Venting**. Open the pot and, wearing heat-resistant mitts, lift out the steamer basket. Lift out the inner pot and discard the water. Quickly return the potatoes to the still-hot inner pot, add the butter and Sriracha, and toss to melt the butter and coat the potatoes evenly.

5 Transfer the potatoes to the prepared pan, spreading them in an even layer. Bake the potatoes for about 20 minutes, until golden brown and crispy.

6 Transfer the potatoes to a serving bowl, sprinkle with salt and cilantro, and serve hot.

Nutrition Information

Per serving: 137 calories, 3 grams fat, 38 grams carbohydrates, 3 grams fiber, 3 grams protein

Serve these mashed potatoes on your holiday table or on a weeknight. They're lightly sweetened and are laced with grated orange zest for a welcome citrusy flavor. A topping of toasted pecans adds a little crunch, elevating this dish beyond its humble beginning.

MASHED SWEET POTATOES

2 pounds sweet potatoes, peeled and cut into 1-inch pieces

2 tablespoons pure maple syrup or coconut nectar

2 tablespoons unsalted butter or vegan buttery spread

¼ teaspoon fine sea salt

¼ teaspoon ground cinnamon

1 teaspoon finely grated orange zest

¼ cup pecans, toasted and chopped, for serving

PREP	5 MINUTES
COOK	15 MINUTES
PR	QPR
SERVES	6

1 Pour 1 cup water into the Instant Pot and place a steamer basket into the pot. Add the sweet potatoes to the steamer basket.

2 Secure the lid and set the Pressure Release to **Sealing**. Select the **Steam** setting and set the cooking time for 4 minutes at high pressure. (The pot will take about 10 minutes to come up to pressure before the cooking program begins.)

3 When the cooking program ends, perform a quick release by moving the Pressure Release to **Venting**. Open the pot and, wearing heatproof mitts, lift out the steamer basket. Lift out the inner pot and discard the water. Quickly return the sweet potatoes to the still-hot inner pot and add the maple syrup, butter, salt, cinnamon, and ½ teaspoon of the orange zest. Using a potato masher, mash the potatoes until smooth and uniform.

4 Spoon the potatoes into a shallow serving bowl and top with the pecans and the remaining ½ teaspoon orange zest. Serve right away.

Notes: This recipe is easily doubled. Use only 1 cup water but double the quantity of all of the other ingredients.

For a savory twist, omit the maple syrup, cinnamon, orange zest, and pecans. Top with sliced green onions and crumbled goat cheese or a dollop of Almond Feta Cheese (page 265).

Nutrition Information

Per serving: 213 calories, 7 grams fat, 36 grams carbohydrates, 5 grams fiber, 3 grams protein

These generously seasoned potato wedges are a good side dish to Honey Mustard Chicken Tenders and Slaw (page 149). You can make the chicken dish while the JoJos are crisping up in the oven.

JOJO POTATOES

2 pounds russet potatoes, cut into 1-inch-thick wedges

1 teaspoon sweet paprika

½ teaspoon garlic powder

½ teaspoon onion powder

¼ teaspoon freshly ground black pepper

⅛ teaspoon cayenne pepper

¾ teaspoon fine sea salt

2 tablespoons cold-pressed avocado oil

PREP	5 MINUTES
COOK	45 MINUTES
PR	QPR
SERVES	6

1 Preheat the oven to 425°F. Line a sheet pan with parchment paper and grease the paper lightly with avocado oil or nonstick cooking spray.

2 Pour 1 cup water into the Instant Pot and place a steamer basket into the pot. Add the potatoes to the basket.

3 Secure the lid and set the Pressure Release to **Sealing**. Select the **Steam** setting and set the cooking time for 2 minutes at high pressure. (The pot will take about 15 minutes to come up to pressure before the cooking program begins.)

4 While the potatoes are steaming, in a small bowl, stir together the paprika, garlic powder, onion powder, black pepper, cayenne, and salt.

5 When the cooking program ends, perform a quick pressure release by moving the Pressure Release to **Venting**. Open the pot and, wearing heat-resistant mitts, lift out the steamer basket and transfer the potatoes to a large bowl. Drizzle the potatoes with the oil and then sprinkle them with the spice mixture. Toss gently until the potatoes are evenly coated with the spice mixture. (It's fine if a few of the wedges are broken during the tossing.)

6 Using tongs, arrange the potato wedges in a single layer on the prepared pan, allowing a little space around each wedge. Bake the potatoes for about 25 minutes, until golden brown and crispy.

7 Transfer the potatoes to a serving dish and serve hot.

Nutrition Information

Per serving: 193 calories, 5 grams fat, 35 grams carbohydrates, 3 grams fiber, 4 grams protein

9

Drinks and Desserts

Rosemary might sound like an unusual addition to a pot of spiced cider, but in the right amount, it adds a woody note that makes this hot, comforting drink uniquely delicious. You'll heat the cider on the Instant Pot's Sauté setting, then leave it on the Keep Warm setting, where it will stay warm for everyone to enjoy.

MULLED APPLE CIDER WITH ORANGES AND ROSEMARY

Zest (in strips) and juice of 1 navel orange

Two 6-inch rosemary sprigs

1 cinnamon stick, broken into large pieces

1 bay leaf

8 cups unfiltered apple cider

PREP	0 MINUTES
COOK	15 MINUTES
PR	N/A
STEEP	30 MINUTES
SERVES	8

1 Put the orange zest, rosemary, cinnamon, and bay leaf into a wire-mesh steamer basket and place the steamer basket into the Instant Pot. Pour in the orange juice and cider.

2 Cover the pot with a tempered glass lid. Select the **Sauté** setting and heat the cider for about 15 minutes, until barely at a simmer (around 190°F). Press the **Cancel** button to turn off the pot, then select the **Keep Warm** setting. Leave the steamer basket in the cider and steep for 30 minutes, then remove the steamer basket and discard the solids.

3 Stir the cider and ladle into mugs. Serve warm.

Note: For traditional mulled cider, replace the orange, rosemary, cinnamon, and bay leaf with a packet of mulling spices.

Nutrition Information

Per serving: 120 calories, 0 grams fat, 30 grams carbohydrates, 0 grams fiber, 0 grams protein

No alcohol is added to this comforting winter sipper. It's made up of just tart cranberry juice, apple juice, spices, and a drizzle of honey. You can find 100 percent cranberry juice in some grocery stores and in natural foods stores. Check the label to make sure you are buying no-sugar-added juice.

HOT CRANBERRY COCKTAIL

2 cinnamon sticks

2 teaspoons whole allspice berries

1 teaspoon whole cloves

1 whole star anise

4 cups unfiltered apple cider

2 cups 100 percent cranberry juice (no sugar added)

2 tablespoons honey or agave nectar

PREP	0 MINUTES
COOK	10 MINUTES
PR	N/A
STEEP	20 MINUTES TO 1 HOUR
SERVES	6

1 Put the cinnamon, allspice, cloves, and star anise into a wire-mesh steamer basket and place the steamer basket into the Instant Pot. Pour in the apple juice and cranberry juice. Add the honey.

2 Cover the pot with a tempered glass lid. Select the **Sauté** setting and set the cooking time for 11 minutes.

3 When the cooking program ends, select the **Keep Warm** setting. Leave the spices in the liquid and steep for at least 20 minutes or up to 1 hour, depending on how strongly you want the drink to be spiced. Remove the steamer basket and discard the spices.

4 Stir the cocktail and ladle it into mugs. Serve warm.

Nutrition Information

Per serving: 138 calories, 0 grams fat, 36 carbohydrates, 1 gram fiber, 0 grams protein

Here is a welcome nonalcoholic, spice-infused winter warmer for snowy days and chilly nights. Sweetened with honey or agave nectar, it is made with black tea but is easily switched to a caffeine-free sipper by swapping in rooibos tea or decaffeinated black tea.

VIRGIN TODDY TONIC

3 cinnamon sticks, broken into large pieces

1 teaspoon whole cloves

6 cups water

4 black tea bags

Zest (in strips) and juice of 1 lemon

¼ cup honey or agave nectar, plus more as needed

PREP	0 MINUTES
COOK	15 MINUTES
PR	N/A
STEEP	4 MINUTES
SERVES	6

1 Place the cinnamon and cloves into the Instant Pot and select the **Sauté** setting. Let the spices heat and toast, stirring occasionally, for about 4 minutes, until the pot displays its "hot" message and the spices are aromatic. Wearing heat-resistant mitts, lift out the inner pot and pour the spices into a wire-mesh steamer basket. Make sure no bits of spices are left in the pot.

2 Return the inner pot to the housing and place the steamer basket into the pot. Pour the water over the spices and cover the pot with a tempered glass lid. (The pot should still be on its **Sauté** setting.)

3 When the water has come to a simmer (after about 10 minutes), uncover the pot and add the tea bags to the steamer basket, nudging them with a wooden spoon or spatula to submerge them in the water. Press the **Cancel** button to turn off the pot, then cover the pot with the glass lid once more. Let the tea steep for 4 minutes.

4 Uncover the pot and, wearing heat-resistant mitts, remove the steamer basket. Add the lemon juice and honey to the pot and stir until fully dissolved. Taste for sweetness, adding more honey if needed.

5 You can serve the toddies right away, or keep them warm, covered, on the **Keep Warm** setting. To serve, ladle into mugs and garnish each mug with a twist of lemon zest.

Notes: You can also sweeten each mug individually if you like, with your sweetener of choice. I like 2 teaspoons honey or agave nectar per mug. For a sugar-free drink, use 8 drops liquid stevia per mug.

For a spicy variation, add a 2-inch piece fresh ginger, peeled and thinly sliced, to the pot along with the spices. Garnish each mug with a tiny pinch of cayenne pepper.

Nutrition Information

Per serving: 45 calories, 0 grams fat, 12 grams carbohydrates, 0 grams fiber, 0 grams protein

Make a batch of Greek yogurt in the Instant Pot, then freeze up a batch of sweet treats. These ice pops will satisfy your dark chocolate ice cream craving without a ton of calories or any unpronounceable ingredients. Cocoa powder and semisweet chocolate chips provide a double dose of chocolate flavor, toning down the tanginess of the yogurt.

FROZEN YOGURT FUDGE ICE POPS

1¼ cups plain 2 percent Greek yogurt, homemade (page 34) or store-bought

¼ cup 2 percent milk

¼ cup agave nectar or coconut nectar

¼ cup natural cocoa powder

½ teaspoon pure vanilla extract

⅛ teaspoon fine sea salt

2 ounces semisweet chocolate chips or baking wafers, melted and cooled

PREP	10 MINUTES
COOK	N/A
PR	N/A
FREEZE	4 HOURS
MAKES	6 ICE POPS

1 In a blender, combine the yogurt, milk, agave nectar, cocoa powder, vanilla, and sea salt. Blend on medium speed for about 30 seconds, until well mixed. Scrape down the sides, add the melted chocolate, and blend for 30 more seconds at high speed, until smooth.

2 Let the mixture settle in the blender for a couple of minutes, tap it against the counter a dozen times to remove the air bubbles, let sit for another 2 minutes, and tap once more.

3 Pour the mixture into ice-pop molds (about 4 ounces each), insert an ice-pop stick in each mold, and freeze for at least 4 hours, until frozen solid.

4 To unmold, dip each mold into warm water for about 5 seconds, then wiggle the ice pop out by the stick. Serve right away or transfer the ice pops to ziplock freezer bags and store in the freezer for up to 6 months.

Notes: Replace the cocoa powder with peanut powder (PB2 or Pbfit brand, see page 13) to make ice pops flavored with chocolate and peanut butter.

For a peppermint variation, substitute ½ teaspoon peppermint extract for the vanilla.

Nutrition Information

Per ice pop: 134 calories, 5 grams fat, 21 grams carbohydrates, 2 grams fiber, 6 grams protein

This is a vegan spin on *trigo con leche*, a traditional Dominican breakfast dish that also makes a satisfying dessert. Quick-cooking, whole-grain bulgur wheat cooks in just 15 minutes under pressure and is then combined with almond milk, coconut cream, spices, and a touch of citrus zest. Coconut nectar is a natural sweetener, and it gives the pudding a rich flavor and toffee hue. I like this pudding served either warm or chilled.

COCONUT BULGUR PUDDING

1 cup coarse bulgur wheat

2 cups water

2 cups unsweetened almond milk

One 5⅓-ounce can coconut cream

¾ teaspoon ground cinnamon, plus more for serving

¼ teaspoon ground nutmeg

2 whole cloves

⅓ cup coconut nectar

¼ cup raisins

2 teaspoons finely grated orange zest

Chopped walnuts, for serving (optional)

PREP	0 MINUTES
COOK	30 MINUTES
PR	10 MINUTES NPR
COOL	1 HOUR
CHILL	3 HOURS TO OVERNIGHT
SERVES	8

1 Combine the bulgur and water in the Instant Pot and swirl the pot a bit, making sure all of the grains are in an even layer and submerged in the water.

2 Secure the lid and set the Pressure Release to **Sealing**. Select the **Pressure Cook** or **Manual** setting and set the cooking time for 15 minutes at high pressure. (The pot will take about 5 minutes to come up to pressure before the cooking program begins.)

3 When the cooking program ends, let the pressure release naturally for 10 minutes, then move the Pressure Release to **Venting** to release any remaining steam. Open the pot and add the almond milk, coconut cream, cinnamon, nutmeg, cloves, coconut nectar, and raisins. Whisk to combine.

4 Press the **Cancel** button to reset the cooking program, then select the **Sauté** setting. Bring the pudding to a simmer (this will take about 3 minutes), then cook, whisking continuously, for about 7 minutes, until it has thickened and begins to sputter as it boils (it will continue to thicken when chilled). Press the **Cancel** button to turn off the pot. Stir in 1 teaspoon of the orange zest.

5 Wearing heat-resistant mitts, lift out the inner pot. Remove and discard the whole cloves. Ladle the pudding into a glass or ceramic serving dish, individual bowls, or ¾-cup ramekins. Cover and let cool for 1 hour on the counter, then refrigerate the pudding for at least 3 hours or up to overnight.

6 Just before serving, top the pudding with a sprinkling of walnuts (if using), a light dusting of cinnamon, and the remaining 1 teaspoon orange zest.

Nutrition Information

Per serving: 162 calories, 5 grams fat, 27 grams carbohydrates, 3 grams fiber, 3 grams protein

Use a robust red wine for poaching your pears, such as a Merlot, Malbec, or Syrah. This will result in some seriously beautiful pears: a deep burgundy exterior that reveals a lovely pale interior when the fruit is cut. Enjoy the sweet, tender pears with a drizzle of some of the wine syrup and a dollop of Greek yogurt. For a nondairy option, serve with a scoop of coconut or soy ice cream.

WINE-POACHED PEARS

One 750 ml bottle robust red wine

¾ cup water

½ cup honey or agave nectar

Two 3-inch cinnamon sticks

2 pounds slightly underripe Bartlett or D'Anjou pears (4 pears)

Plain 2 percent Greek yogurt, homemade (page 34) or store-bought, for serving

PREP	0 MINUTES
COOK	45 MINUTES
PR	QPR
CHILL	4 HOURS TO 2 DAYS
SERVES	4

1 Combine the wine, water, honey, and cinnamon sticks in the Instant Pot. Select the **Sauté** setting and bring the liquid to a simmer.

2 While the liquid is coming to a simmer, peel the pears, quarter them lengthwise, and cut away the core. When the poaching liquid is simmering (it will take about 10 minutes to come to a simmer), add the pears.

3 Secure the lid and set the Pressure Release to **Sealing**. Press the **Cancel** button to reset the cooking program, then select the **Pressure Cook** or **Manual** setting and set the cooking time for 1 minute at high pressure. (The pot will take about 5 minutes to come up to pressure before the cooking program begins.)

4 When the cooking program ends, perform a quick release by moving the Pressure Release to **Venting**. Open the pot and, using a slotted spoon, transfer the pears and cinnamon sticks to a medium bowl.

5 Press the **Cancel** button to reset the cooking program once again, then select the **Sauté** setting. Leave the pot uncovered and allow the liquid to reduce for the full 30 minutes of the **Sauté** program. The liquid should reduce by about half, leaving you with about 1½ cups syrupy liquid. Pour the reduced liquid over the pears, then cover and refrigerate them for at least 4 hours or up to 2 days.

6 Serve the chilled pears in bowls. Top each serving with 2 tablespoons of the wine syrup and a dollop of yogurt.

Note: You can use the leftover syrup as a yogurt topping, or mix it with club soda for a fizzy, relatively low-alcohol spritzer.

Nutrition Information

Per serving (4 pear quarters plus 2 tablespoons wine syrup): 230 calories, 0 grams fat, 47 grams carbohydrates, 6 grams fiber, 2 grams protein

Have your dessert and eat your vegetables, too. This applesauce has a secret ingredient: a full pound of beets are cooked with the apples and then mixed right in. Cinnamon and raisins add spice and sweetness, and the beets turn the dish a beautiful, vibrant pink. (You can use golden beets if you prefer. They are a lot less messy to peel, and the applesauce will have a more traditional appearance.) Mash the apples and beets with a potato masher for a rustic texture or use an immersion blender for a smooth puree.

PINK APPLESAUCE

3 pounds apples (such as Fuji, Gala, or Granny Smith), peeled, quartered, and cored

1 pound red beets, peeled and cut into ¼-inch-thick wedges

½ cup water

⅓ cup raisins

½ teaspoon ground cinnamon

PREP	0 MINUTES
COOK	30 MINUTES
PR	20 MINUTES NPR
MAKES	6 CUPS

1 Combine the apples, beets, water, raisins, and cinnamon in the Instant Pot.

2 Secure the lid and set the Pressure Release to **Sealing**. Select the **Steam** setting and set the cooking time for 7 minutes at high pressure. (The pot will take about 20 minutes to come up to pressure before the cooking program begins.)

3 When the cooking program ends, let the pressure release naturally (this will take about 20 minutes). Open the pot and, wearing heat-resistant mitts, lift out the inner pot. For chunky applesauce, use a potato masher to break up the apples and beets. For a smooth puree, use an immersion blender to blend until smooth.

4 Serve right away, or let cool, transfer to an airtight container, and refrigerate for up to 1 week. Applesauce also freezes well, so you don't have to worry about using up the whole batch at once. Freeze 2-cup portions flat in 1-quart ziplock plastic freezer bags for up to 6 months. The bags stack nice and even and take up hardly any space in the freezer.

Notes: If you like, omit the raisins and add a handful of chopped dried apples instead. The dried fruit absorbs the extra water needed for pressure cooking in the Instant Pot, so you don't end up with a watery applesauce if you opt for dried apples over raisins.

Make sure to peel the beets thoroughly to avoid any fibrous skin getting into the sauce. If you prefer not to peel the beets before cooking them, you can steam them whole according to the chart on page 267 and then puree them with the cooked apples.

Nutrition Information

Per ½ cup: 59 calories, 0 grams fat, 18 grams carbohydrates, 2 grams fiber, 1 gram protein

My mother learned how to make compote from her mom, and now I love it, too. This Instant Pot version is done in an hour, rather than the overnight fridge soak my family traditionally used. Dried fruits are immersed in water with cinnamon, and the water becomes sweet and spiced as the fruit rehydrates.

DRIED FRUIT COMPOTE

8 ounces dried peach halves, quartered

8 ounces dried Turkish apricots

½ cup dried cranberries

¼ cup dark raisins

¼ cup golden raisins

2 cinnamon sticks

3 cups water

4 cups plain 2 percent Greek yogurt, homemade (page 34) or store-bought, for serving

PREP	0 MINUTES
COOK	10 MINUTES
PR	1 HOUR NPR
SERVES	12

1 Combine the peaches, apricots, cranberries, raisins, and cinnamon sticks in the Instant Pot and pour the water over them.

2 Secure the lid and set the Pressure Release to **Sealing**. Select the **Pressure Cook** or **Manual** setting and set the cooking time for 0 (zero) minutes at low pressure. (The pot will take about 10 minutes to come up to pressure before the cooking program begins.)

3 When the cooking program ends, let the pressure release naturally and leave the pot covered on the **Keep Warm** setting for 1 hour.

4 Open the pot and remove and discard the cinnamon sticks. The compote can be served warm or chilled. Spoon the yogurt into bowls and top with the compote.

Note: My mom recommends adding peeled and sliced apples or oranges to the cooked compote and enjoying it chilled.

Nutrition Information

Per serving: 136 calories, 0 grams fat, 34 grams carbohydrates, 3 grams fiber, 2 grams protein

When you steam this bread pudding in the Instant Pot, it stays perfectly moist, unlike some baked bread puddings. Instead of using cinnamon raisin bread, which is usually made with white flour, you'll create the flavor by tossing whole-wheat bread with cinnamon, raisins, milk, eggs, and a touch of sweetener. A drizzle of cream cheese glaze is a decadent and dessert-worthy finishing touch.

CINNAMON RAISIN BREAD PUDDING

4 large eggs

1 cup 2 percent milk

3 tablespoons agave nectar or honey

1 teaspoon ground cinnamon

¼ teaspoon fine sea salt

6 cups cubed whole-wheat French bread, in 1-inch cubes

⅓ cup raisins

Glaze

¼ cup cream cheese, at room temperature

½ cup confectioners' sugar

½ teaspoon pure vanilla extract

1 Grease a 7-cup round heatproof glass dish with butter or nonstick cooking spray.

2 In a blender, combine the eggs, milk, agave nectar, cinnamon, and salt. Blend on low speed for about 30 seconds, until well mixed, stopping to scrape down the sides as needed.

3 Put the cubed bread and raisins into a large bowl. Pour in the egg mixture and stir to combine, pressing the bread down to make sure all of the pieces are moistened. Transfer the mixture to the prepared dish, making sure the raisins are distributed evenly throughout. Cover the container tightly with aluminum foil. Let rest at room temperature for 10 minutes or refrigerate for up to 24 hours.

4 When you're ready to cook the bread pudding, pour 1 cup water into the Instant Pot. Place the covered dish on a long-handled silicone steam rack, then, holding the handles of the steam rack, lower it into the pot. (If you don't have the long-handled rack, use the wire metal steam rack and a homemade sling as described on page 10.)

5 Secure the lid and set the Pressure Release to **Sealing**. Select the **Pressure Cook** or **Manual** setting and set the cooking time for 30 minutes at high pressure. (The pot will take about 10 minutes to come up to pressure from room temperature, or 15 from the fridge.)

Nutrition Information

Per serving: 287 calories, 7 grams fat, 45 grams carbohydrates, 1 gram fiber, 9 grams protein

PREP	5 MINUTES
REST	10 MINUTES TO 24 HOURS
COOK	45 MINUTES
PR	10 MINUTES NPR
SERVES	6

6 While the bread pudding is cooking, make the glaze: In a small bowl, whisk together the cream cheese, confectioners' sugar, and vanilla.

7 When the cooking program ends, let the pressure release naturally for 10 minutes, then move the Pressure Release to **Venting** to release any remaining steam. Open the pot and, wearing heat-resistant mitts, grasp the handles of the steam rack and lift the dish out of the pot. Uncover the pudding, taking care not to get burned by the steam or to drip condensation onto the surface. Spoon the cream cheese glaze evenly over the pudding.

8 Using a large serving spoon, scoop the pudding onto plates. Serve warm.

Note: You can also make this pudding with whole-wheat English muffins.

Serve this moist, honey-sweetened cake at teatime or for dessert. Whole-wheat pastry flour performs much more like white flour than traditional whole-wheat flour, making it the better choice for delicately crumbed cakes like this one (or to make the cake gluten-free, substitute a gluten-free flour blend). Bob's Red Mill and Giusto's are my go-to brands for whole-wheat pastry flour.

GLAZED HONEY-LEMON CAKE

Cake

2 cups whole-wheat pastry flour or gluten-free flour blend

1½ teaspoons baking powder

½ teaspoon baking soda

¼ teaspoon fine sea salt

2 large eggs

6 tablespoons unsalted butter, melted and cooled

⅓ cup honey

1½ teaspoons finely grated lemon zest

¼ cup fresh lemon juice

Lemon Glaze

⅓ cup confectioners' sugar

½ teaspoon finely grated lemon zest

1½ teaspoons fresh lemon juice

PREP	10 MINUTES
COOK	50 MINUTES
PR	10 MINUTES NPR
COOL	10 MINUTES
SERVES	8

1 To make the cake: Pour 1 cup water into the Instant Pot. Grease a 7-inch round Bundt pan with butter or nonstick cooking spray and dust with flour, shaking and rotating the pan to coat it evenly. Tap out the excess.

2 In a medium bowl, whisk together the flour, baking powder, baking soda, and salt. Make a well in the center of the dry ingredients. Add the eggs to the well and whisk to break up the yolks a bit. Add the butter, honey, and lemon zest and juice and whisk just until the dry ingredients are fully incorporated. The batter will be quite thick.

3 Spoon the batter into the prepared pan and spread it in an even layer. Tap the pan firmly against the countertop a few times to remove any air bubbles in the batter. Cover the pan tightly with aluminum foil. Place the pan on a long-handled silicone steam rack, then, holding the handles of the steam rack, lower the pan into the pot. (If you don't have the long-handled rack, use the wire metal steam rack and a homemade sling as described on page 10.)

4 Secure the lid and set the Pressure Release to **Sealing**. Select the **Cake**, **Pressure Cook**, or **Manual** setting and set the cooking time for 45 minutes at high pressure. (The pot will take about 5 minutes to come up to pressure before the cooking program begins.)

5 While the cake is cooking, make the glaze: In a small bowl, stir together the confectioners' sugar and lemon zest and juice until smooth.

CONTINUED

GLAZED HONEY-LEMON CAKE

CONTINUED

6 When the cooking program ends, let the pressure release naturally for 10 minutes, then move the Pressure Release to **Venting** to release any remaining steam. Open the pot and, wearing heat-resistant mitts, grab the handles of the steam rack, lift the pan out of the pot, and set the pan on a cooling rack. Uncover the pan, taking care not to get burned by the steam or to drip condensation onto the surface. Let the cake cool in the pan for 5 minutes, then invert the pan onto the cooling rack and carefully lift off the pan. Let the cake cool for 5 more minutes.

7 Set the rack with the cake over a large plate to catch any drips. Stir the glaze once more, then spoon the glaze evenly all over the cake.

8 Serve the cake warm or let cool to room temperature, then transfer to a serving plate. Cut into wedges and serve.

Note: The cake will keep, covered with plastic wrap or in a tightly lidded container, on the counter for up to 3 days. If serving on day two or three, pop a slice in the microwave for 5 to 10 seconds to revive it.

Nutrition Information

Per serving: 260 calories, 10 grams fat, 40 grams carbohydrates, 4 grams fiber, 5 grams protein

You would never guess this cake is gluten-free. It is rich, chocolaty, moist, and delicious warm or at room temperature. It'll keep, tightly covered, on the countertop for a few days, and a next-day slice is best when revived for about 10 seconds in the microwave.

GLUTEN-FREE CHOCOLATE CAKE

1¼ cups gluten-free flour blend

⅓ cup natural cocoa powder

¾ teaspoon baking powder

½ teaspoon baking soda

¼ teaspoon fine sea salt

3 large eggs

⅓ cup agave nectar or honey

½ cup plain 2 percent yogurt, homemade (page 34) or store-bought

1 teaspoon pure vanilla extract

4 tablespoons unsalted butter, melted and cooled

½ cup semisweet chocolate chips

PREP	10 MINUTES
COOK	50 MINUTES
PR	10 MINUTES NPR
COOL	25 MINUTES
SERVES	8

1 Pour 1 cup of water into the Instant Pot. Grease a 7-inch round Bundt pan with butter or nonstick cooking spray.

2 In a large bowl, whisk together the flour, cocoa powder, baking powder, baking soda, and salt. Make a well in the center of the dry ingredients.

3 In a medium bowl, whisk together the eggs, agave nectar, yogurt, and vanilla until well blended, then whisk in the butter. Pour the wet mixture into the well in the dry ingredients. Stir the wet mixture into the dry mixture just until the dry ingredients are fully incorporated. Fold in the chocolate chips.

4 Pour the batter into the prepared pan. Tap the pan firmly against the countertop a few times to remove any air bubbles in the batter. Cover the pan tightly with aluminum foil. Place the pan on a long-handled silicone steam rack, then, holding the handles of the steam rack, lower the pan into pot.

5 Secure the lid and set the Pressure Release to **Sealing**. Select the **Cake**, **Pressure Cook**, or **Manual** setting and set the cooking time for 40 minutes at high pressure. (The pot will take about 10 minutes to come up to pressure before the cooking program begins.)

6 When the cooking program ends, let the pressure release naturally for 10 minutes, then move the Pressure Release to **Venting** to release any remaining steam. Open the pot and, wearing heat-resistant mitts, grasp the handles of the steam rack, lift the pan out of the pot, and transfer the pan to a cooling rack. Uncover the cake, taking care not to get burned by the steam or to drip condensation onto the surface. Let the cake cool in the pan for 5 minutes, then invert the pan onto the cooling rack and carefully lift off the pan. Let the cake cool for at least 20 minutes before serving.

7 Transfer the cake to a serving plate and cut into wedges. Serve warm or at room temperature.

Nutrition Information

Per serving: 275 calories, 14 grams fat, 35 grams carbohydrates, 2 grams fiber, 6 grams protein

This cheesecake has all of the rich, creamy goodness of a traditional cheesecake but with a little less fat, a little more protein, and no cane sugar in the filling. The Greek yogurt adds a light tanginess that nicely offsets the sweetness of the just-thick-enough graham cracker crust. At about 250 calories a slice, this cheesecake is an indulgence you can easily fit into a healthy eating lifestyle. The fresh berries on the side add both color and plenty of vitamin C.

GREEK YOGURT CHEESECAKE

Crust

6 graham cracker sheets, broken roughly into crackers

1½ tablespoons unsalted butter, melted

Filling

One 8-ounce package cream cheese, at room temperature

¾ cup plain 2 percent Greek yogurt, homemade (page 34) or store-bought, at room temperature

⅓ cup agave nectar or honey

1 teaspoon pure vanilla extract

3 large eggs, at room temperature

1 cup fresh raspberries or sliced strawberries, for serving

1 Line the base of a 7-inch springform or cheesecake pan with parchment paper. Grease the sides of the pan and the parchment with butter.

2 To make the crust: In a food processor, process the graham crackers to fine crumbs. Add the butter and process using 1-second pulses until the mixture resembles damp sand.

3 Transfer the crumb mixture to the prepared pan and press it firmly into an even layer on the bottom and about ½ inch up the sides of the pan. Use a paper towel to wipe any crumbs out of the food processor.

4 To make the filling: In the food processor, combine the cream cheese, yogurt, agave nectar, and vanilla and process using 1-second pulses just until smooth. Add the eggs one at a time, using two 1-second pulses to mix in each egg. It's fine if some streaks of egg yolk remain.

5 Pour the filling into the crust. Gently tap the pan on the counter a few times to remove some of the air bubbles in the filling. Cover the pan tightly with aluminum foil.

6 Pour 1 cup water into the Instant Pot. Place the pan on a long-handled silicone steam rack, then, holding the handles of the steam rack, lower it into the pot. (If you don't have the long-handled rack, use the wire metal steam rack and a homemade sling as described on page 10.)

7 Secure the lid and set the Pressure Release to **Sealing**. Select the **Cake**, **Pressure Cook**, or **Manual** setting and set the cooking time for 34 minutes at high pressure. (The pot will take about 5 minutes to come up to pressure before the cooking program begins.)

Nutrition Information

Per serving (cheesecake only): 254 calories, 15 grams fat, 21 grams carbohydrates, 0 grams fiber, 7 grams protein

PREP	10 MINUTES
COOK	40 MINUTES
PR	20 MINUTES NPR
COOL	2 HOURS
CHILL	12 TO 24 HOURS
SERVES	8

8 When the cooking program ends, let the pressure release naturally for 20 minutes, then move the Pressure Release to **Venting**. Open the pot and, wearing heat-resistant mitts, grasp the handles of the steam rack and lift the pan out of the pot. Uncover the cheesecake, taking care not to get burned from the steam or to drip condensation onto the surface. Use a paper towel to dab off any excess moisture that may have settled on top of the cheesecake. The cake will be a bit puffed up and uneven at first, but it will settle and even out as it cools.

9 Leave the cheesecake to cool on the counter for 2 hours, then cover and refrigerate. Let chill for at least 12 hours or up to 24 hours before serving.

10 To unmold the cheesecake, unclasp the collar of the pan and lift it off, then use the parchment border to tug the cheesecake off the base of the pan and onto a plate. Cut the cake into wedges and serve with the berries on the side.

There are just five ingredients in this dense, decadent, naturally gluten-free dark chocolate torte. It's easy and quick to make, too, with everything whisked together in one bowl, then transferred to a springform pan and cooked under pressure for just a half hour. The texture falls somewhere between brownies and fudge, so a small wedge is enough to satisfy your sweet tooth. Serve it at a dinner party and nobody will guess that (a) it took so little effort and (b) you made it in an Instant Pot.

FLOURLESS CHOCOLATE TORTE

10 ounces semisweet chocolate chips or baking wafers

6 tablespoons unsalted butter, at room temperature, cubed

4 large eggs, at room temperature

3 tablespoons honey or agave nectar

¼ teaspoon fine sea salt

Raspberries or sliced strawberries, for serving

Whipped cream, for serving

1 Pour 1 cup water into the Instant Pot. Line a 7-inch springform pan with an 8-inch parchment round, clamping the collar in place so that a little of the parchment is sticking evenly out the sides of the pan. Grease the sides of the pan with butter.

2 Put the chocolate chips into a medium microwave-safe bowl. Heat the chocolate chips in a microwave in 30-second intervals, stirring after each interval, just until melted. While the chocolate is still warm, add the butter and whisk vigorously for about 1½ minutes, until the butter melts and is evenly combined with the chocolate. Add the eggs one at a time, whisking after each addition until thoroughly combined. Whisk in the honey and salt for about 1 minute, until the batter is completely smooth and glossy.

3 Pour the batter into the prepared pan. Tap the pan against the counter a few times to remove any air bubbles in the batter. Cover the pan tightly with aluminum foil. Place the pan on a long-handled silicone steam rack, then, holding the handles of the steam rack, lower the pan into the pot. (If you don't have the long-handled rack, use the wire metal steam rack and a homemade sling as described on page 10.)

4 Secure the lid and set the Pressure Release to **Sealing**. Select the **Cake**, **Pressure Cook**, or **Manual** setting and set the cooking time for 30 minutes at high pressure. (The pot will take about 5 minutes to come up to pressure before the cooking program begins.)

Nutrition Information

Per serving (torte only): 240 calories, 17 grams fat, 24 grams carbohydrates, 4 grams fiber, 5 grams protein

PREP	15 MINUTES
COOK	35 MINUTES
PR	15 MINUTES NPR
COOL	2 HOURS
CHILL	10 TO 24 HOURS
SERVES	10

5 When the cooking program ends, let the pressure release naturally for 15 minutes, then move the Pressure Release to **Venting** to release any remaining steam. Open the pot and, wearing heat-resistant mitts, grasp the handles of the steam rack, lift the pan out of the pot, and set the pan on a cooling rack. Uncover the cake, taking care not to get burned by the steam or to drip condensation onto the surface. Let the cake cool on the counter for 2 hours, re-cover with a dry sheet of aluminum foil, and then transfer to the refrigerator and chill for at least 10 hours or up to 24 hours.

6 To unmold the torte, run a knife around the edge to release it from the pan sides, then unclasp the collar and lift it off. Use the parchment border to tug the torte off the base of the pan and onto a serving plate.

7 Cut the torte into wedges and serve with the berries and whipped cream.

10

Pantry

LOW-SODIUM CHICKEN BONE BROTH

MAKES ABOUT 8 CUPS

1 chicken carcass plus any drumstick, thigh, breast, and wing bones you've saved

2 celery stalks, cut into 3-inch lengths

2 carrots, halved lengthwise, then cut crosswise into 3-inch lengths

1 yellow onion, cut into wedges

6 fresh flat-leaf parsley sprigs

¾ teaspoon fine sea salt

2 teaspoons raw cider vinegar

1½ cups drippings (saved from Whole Chicken in a Hurry, page 167) or 1½ cups water, ½ teaspoon poultry seasoning, and ½ teaspoon fine sea salt

6½ cups water

1 Combine the chicken carcass and bones, celery, carrots, onion, parsley, and salt in the Instant Pot. Add the vinegar, drippings, and water, pouring the drippings and water slowly to prevent splashing.

2 Secure the lid and set the Pressure Release to **Sealing**. Select the **Soup/Broth** setting and set the cooking time for 40 minutes at high pressure. (It will take about 25 minutes for the pot to come up to pressure before the cooking program begins.)

3 When the cooking program ends, let the pressure release naturally for at least 40 minutes, then move the Pressure Release to **Venting** to release any remaining steam. If you like, you can leave the pot on the **Keep Warm** setting for up to 10 hours.

4 Place a fine-mesh strainer over a large heatproof bowl or pitcher. For a clearer broth, line the strainer with a double layer of cheesecloth.

5 Open the pot and, wearing heat-resistant mitts, lift out the inner pot and pour the broth into the strainer. Discard the contents of the strainer.

6 Let the broth cool to room temperature. (To speed up the cooling process, prepare an ice bath and set the bowl in the ice bath.)

7 The broth can be used right away, stored in an airtight container in the refrigerator for up to 5 days, or frozen for up to 6 months.

Note: There may be a little fat in the broth. I don't mind it, and I think it actually adds a nice richness and flavor. Feel free to skim it off the top with a ladle or spoon if you prefer. If you are not using the broth immediately, the fat will solidify on the surface once the broth is refrigerated and will be easy to scrape off.

Nutritional Information

Per 1 cup: 35 calories, 0 grams fat, 0.5 grams carbohydrates, 0 grams fiber, 8 grams protein

LOW-SODIUM ROASTED BEEF BONE BROTH

MAKES ABOUT 8 CUPS

2 pounds beef bones (such as knucklebones, shanks, or oxtails)

3 celery stalks, cut into 3-inch lengths

2 large carrots, halved lengthwise and cut crosswise into 3-inch lengths

1 large yellow onion, cut into wedges

1 teaspoon salt

½ teaspoon black peppercorns

1 bay leaf

8 cups water

1 Preheat the oven to 400°F. Line a sheet pan with aluminum foil.

2 Arrange the beef bones in a single layer on the prepared pan. Roast for about 45 minutes, until browned.

3 Using tongs, transfer the roasted bones to the Instant Pot. Add the celery, carrots, onion, salt, peppercorns, and bay leaf. Pour in the water slowly, to avoid splashing, making sure the pot is no more than two-thirds full.

4 Secure the lid and set the Pressure Release to **Sealing**. Select the **Soup/Broth** setting and set the cooking time for 2 hours at high pressure. (The pot will take about 30 minutes to come up to pressure before the cooking program begins.)

5 When the cooking program ends, let the pressure release naturally (this will take about 45 minutes). Place a wire-mesh strainer over a large stainless-steel bowl. For a clearer broth, line the strainer with a double layer of cheesecloth. Open the pot and, using tongs, remove the beef bones. Wearing heat-resistant mitts, lift out the inner pot and pour the broth through the prepared strainer into the bowl. Discard the vegetables and bones. You can pick the meat off the bones if you like, but it will have given up most of its flavor to the broth. Pour the broth into a fat separator to remove the fat, or chill the broth in the refrigerator until the fat solidifies on top, then scoop off the fat from the surface with a large spoon. Let the broth cool to room temperature. (To speed up the cooling process, set the bowl in a larger bowl containing an ice bath.)

6 The broth can be used right away, stored in an airtight container in the refrigerator for up to 5 days, or frozen for up to 6 months.

Nutrition Information

Per 1 cup: 30 calories, 0 grams fat, 0 grams carbohydrates, 0 grams fiber, 6 grams protein

LOW-SODIUM VEGETABLE BROTH

MAKES ABOUT 8 CUPS

1 tablespoon extra-virgin olive oil

1 large yellow onion, diced

4 garlic cloves, smashed

2 large carrots, diced

4 celery stalks, diced

2 teaspoons fine sea salt

2 teaspoons tomato paste

2 tablespoons nutritional yeast

8 cups water

1 teaspoon black peppercorns

2 bay leaves

One 3-ounce bunch flat-leaf parsley

1 Select the **Sauté** setting on the Instant Pot and heat the oil for 1 minute. Add the onion, garlic, carrots, celery, and salt and sauté for about 10 minutes, until the vegetables give up some of their liquid and begin to brown. Stir in the tomato paste and nutritional yeast, then add 1 cup of the water and use a wooden spoon or spatula to nudge any browned bits from the bottom of the pot. Add the peppercorns, bay leaves, parsley, and the remaining 7 cups water, making sure not to fill the pot more than two-thirds full.

2 Secure the lid and set the Pressure Release to **Sealing**. Press the **Cancel** button to reset the cooking program, then select the **Soup/Broth** setting and set the cooking time for 10 minutes at high pressure. (The pot will take about 20 minutes to come up to pressure before the cooking program begins.)

3 When the cooking program ends, let the pressure release naturally for 30 minutes, then move the Pressure Release to **Venting** to release any remaining steam.

4 Place a fine-mesh strainer over a large heatproof bowl or pitcher. For a clearer broth, line the strainer with a double layer of cheesecloth.

5 Open the pot and, wearing heat-resistant mitts, lift out the inner pot and pour the broth through the prepared strainer into the bowl. Discard the contents of the strainer. Let the broth cool to room temperature. (To speed up the cooling process, prepare an ice bath and set the bowl in the ice bath.)

6 The broth can be used right away, stored in an airtight container in the refrigerator for up to 5 days, or frozen for up to 6 months.

Nutrition Information

Per 1 cup: 36 calories, 2 grams fat, 2 grams carbohydrates, 0 grams fiber, 2 grams protein

ROASTED GARLIC

MAKES 12 SERVINGS

3 garlic heads, left whole

1 tablespoon extra-virgin olive oil

¼ teaspoon fine sea salt

⅛ teaspoon freshly ground black pepper

1 Pour 1 cup water into the Instant Pot and place the wire metal steam rack into the pot. Cut off the top ½ inch from each garlic head, exposing the cloves. Place the heads, cut side up, on the steam rack.

2 Secure the lid and set the Pressure Release to **Sealing**. Select the **Steam** setting and set the cooking time for 10 minutes at high pressure. (The pot will take about 5 minutes to come up to pressure before the cooking program begins.)

3 While the garlic is steaming, preheat the oven or toaster oven to 425°F. Line a small sheet pan with aluminum foil.

4 When the cooking program ends, perform a quick release by moving the Pressure Release to **Venting**. Open the pot and, using a pair of tongs, transfer the garlic to the prepared pan.

5 Drizzle the oil over the garlic, then sprinkle with the salt and pepper. Roast for 12 to 15 minutes, until golden brown. Remove the garlic from the oven and set aside to cool.

6 Check the garlic heads to see if they have cooled enough for you to handle them comfortably (about 10 minutes). Once they have, separate them into cloves and squeeze the base of each clove to free the flesh from the skins.

Nutrition Information

12 cloves of garlic per bulb = 3 cloves per serving:
25 calories, 1 gram fat, 3 grams carbohydrates, 0 grams fiber, 1 gram protein

SALSA PICANTE

MAKES 2½ CUPS

2 guajillo chiles, stemmed and seeded
Boiling water
¼ cup cold water
½ small yellow onion, diced
1 garlic clove, minced
1 jalapeño chile, seeded and diced
2 tablespoons chopped fresh cilantro
2 tablespoons fresh lime juice
½ teaspoon fine sea salt
One 14½-ounce can diced tomatoes and their liquid

1 In a small heatproof bowl, combine the chiles and boiling water to cover. Cover the bowl with a silicone lid or plastic wrap and let the chiles soak for 20 minutes.

2 Transfer the soaked chiles to a cutting board and discard the soaking water. Roughly chop the chiles, then add them to a food processor or blender. Add the cold water, onion, garlic, jalapeño, cilantro, lime juice, and salt. Process for about 1 minute at medium speed, until the salsa is thoroughly blended, stopping to scrape down the sides halfway through. Add the tomatoes and process in two or three 1-second pulses, so the tomatoes stay a bit chunky.

3 The salsa can be used right away or stored in an airtight container in the refrigerator for up to 1 week.

Nutrition Information

Per 2 tablespoons: 10 calories, 0 grams fat, 2 grams carbohydrates, 0 grams fiber, 0 grams protein

TAHINI DRESSING

MAKES ¾ CUP

⅓ cup tahini
¼ cup water
2 tablespoons fresh lemon juice
¼ teaspoon fine sea salt
⅛ teaspoon ground cumin

1 In a small bowl, whisk together the tahini, water, lemon juice, salt, and cumin until smooth. The dressing will thicken as it sits, so if you like a thinner dressing, blend in another 2 teaspoons water.

2 The dressing can be used right away or stored in an airtight container in the refrigerator for up to 5 days.

Nutrition Information

Per 2 tablespoons: 85 calories, 8 grams fat, 3 grams carbohydrates, 1 gram fiber, 3 grams protein

TZATZIKI

MAKES ABOUT 1½ CUPS

1 cup plain 2 percent Greek yogurt, homemade (page 34) or store-bought

1 Persian cucumber, finely diced

1 tablespoon chopped fresh mint

1 garlic clove, pressed or grated

½ teaspoon fine sea salt

1 In a medium bowl, stir together the yogurt, cucumber, mint, garlic, and salt, mixing well.

2 The tzatziki can be used right away or stored in an airtight container in the refrigerator for up to 3 days.

Nutrition Information

Per ¼ cup: 32 calories, 1 gram fat, 2 grams carbohydrates, 0 grams fiber, 4 grams protein

BASIL OIL

MAKES ½ CUP

2 cups water

1 cup firmly packed fresh basil leaves

½ cup cold-pressed avocado oil

¼ teaspoon fine sea salt

1 Line a dinner plate with paper towels. In a small saucepan, bring the water to a boil over high heat. Add the basil leaves and turn off the heat. Let sit for 30 seconds, then, using a slotted spoon, transfer the basil leaves to the prepared plate. Squeeze any excess liquid from the leaves and transfer them to a widemouthed 1-pint Mason jar. Add the oil and salt to the jar, then use an immersion blender to process for about 1 minute, until the basil leaves are mostly blended into the oil (it's fine if there are still little bits of leaf).

2 The oil can be used right away or stored in an airtight container in the refrigerator for up to 1 week.

Nutrition Information

Per 1 tablespoon: 124 calories, 14 grams fat, 0 grams carbohydrates, 0 grams fiber, 0 grams protein

DILL PICKLE CHIPS

MAKES 4 PINTS

2 quarts water

5 tablespoons pickling salt (I prefer Ball brand)

2 pounds pickling cucumbers, cut into ⅛-inch-thick rounds

Pickling Brine

2⅔ cups water

2 cups distilled white vinegar

1 tablespoon agave nectar

2 tablespoons pickling salt

2 teaspoons pickling spice

2 teaspoons dill seeds

8 fresh dill sprigs

1 In a large bowl, combine the water and pickling salt and stir to dissolve the salt. Add the cucumbers to the bowl and let stand at room temperature for 4 hours.

2 To make the pickling brine: Combine the water, vinegar, agave nectar, pickling salt, and pickling spice in the Instant Pot and stir to dissolve the salt. Select the high **Sauté** setting and set the cooking time for 12 minutes. When the timer goes off, the brine should be boiling.

3 While the brine is heating, combine the dill seeds and dill sprigs in a single 2-quart airtight container, or divide the ingredients equally among four 1-pint or two 1-quart canning jars. Drain the cucumbers in a colander, then pack them into the container(s).

4 Wearing heat-resistant mitts, lift out the inner pot. Using a jam funnel and ladle, fill the container(s) with the hot brine, covering the cucumbers but leaving ½-inch headspace if using canning jars. Lightly tap the container(s) against the counter and then rotate gently to remove any air bubbles. Cover the container(s). Discard any extra brine. Let the pickles cool to room temperature, then store in the refrigerator for 3 days before serving.

5 The pickles will keep, refrigerated, for up to 1 month.

Nutrition Information

Per 1 ounce serving (about 8 chips): 5 calories, 0 grams fat, 1 gram carbohydrates, 0 grams fiber, 0 grams protein

CASHEW SOUR CREAM

MAKES 1 CUP

½ cup raw whole cashews, soaked in water to cover for 2 hours at room temperature or up to overnight in the refrigerator, drained

¼ cup cold-pressed avocado oil

2 tablespoons water

2 tablespoons fresh lemon juice

1 tablespoon nutritional yeast

½ teaspoon fine sea salt

1 In a widemouthed 1-pint jar, combine the cashews, oil, water, lemon juice, nutritional yeast, and salt. Using an immersion blender, blend the mixture for about 2 minutes, until smooth.

2 The sour cream can be used right away or stored in an airtight container in the refrigerator for up to 1 week.

Nutrition Information

Per 1 tablespoon: 52 calories, 5 grams fat, 1 gram carbohydrates, 0 grams fiber, 1 gram protein

VEGAN PARMESAN CHEESE

MAKES 1 CUP

1 cup raw cashews

¼ cup nutritional yeast

1 teaspoon garlic powder

¾ teaspoon fine sea salt

1 In a food processor, combine the cashews, nutritional yeast, garlic powder, and salt. Process using about ten 1-second pulses, until the mixture resembles grated Parmesan cheese.

2 The vegan Parmesan can be used right away or stored in an airtight container in the refrigerator for up to 3 months.

Nutrition Information

Per 1 tablespoon: 46 calories, 3 grams fat, 3 grams carbohydrates, 1 gram fiber, 2 grams protein

ALMOND FETA CHEESE

MAKES 1½ CUPS

1¼ cups slivered or whole blanched almonds

¼ cup fresh lemon juice

¼ cup extra-virgin olive oil

2 tablespoons water

1 teaspoon nutritional yeast

1 teaspoon fine sea salt

1 In a food processor, combine the almonds, lemon juice, oil, water, nutritional yeast, and salt and process for 30 seconds. Scrape down the sides of the processor and then process for 1 more minute, until the mixture is almost smooth. There will still be a bit of texture from the almonds.

2 The almond feta can be used right away, or it can be transferred to an airtight container (pack it down and spread it in an even layer) and refrigerated for up to 1 week. It will be soft and easy to spoon straight out of the food processor and will firm up in the refrigerator.

Nutritional Information

Per 2 tablespoons: 117 calories, 11 grams fat, 3 grams carbohydrates, 1 gram fiber, 3 grams protein

COOKING CHARTS

Refer to these charts* to determine the cooking times for lots of foods. When converting recipes for the Instant Pot, use the longest-cooking ingredient to determine the cooking time.

Meat	Cooking Time (in minutes)	Pressure Release
Beef, stew meat	25 to 30	natural
Beef, pot roast, steak, rump, round, chuck, blade, or brisket, large chunks	35 to 40	natural
Beef, pot roast, rump, round, chuck, or brisket, small chunks	25 to 30	natural
Beef, pot roast, rump, round, chuck, or brisket, whole, up to 4 pounds	20 to 25/pound	natural
Beef, short ribs	30 to 35	natural
Beef, shanks (crosscut)	30 to 35	natural
Beef, oxtail	50 to 55	natural
Chicken, breasts, with bones	10 to 15	quick
Chicken, breasts, boneless, skinless	8	quick
Chicken, drumsticks, legs, or thighs, with bones	15	quick
Chicken, thighs, boneless	10	quick
Chicken, whole	20 to 25	quick
Chicken, whole, cut up with bones	10 to 15	quick
Ham slice	9 to 12	quick
Lam, stew meat	20 to 25	natural
Pork, loin roast	20/pound	natural
Pork, butt roast	15/pound	natural
Pork, ribs	20 to 25	natural
Turkey, breast, boneless	15 to 20	quick
Turkey, breast, whole, with bones	25 to 30	quick
Turkey, drumsticks (leg)	15 to 20	quick

*Charts adapted from information provided by Instant Pot

Rice and Other Grains	Water Quantity (rice/grain to water ratio)	Cooking Time (in minutes)
Barley, pearl	1:1½ to 2	25 to 30
Barley, pot	1:3 to 4	25 to 30
Congee, thick	1:4 to 5	15 to 20
Congee, thin	1:6 to 7	15 to 20
Couscous (not quick-cooking)	1:2	5 to 8
Millet	1:1⅔	10 to 12
Oats, old-fashioned (rolled)	1:1⅔	6
Oats, steel-cut	1:3	10 to 12
Polenta, coarse	1:4	10 to 15
Quinoa	1:1 to 1¼	8
Rice, basmati	1:1 to1¼	4 to 8
Rice, brown	1:1 to 1¼	20 to 25
Rice, jasmine	1:1 to 1¼	4 to 10
Rice, white	1:1 to 1¼	8
Rice, wild	1:1⅓ to 1½	25 to 30
Whole-grain wheat berries, spelt, farro, or kamut	1:1½ to 2	25 to 30

Beans	Soaked, Cooking Time (in minutes)	Unsoaked, Cooking Time (in minutes)
Black	6 to 8	20 to 25
Black-eyed pea	4 to 5	20 to 25
Cannellini	6 to 9	30 to 35
Chickpea (garbanzo)	10 to 15	35 to 40
Corona, gigante	10 to 15	25 to 30
Flageolet	6 to 9	20 to 25
Great Northern	12 to 14	25 to 30
Kidney	7 to 8	15 to 20
Lima	6 to 10	12 to 14
Navy	7 to 8	20 to 25
Pinquito	5 to 7	20 to 25
Pinto	6 to 9	25 to 30
Red	6 to 8	2 to 25

Lentils	Soaked, Cooking Time (in minutes)	Unsoaked, Cooking Time (in minutes)
Beluga (black)	n/a	15 to 20
Green	n/a	15 to 20
Puy (French)	n/a	15 to 20
Red (split)	n/a	15 to 18
Small brown (Spanish)	n/a	15 to 20
Yellow (split)	n/a	15 to 18

Vegetables	Fresh, Cooking Time (in minutes)	Frozen, Cooking Time (in minutes)
Artichokes, whole, trimmed without leaves removed	9 to 11	11 to 13
Artichokes, hearts	4 to 5	5 to 6
Asparagus, whole or cut	0 to 2	2 to 3
Beets, small, whole	11 to 13	13 to 15
Beets, large, whole	20 to 25	25 to 30
Broccoli, florets	0 to 2	2 to 3
Broccoli, stalks	1 to 3	3 to 4
Brussels sprouts, whole	2 to 4	4 to 5
Cabbage, red, purple or green, shredded	1 to 2	2 to 3
Cabbage, red, purple or green, wedges	2 to 3	3 to 4
Carrots, sliced or shredded	1 to 2	2 to 3
Carrots, whole or chunks	2 to 3	3 to 4
Cauliflower, florets	1 to 2	3 to 4
Celery, chunks	2 to 3	3 to 4
Corn, kernels	1 to 2	2 to 3
Corn, on the cob	3 to 4	4-5
Eggplant, slices or chunks	2 to 3	3 to 4
Endives, whole	1 to 2	2 to 3
Escarole, chopped	1 to 2	2 to 3
Green beans, whole	3 to 5	4 to 7
Greens (beet greens, collards, kale, spinach, Swiss chard, turnip greens), chopped	3 to 6	4 to 7
Leeks, chopped	2 to 4	3 to 5
Mixed vegetables, chopped (frozen blend)	2 to 3	3 to 4
Okra, sliced	2 to 3	3 to 4
Onions, sliced	2 to 3	3 to 4
Parsnips, sliced	1 to 2	2 to 3
Parsnips, chunks	2 to 4	4 to 6
Peas, sugar snap or snow, whole	0 to 1	2 to 3
Peas, green (English), shelled	0 to 1	2 to 3
Potatoes, in cubes	3 to 5	7 to 9
Potatoes, whole, baby	10 to 12	12 to 14
Potatoes, whole, large	12 to 15	15 to 19
Pumpkin, small slices or chunks	4 to 5	6 to 7
Rutabagas, slices	3 to 5	4 to 6
Rutabagas, chunks	4 to 6	6 to 8
Spinach	0 to 1	2 to 3
Squash, acorn, slices or chunks	6 to 7	8 to 9
Squash, butternut, slices or chunks	6 to 7	8 to 9
Sweet peppers, slices or chunks	0 to 2	3 to 4
Sweet potatoes, cubed	3 to 5	5 to 7
Sweet potatoes, whole, small	10 to 12	12 to 14
Sweet potatoes, whole, large	12 to 15	15 to 19
Tomatoes, quartered	2 to 3	4 to 5
Tomatoes, whole	3 to 5	5 to 7
Turnips, chunks	2 to 4	4 to 6
Yams, cubed	3 to 5	5 to 7
Yams, whole, small	12 to 15	15 to 19
Zucchini, slices or chunks	2 to 3	3 to 4

DIETARY CHART

Recipe	Vegan	Vegetarian	Gluten-Free	Dairy- Free	Notes/Substitutions*
CHAPTER 1: BREAKFAST					
Butternut Squash Steel-Cut Oatmeal	√	√	√	√	Gluten-free oats
Banana Oatmeal with Strawberry-Chia Jam	√	√	√	√	Gluten-free oats
Barley Bowls with Crispy Eggs and Tamari		√		√	
Quinoa Muesli Breakfast Bowls	√	√	√	√	
Soft- or Hard-Boiled Eggs		√	√	√	
Soft-Boiled Eggs in Yogurt Sauce		√	√		Gluten-free bread for serving
Corn and Zucchini Omelet with Smoked Salmon			√		
Crustless Ham and Swiss Quiche			√		
Sweet Potato and Arugula Frittata		√	√	√	
Broccoli-Cheddar Egg Muffins		√	√		
Yogurt		√	√		
Yogurt Bowl with Ginger Almond Granola		√	√		Gluten-free oats
Chocolate and PB Yogurt Smoothie		√	√		
Whole-Wheat Matzo Brei		√		√	
Apple-Cinnamon French Toast Casserole		√			
Yeasted Buckwheat Waffles		√	√	√	
CHAPTER 2: BEANS, GRAINS, AND PASTAS					
Basic Beans	√	√	√	√	
Mixed Bean Salad	√	√	√	√	
Toasted Sesame Miso Hummus	√	√	√	√	
Balsamic and Butter Lentils	√	√	√	√	Gluten-free balsamic vinegar
Refried Black Beans	√	√	√	√	
Basic Rice	√	√	√	√	
Cajun-Spiced Red Beans and Rice	√	√	√	√	
Spinach and Pea Risotto		√	√		
Double Mushroom Risotto		√	√		
Brown Rice Nori Rolls	√	√	√	√	
Chickpea and Brown Rice Tabbouleh	√	√	√	√	
Wild Rice Salad with Cranberries and Oranges	√	√	√	√	
Basic Whole Grains	√	√	√	√	Some varieties of grains contain gluten
Quinoa with Pears and Walnuts	√	√	√	√	

* Check the recipe Notes to see if any substitutions are needed to make a recipe vegan, vegetarian, gluten-free, or dairy-free.

Recipe	Vegan	Vegetarian	Gluten-Free	Dairy- Free	Notes/Substitutions*
Farro Salad with Romaine, Raisins, and Almond Feta	√	√		√	
Vegan Mac 'n' Greens	√	√		√	
Winter White Pasta Salad		√			
Whole-Wheat Penne Arrabbiata	√	√		√	
CHAPTER 3: SOUPS AND CHILIS					
Beet Borscht	√	√	√	√	
Winter Squash Miso Soup	√	√	√	√	Gluten-free miso paste
Cream of Zucchini Soup	√	√	√	√	
Tomato–Red Pepper Bisque with Basil Oil	√	√	√	√	
Green Minestrone	√	√	√	√	
Pasta, Bean, and Sausage Soup				√	
Red Lentil and Spinach Soup	√	√	√	√	
Greek Lentil Soup	√	√	√	√	
Hearty Multibean Soup	√	√	√	√	
Sweet Potato Soup	√	√	√	√	
Roasted Garlic and Potato Soup	√	√	√	√	
Cabbage and Potato Soup	√	√	√	√	
Vegan Red Pozole	√	√	√	√	
Vegetable Beef Soup			√	√	
Chicken Drumstick Soup			√	√	
Chicken Pho			√	√	
Vegan Soy Curls Chili	√	√	√	√	
Tomatillo Chicken Chili			√	√	
Tri-Tip and Bean Chili			√	√	
CHAPTER 4: VEGETARIAN					
Avocado Egg Salad Sandwiches		√		√	
Seitan Chickpea Chorizo Sausages	√	√		√	
Falafel-Spiced Chickpea Pockets	√	√		√	
Mixed-Vegetable Korma	√	√	√	√	
BBQ Jackfruit Bowls with Alabama Sauce	√	√	√	√	
Josephine's Special	√	√		√	Gluten-free Worcestershire sauce
Tamale Casserole	√	√		√	
Vegan Salisbury Steak	√	√		√	
Cheesy Loaded Potato Casserole		√	√		
"Chick'n" and Brown Rice Pilaf	√	√	√	√	
Black-Eyed Peas and Kale	√	√	√	√	
Sesame Peanut Noodles with Seared Tofu	√	√		√	

Recipe	Vegan	Vegetarian	Gluten-Free	Dairy- Free	Notes/Substitutions*
Korean Hot Pot with Tofu and Mushrooms	√	√	√	√	Gluten-free doenjang (or substitute gluten-free miso paste)
Garden Patch Jambalaya	√	√	√	√	
Steamed Butternut or Spaghetti Squash					
Spaghetti Squash Marinara with Vegan Parmesan	√	√	√	√	
CHAPTER 5: SEAFOOD					
Mussels with Tomatoes and White Wine Broth			√	√	
Shrimp and Avocado Toast				√	
Shrimp Ceviche with Sweet Potatoes and Corn			√	√	
Cioppino Pasta				√	
Seafood Risotto			√	√	
New England Fish Chowder			√		
Cod and Shrimp Stew with Tomatoes and Saffron			√	√	
Fish Taco Salad with Mango Salsa			√	√	
Salmon and Spinach Patties			√	√	
Poached Salmon with Basil Vinaigrette			√	√	
Thai Green Curry Tilapia			√	√	
CHAPTER 6: POULTRY					
Sweet and Spicy Chicken Wings			√	√	
Honey Mustard Chicken Tenders and Slaw					
Buffalo Chicken Lettuce Cups			√	√	Gluten-free Worcestershire sauce
Antipasto Chicken Chopped Salad			√	√	
Za'atar-Spiced Chicken Salad with Tahini Dressing			√	√	Gluten-free za'atar, flat-bread
Greek Chicken Meatballs			√	√	
Dairy-Free Pesto Chicken Penne			√	√	
Chicken, Chickpea, and Carrot Plov			√	√	
Spicy Sesame Peanut Chicken			√	√	
Salsa Chicken and Supercharged Rice			√	√	
Southern Smothered Chicken			√		
Chicken Cutlets in Tuscan Cream Sauce			√		
Chicken and Mushroom Goulash			√	√	
Whole Chicken in a Hurry			√	√	
Tandoori-Spiced Chicken Thighs			√		

Recipe	Vegan	Vegetarian	Gluten-Free	Dairy- Free	Notes/Substitutions*
Paella Turkey Meatballs			√	√	
Chipotle Turkey Sloppy Joes			√	√	Gluten-free chipotle en adobo, gluten-free hamburger buns
CHAPTER 7: PORK, LAMB, AND BEEF					
Pork Chops Marsala			√	√	
Pork Chops with Cumin and Coriander			√	√	
Pork Loin with Balsamic and Cherries			√	√	Gluten-free balsamic vinegar
Crispy Pulled Pork Gyros			√		Gluten-free flatbread
Ground Pork Bolognese			√	√	For dairy-free, use Vegan Parmesan Cheese (page 265)
Honey-Dijon Baby Back Ribs			√	√	
Spanish-Style Pork and White Beans			√	√	
Braised Loin Shoulder with Chinese Black Bean Sauce				√	
Pork Loin with Lemon, Capers, and Artichokes			√	√	
Irish Lamb Stew				√	
Cabbage Roll Casserole			√	√	
Ground Beef Tostada Salads			√	√	
Florentine Beef Meat Loaf				√	
Beef Tips with Onion and Mushroom Gravy			√	√	Gluten-free Worcestershire sauce
Sweet Potato Cottage Pie				√	Gluten-free Worcestershire sauce
Shredded BBQ Pot Roast			√	√	Gluten-free barbecue sauce
Cincinnati Chili Mac				√	
Beef and Spinach Lasagna					
Indian-Style Beef Curry			√		
CHAPTER 8: VEGETABLES AND SIDE DISHES					
Pan-Grilled Artichokes with Curry Dip		√	√		
Asparagus with Vegan Aioli	√	√	√	√	
Baby Carrots with Honey Lemon Butter	√	√	√	√	
Broccoli with Crispy Garlic Chips	√	√	√	√	
Everything Brussels Sprouts	√	√	√	√	
Cauliflower Carrot Mash	√	√	√	√	
Cauliflower Florets with Herbed Butter	√	√	√	√	
Celery Root Salad	√	√	√	√	
Italian Braised Green Beans and Tomatoes	√	√	√	√	
Chimichurri Corn on the Cob	√	√	√	√	

Recipe	Vegan	Vegetarian	Gluten-Free	Dairy- Free	Notes/Substitutions*
Crunchy Vegetable Dip		√	√		
Bacon-Braised Beets and Greens			√	√	
Vegan Creamed Spinach	√	√	√	√	
Giardiniera Salad	√	√	√	√	
Zucchini with Olive Oil and Parsley	√	√	√	√	
Steamed Potatoes (Regular and Sweet)	√	√	√	√	
Beet, Carrot, and Potato Salad	√	√	√	√	
Crispy Sriracha Potatoes	√	√	√	√	
Mashed Sweet Potatoes	√	√	√	√	
JoJo Potatoes	√	√	√	√	
CHAPTER 9: DRINKS AND DESSERTS					
Mulled Apple Cider with Oranges and Rosemary	√	√	√	√	
Hot Cranberry Cocktail	√	√	√	√	
Virgin Toddy Tonic	√	√	√	√	
Frozen Yogurt Fudge Ice Pops		√	√		
Coconut Bulgur Pudding	√	√		√	
Wine-Poached Pears	√	√	√	√	
Pink Applesauce	√	√	√	√	
Dried Fruit Compote	√	√	√	√	
Cinnamon Raisin Bread Pudding		√			
Glazed Honey-Lemon Cake		√	√		
Gluten-Free Chocolate Cake		√	√		
Greek Yogurt Cheesecake		√			
Flourless Chocolate Torte		√	√		
CHAPTER 10: PANTRY					
Low-Sodium Chicken Bone Broth			√	√	
Low-Sodium Roasted Beef Bone Broth			√	√	
Low-Sodium Vegetable Broth	√	√	√	√	
Roasted Garlic					
Salsa Picante	√	√	√	√	
Tahini Dressing					
Tzatziki					
Basil Oil					
Dill Pickle Chips	√	√	√	√	
Cashew Sour Cream	√	√	√	√	
Vegan Parmesan Cheese	√	√	√	√	
Almond Feta Cheese	√	√	√	√	

ACKNOWLEDGMENTS

I am so excited to bring *The Ultimate Instant Pot Healthy Cookbook* to life, and it would not be here without the dedication and hard work of many people. I can't thank you all enough, but I will make a start here.

To longtime friend Lizzie Paulsen, thank you so much for your contributions to this book. From double-checking (and fact-checking) my first drafts to calculating nutrition information to recipe testing, you truly went above and beyond to help a friend. I am so lucky to have you in my life for two dozen years and counting.

To my agent, Alison Fargis, and the rest of the team at Stonesong, I am ever grateful for all you do to keep me writing these beautiful cookbooks. It is a privilege to have you in my corner.

To the team at Ten Speed Press, thank you for continuing to share the Instant Pot love with me. Thanks to senior editor Lisa Westmoreland; director of marketing Windy Dorresteyn and publicity director Kristin Casemore; project editor Leigh Saffold; copy editor Sharon Silva; senior art director Betsy Stromberg; food stylist Nathan Carrabba and assistant food stylists Rachel Bieber and Katherine Knowlton; prop stylist Claire Mack; and photographer Jennifer Davick and assistant Bernard Manning. I have truly lucked out in life to be able to work with such talented and kind people.

To Robert Wang and the rest of the team at Instant Pot, thank you for giving your stamp of approval to both my *Essential* and *Ultimate* series of books. Since I began my cookbook writing career, countless millions of Instant Pots have landed on kitchen counters the world over, and I have you and your genius appliance to thank for my success.

To my friend and editor at Simply Recipes, Emma Christensen, thank you for endless support and general awesomeness as a friend and colleague. I am beyond lucky to have met you for so many reasons. And to the rest of the team at Simply Recipes, I am so glad we got to connect and bond at our retreat this year. Till next time!

To my parents, Cindy and Larry Harris, thank you for your recipe-testing help on this book, especially with the Flourless Chocolate Torte. Thanks to your input, we ended up with a truly decadent dessert worthy of my chocolate-loving dad's affection. To my Grandma Rachel, thank you for teaching me to save the drippings—they really do make a great soup. Oh, and congratulations on being the latest nonagenarian to join the Instant Pot club!

Last but not least, thank you to my husband, Brendan, for, well, everything. You're my best friend and fellow adventurer in life, and I would not be where I am if it weren't for your quiet confidence in me.

ABOUT THE AUTHOR

Coco Morante is the author of the bestselling *The Essential Instant Pot Cookbook*, *The Ultimate Instant Pot Cookbook*, and *The Essential Vegan Instant Pot Cookbook*. She is a recipe developer, facilitator of the Instant Pot Recipes Facebook page, and creator of the blog *Lefty Spoon*. Her recipes and writing have been featured in numerous print and online publications, including *People*, Epicurious, POPSUGAR, Food Republic, TASTE, The Kitchn, Simply Recipes, and *Edible Silicon Valley*.

Coco lives in Portland, Oregon, with her husband, Brendan, and their beagle, Beagle Brendan.

INDEX

A

Aioli, Vegan, 208
Alabama Sauce, 110
almonds
  Almond Feta Cheese, 265
  Farro Salad with Romaine, Raisins, and Almond Feta, 65
  Ginger-Almond Granola, 36
  Wild Rice Salad with Cranberries and Oranges, 59
Antipasto Chicken Chopped Salad, 152
apples
  Apple-Cinnamon French Toast Casserole, 39
  Mulled Apple Cider with Oranges and Rosemary, 238
  Pink Applesauce, 245
  Quinoa Muesli Breakfast Bowls, 24
apricots
  Dried Fruit Compote, 246
aquafaba, 47
  Vegan Aioli, 208
artichokes, 267
  Pan-Grilled Artichokes with Curry Dip, 206–7
  Pork Loin with Lemon, Capers, and Artichokes, 186–87
Arugula Frittata, Sweet Potato and, 31
asparagus, 267
  Asparagus with Vegan Aioli, 208
  Garden Patch Jambalaya, 124
avocados
  Avocado Egg Salad Sandwiches, 103
  Shrimp and Avocado Toast, 132

B

bacon
  Bacon-Braised Beets and Greens, 223
  Ground Pork Bolognese, 180
  Spanish-Style Pork and White Beans, 184
Banana Oatmeal with Strawberry-Chia Jam, 20
barley, 266
  Barley Bowls with Sunny Eggs and Tamari, 23
basil
  Basil Oil, 264
  Basil Vinaigrette, 144
  Pesto, 156
beans, 12, 266
  Basic Beans, 44
  Cajun-Spiced Red Beans and Rice, 53
  Cincinnati Chili Mac, 198–99
  Fish Taco Salads with Fresh Mango Salsa, 140–41
  Ground Beef Tostada Salads, 190
  Hearty Multibean Soup, 87
  Mixed-Bean Salad, 45
  Pasta, Bean, and Sausage Soup, 82
  Refried Black Beans, 49
  Spanish-Style Pork and White Beans, 184
  Tamale Casserole, 113
  Tomatillo Chicken Chili, 98
  Tri-Tip and Bean Chili, 99
  Vegan Red Pozole, 91
  Vegan Salisbury Steak, 114–15
  Vegan Soy Curls Chili, 97
  See also black-eyed peas; chickpeas; green beans
beef, 266
  Beef and Spinach Lasagna, 200–201
  Beef Tips with Onion and Mushroom Gravy, 194
  Cabbage Roll Casserole, 189
  Cincinnati Chili Mac, 198–99
  Florentine Beef Meat Loaf, 193
  Ground Beef Tostada Salads, 190
  Indian-Style Beef Curry, 202–3
  Low-Sodium Roasted Beef Bone Broth, 260–61
  Meat Sauce, 200–201
  Shredded BBQ Pot Roast, 196–97
  Sweet Potato Cottage Pie, 195
  Tri-Tip and Bean Chili, 99
  Vegetable Beef Soup, 92
beets, 267
  Bacon-Braised Beets and Greens, 223
  Beet Borscht, 75
  Beet, Carrot, and Potato Salad, 231
  Pink Applesauce, 245
black-eyed peas, 266
  Black-Eyed Peas and Kale, 120
Borscht, Beet, 75
bread
  Apple-Cinnamon French Toast Casserole, 39
  Cinnamon Raisin Bread Pudding, 248–49
  Shrimp and Avocado Toast, 132
  See also pitas; sandwiches
broccoli, 267
  Broccoli-Cheddar Egg Muffins, 33
  Broccoli with Crispy Garlic Chips, 210
  Garden Patch Jambalaya, 124
  Mixed-Vegetable Korma, 108–9
  Vegan Mac 'n' Greens, 66–67
broths
  alternatives to making, 11–12, 14
  Low-Sodium Chicken Bone Broth, 260
  Low-Sodium Roasted Beef Bone Broth, 260–61
  Low-Sodium Vegetable Broth, 261
brussels sprouts, 267
  Everything Brussels Sprouts, 213
Buckwheat Waffles, Yeasted, 40
Buffalo Chicken Lettuce Cups, 150–51
Buffalo Sauce, 150
bulgur wheat
  Coconut Bulgur Pudding, 243
  Sunshine Salad with Bulgur, Kale, and Mango, 62

C

cabbage, 267
  BBQ Jackfruit Bowls with Alabama Sauce, 110–11
  Beet Borscht, 75
  Cabbage and Potato Soup, 90
  Cabbage Roll Casserole, 189
  Fish Taco Salads with Fresh Mango Salsa, 140–41
  Salsa Chicken and Supercharged Rice, 161
  Slaw, 149
  Vegan Red Pozole, 91
Cajun-Spiced Red Beans and Rice, 53
cakes
  Flourless Chocolate Torte, 256–57
  Glazed Honey-Lemon Cake, 251–52
  Gluten-Free Chocolate Cake, 253
  Greek Yogurt Cheesecake, 254–55
carrots, 267
  Baby Carrots with Honey Lemon Butter, 209
  Beet, Carrot, and Potato Salad, 231
  Cauliflower Carrot Mash, 214
  Chicken, Chickpea, and Carrot Plov, 157
cashews
  Alabama Sauce, 110
  Cashew Sour Cream, 265
  Mixed-Vegetable Korma, 108–9
  Ranch Dressing, 150
  Vegan Creamed Spinach, 225
  Vegan Mac 'n' Greens, 66–67
  Vegan Parmesan Cheese, 265
cauliflower, 267
  Cauliflower Carrot Mash, 214
  Cauliflower Florets with Herbed Butter, 217
  Giardiniera Salad, 226
  Green Minestrone, 81
  Winter White Pasta Salad, 69
celery, 267
Celery Root Salad, 218
Champagne Vinaigrette, 218
cheese
  Beef and Spinach Lasagna, 200–201
  Broccoli-Cheddar Egg Muffins, 33
  Cheesy Loaded Potato Casserole, 116–17
  Chicken Cutlets in Tuscan Cream Sauce, 165
  Cincinnati Chili Mac, 198–99
  Crustless Ham and Swiss Quiche, 30
  Greek Yogurt Cheesecake, 254–55
  Sweet Potato Cottage Pie, 195
cheese substitutes
  Almond Feta Cheese, 265
  Vegan Parmesan Cheese, 265
Cherries, Pork with Balsamic and, 177
chia seeds, 12
  Strawberry-Chia Jam, 20

chicken, 266
Antipasto Chicken Chopped Salad, 152
Buffalo Chicken Lettuce Cups, 150–51
Chicken and Mushroom Goulash, 166
Chicken, Chickpea, and Carrot Plov, 157
Chicken Cutlets in Tuscan Cream Sauce, 165
Chicken Drumstick Soup, 94
Chicken Pho, 95
Dairy-Free Pesto Chicken Penne, 156
Greek Chicken Meatballs, 155
Honey Mustard Chicken Tenders and Slaw, 149
Low-Sodium Chicken Bone Broth, 260
Salsa Chicken and Supercharged Rice, 161
Southern Smothered Chicken, 162
Spicy Sesame Peanut Chicken, 158
Sweet and Spicy Chicken Wings, 148
Tandoori-Spiced Chicken Thighs, 168
Tomatillo Chicken Chili, 98
Whole Chicken in a Hurry, 167
Za'atar-Spiced Chicken Salad with Tahini Dressing, 153
"Chick'n" and Brown Rice Pilaf, 119
chickpeas, 266
Chicken, Chickpea, and Carrot Plov, 157
Chickpea and Brown Rice Tabbouleh, 58
Falafel-Spiced Chickpea Pita Pockets, 107
Seitan Chickpea Chorizo Sausages, 104
Toasted Sesame Miso Hummus, 47
chilis
Cincinnati Chili Mac, 198–99
Tomatillo Chicken Chili, 98
Tri-Tip and Bean Chili, 99
Vegan Soy Curls Chili, 97
Chimichurri Corn on the Cob, 220
chocolate
Chocolate and PB Yogurt Smoothie, 37
Flourless Chocolate Torte, 256–57
Frozen Yogurt Fudge Ice Pops, 242
Gluten-Free Chocolate Cake, 253
Chowder, New England Fish, 137
Cider, Mulled Apple, with Oranges and Rosemary, 238
Cincinnati Chili Mac, 198–99
Cinnamon Raisin Bread Pudding, 248–49
Cioppino Pasta, 134
coconut
aminos, 13
butter, 12
Coconut Bulgur Pudding, 243
cod
Cod and Shrimp Stew with Tomatoes and Saffron, 139
New England Fish Chowder, 137
collards, 267
cooking charts, 266–67
corn, 267
BBQ Jackfruit Bowls with Alabama Sauce, 110–11
Chimichurri Corn on the Cob, 220
Corn and Zucchini Omelet with Smoked Salmon, 28
Mixed-Vegetable Korma, 108–9
Shrimp Ceviche with Sweet Potatoes and Corn, 133
Tamale Casserole, 113
Tri-Tip and Bean Chili, 99
Vegetable Beef Soup, 92
See also hominy
Cottage Pie, Sweet Potato, 195
couscous, 266
cranberries
Dried Fruit Compote, 246
Hot Cranberry Cocktail, 239
Wild Rice Salad with Cranberries and Oranges, 59
cucumbers
Chickpea and Brown Rice Tabbouleh, 58
Dill Pickle Chips, 264–65
Tzatziki, 264
Za'atar-Spiced Chicken Salad with Tahini Dressing, 153
curries
Indian-Style Beef Curry, 202–3
Thai Green Curry Tilapia, 145
Curry Dip, 206
curry paste, 12

D

desserts
Cinnamon Raisin Bread Pudding, 248–49
Coconut Bulgur Pudding, 243
Dried Fruit Compote, 246
Flourless Chocolate Torte, 256–57
Frozen Yogurt Fudge Ice Pops, 242
Glazed Honey-Lemon Cake, 251–52
Gluten-Free Chocolate Cake, 253
Greek Yogurt Cheesecake, 254–55
Pink Applesauce, 245
Wine-Poached Pears, 244
dietary chart, 268–72
Dill Pickle Chips, 264–65
dips
Crunchy Vegetable Dip, 222
Curry Dip, 206
Toasted Sesame Miso Hummus, 47
doenjang, 12
dressings
Ranch Dressing, 150
Tahini Dressing, 262
See also vinaigrettes
drinks
Chocolate and PB Yogurt Smoothie, 37
Hot Cranberry Cocktail, 239
Mulled Apple Cider with Oranges and Rosemary, 238
Virgin Toddy Tonic, 241

E

eggplant, 267
eggs
Avocado Egg Salad Sandwiches, 103
Barley Bowls with Sunny Eggs and Tamari, 23
Broccoli-Cheddar Egg Muffins, 33
Corn and Zucchini Omelet with Smoked Salmon, 28
Crustless Ham and Swiss Quiche, 30
Soft-Boiled Eggs in Yogurt Sauce, 27
Soft- or Hard-Boiled Eggs, 25
Sweet Potato and Arugula Frittata, 31
Whole-Wheat Matzo Brei, 38
endives, 267
escarole, 267

F

Falafel-Spiced Chickpea Pita Pockets, 107
farro, 266
Farro Salad with Romaine, Raisins, and Almond Feta, 65
fish
Cod and Shrimp Stew with Tomatoes and Saffron, 139
Corn and Zucchini Omelet with Smoked Salmon, 28
Fish Taco Salads with Fresh Mango Salsa, 140–41
New England Fish Chowder, 137
Poached Salmon with Basil Vinaigrette, 144
Salmon and Spinach Patties, 142–43
Thai Green Curry Tilapia, 145
Florentine Beef Meat Loaf, 193
French Toast Casserole, Apple-Cinnamon, 39
Frittata, Sweet Potato and Arugula, 31
fruits, dried, 12
Dried Fruit Compote, 246
See also raisins
furikake, 12

G

Garden Patch Jambalaya, 124
garlic
Broccoli with Crispy Garlic Chips, 210
Roasted Garlic, 261–62
Roasted Garlic and Potato Soup, 89
Giardiniera Salad, 226
Ginger-Almond Granola, 36
Goulash, Chicken and Mushroom, 166
grains, 12
Basic Whole Grains, 60
cooking times for, 61, 266
See also individual grains
Granola, Ginger-Almond, 36
Greek Chicken Meatballs, 155

Greek Lentil Soup, 84
Greek Yogurt Cheesecake, 254–55
green beans, 267
  Italian Braised Green Beans and Tomatoes, 219
  Mixed-Vegetable Korma, 108–9
  Thai Green Curry Tilapia, 145
  Vegetable Beef Soup, 92
greens, 267
  Bacon-Braised Beets and Greens, 223
  Vegan Mac 'n' Greens, 66–67
  See also individual greens
Gyros, Crispy Pulled Pork, 179

H

ham, 266
  Crustless Ham and Swiss Quiche, 30
healthy meals, putting together, 1, 15
herb blends, 13
hominy
  Vegan Red Pozole, 91
Hummus, Toasted Sesame Miso, 47

I

Ice Pops, Frozen Yogurt Fudge, 242
Indian-Style Beef Curry, 202–3
Instant Pot
  benefits of, 1
  cooking charts for, 266–67
  lid of, 5, 6
  maximum fill levels for, 7, 9
  operation keys for, 4–5
  pot-in-pot cooking with, 9
  preparation and cooking times for, 9
  releasing pressure from, 5–7
  settings for, 2–4, 14
  sizes of, 2
  steam racks for, 10, 11
  tools and accessories for, 9–11
Irish Lamb Stew, 188
Italian Vinaigrette, 152

J

jackfruit, 12
  BBQ Jackfruit Bowls with Alabama Sauce, 110–11
Jam, Strawberry-Chia, 20
Jambalaya, Garden Patch, 124
JoJo Potatoes, 235
Josephine's Special, 112

K

kale, 267
  Black-Eyed Peas and Kale, 120
  Green Minestrone, 81
  Sunshine Salad with Bulgur, Kale, and Mango, 62
kamut, 266
Korean Hot Pot with Tofu and Mushrooms, 123
Korma, Mixed-Vegetable, 108–9

L

lamb, 266
  Irish Lamb Stew, 188
Lasagna, Beef and Spinach, 200–201
leeks, 267
lentils, 267
  Balsamic and Butter Lentils, 48
  Greek Lentil Soup, 84
  Red Lentil and Spinach Soup, 83
lettuce
  Antipasto Chicken Chopped Salad, 152
  BBQ Jackfruit Bowls with Alabama Sauce, 110–11
  Buffalo Chicken Lettuce Cups, 150–51
  Farro Salad with Romaine, Raisins, and Almond Feta, 65
  Fish Taco Salads with Fresh Mango Salsa, 140–41
  Ground Beef Tostada Salads, 190
  Za'atar-Spiced Chicken Salad with Tahini Dressing, 153

M

mangoes
  Fresh Mango Salsa, 140
  Sunshine Salad with Bulgur, Kale, and Mango, 62
Marinara Sauce, 126
Matzo Brei, Whole-Wheat, 38
meatballs
  Greek Chicken Meatballs, 155
  Paella Turkey Meatballs, 170
Meat Loaf, Florentine Beef, 193
Meat Sauce, 200–201
millet, 266
Minestrone, Green, 81
miso paste, 12
  Toasted Sesame Miso Hummus, 47
  Winter Squash Miso Soup, 76
Muffins, Broccoli-Cheddar Egg, 33
mushrooms
  Beef Tips with Onion and Mushroom Gravy, 194
  Chicken and Mushroom Goulash, 166
  Chicken Cutlets in Tuscan Cream Sauce, 165
  Double Mushroom Risotto, 55
  Josephine's Special, 112
  Korean Hot Pot with Tofu and Mushrooms, 123
  Mushroom Sauce, 114–15
  Pork Chops Marsala, 174–75
  Vegan Salisbury Steak, 114–15
Mussels with Tomatoes and White Wine Broth, 131
Mustard Sauce, 149

N

New England Fish Chowder, 137
noodles. *See* pasta and noodles
Nori Rolls, Brown Rice, 56–57

O

oats, 266
  Banana Oatmeal with Strawberry-Chia Jam, 20
  Butternut Squash Steel-Cut Oatmeal, 19
  Ginger-Almond Granola, 36
oils, 13
  Basil Oil, 264
  Paprika Oil, 27
okra, 267
onions, 267
  Beef Tips with Onion and Mushroom Gravy, 194
oranges
  Mulled Apple Cider with Oranges and Rosemary, 238
  Wild Rice Salad with Cranberries and Oranges, 59

P

Paella Turkey Meatballs, 170
Paprika Oil, 27
parsnips, 267
pasta and noodles
  alternatives to, 13
  Beef and Spinach Lasagna, 200–201
  Chicken Pho, 95
  Cincinnati Chili Mac, 198–99
  Cioppino Pasta, 134
  Dairy-Free Pesto Chicken Penne, 156
  Ground Pork Bolognese, 180
  Pasta, Bean, and Sausage Soup, 82
  Sesame Peanut Noodles with Seared Tofu, 121
  Vegan Mac 'n' Greens, 66–67
  Whole-Wheat Penne Arrabbiata, 70
  Winter White Pasta Salad, 69
peaches
  Dried Fruit Compote, 246
peanut butter
  Sesame Peanut Noodles with Seared Tofu, 121
  Sesame Peanut Sauce, 158
peanut powder, 13
  Chocolate and PB Yogurt Smoothie, 37
pears
  Quinoa with Pears and Walnuts, 64
  Wine-Poached Pears, 244

peas, 267
  Antipasto Chicken Chopped Salad, 152
  Beet, Carrot, and Potato Salad, 231
  Dairy-Free Pesto Chicken Penne, 156
  Garden Patch Jambalaya, 124
  Green Minestrone, 81
  Paella Turkey Meatballs, 170
  Spinach and Pea Risotto, 54
  Vegan Mac 'n' Greens, 66–67
  Vegetable Beef Soup, 92
peppers, 267
  Giardiniera Salad, 226
  Tomato–Red Pepper Bisque with Basil Oil, 78
Pesto, 156
Pho, Chicken, 95
Pickle Chips, Dill, 264–65
pitas
  Crispy Pulled Pork Gyros, 179
  Falafel-Spiced Chickpea Pita Pockets, 107
Plov, Chicken, Chickpea, and Carrot, 157
polenta, 266
pork, 266
  Braised Pork Shoulder with Chinese Black Bean Sauce, 185
  Crispy Pulled Pork Gyros, 179
  Ground Pork Bolognese, 180
  Honey Dijon Baby Back Ribs, 183
  Pork Chops Marsala, 174–75
  Pork Chops with Cumin and Coriander, 176
  Pork Loin with Lemon, Capers, and Artichokes, 186–87
  Pork with Balsamic and Cherries, 177
  Spanish-Style Pork and White Beans, 184
  See also bacon; ham
portion control, 15
potatoes, 267
  Beet Borscht, 75
  Beet, Carrot, and Potato Salad, 231
  Cabbage and Potato Soup, 90
  Cheesy Loaded Potato Casserole, 116–17
  Chicken and Mushroom Goulash, 166
  Cod and Shrimp Stew with Tomatoes and Saffron, 139
  Crispy Sriracha Potatoes, 232
  Green Minestrone, 81
  Irish Lamb Stew, 188
  JoJo Potatoes, 235
  New England Fish Chowder, 137
  Pork Loin with Lemon, Capers, and Artichokes, 186–87
  Roasted Garlic and Potato Soup, 89
  Steamed Potatoes, 229
  Vegetable Beef Soup, 92
pot-in-pot cooking, 9
Pozole, Vegan Red, 91
puddings
  Cinnamon Raisin Bread Pudding, 248–49
  Coconut Bulgur Pudding, 243
pumpkin, 267

Q

Quiche, Crustless Ham and Swiss, 30
quinoa, 266
  Quinoa Muesli Breakfast Bowls, 24
  Quinoa with Pears and Walnuts, 64

R

raisins
  Cinnamon Raisin Bread Pudding, 248–49
  Coconut Bulgur Pudding, 243
  Dried Fruit Compote, 246
  Farro Salad with Romaine, Raisins, and Almond Feta, 65
  Ginger-Almond Granola, 36
  Pink Applesauce, 245
  Quinoa with Pears and Walnuts, 64
Ranch Dressing, 150
rice, 266
  Basic Rice, 50–51
  BBQ Jackfruit Bowls with Alabama Sauce, 110–11
  Brown Rice Nori Rolls, 56–57
  Cabbage Roll Casserole, 189
  Cajun-Spiced Red Beans and Rice, 53
  Chicken, Chickpea, and Carrot Plov, 157
  "Chick'n" and Brown Rice Pilaf, 119
  Chickpea and Brown Rice Tabbouleh, 58
  Double Mushroom Risotto, 55
  Garden Patch Jambalaya, 124
  Greek Chicken Meatballs, 155
  Paella Turkey Meatballs, 170
  Salsa Chicken and Supercharged Rice, 161
  Seafood Risotto, 136
  Spinach and Pea Risotto, 54
risotto
  Double Mushroom Risotto, 55
  Seafood Risotto, 136
  Spinach and Pea Risotto, 54
rutabagas, 267

S

salads
  Antipasto Chicken Chopped Salad, 152
  Avocado Egg Salad Sandwiches, 103
  Beet, Carrot, and Potato Salad, 231
  Celery Root Salad, 218
  Chickpea and Brown Rice Tabbouleh, 58
  Farro Salad with Romaine, Raisins, and Almond Feta, 65
  Fish Taco Salads with Fresh Mango Salsa, 140–41
  Giardiniera Salad, 226
  Ground Beef Tostada Salads, 190
  Mixed-Bean Salad, 45
  Slaw, 149
  Wild Rice Salad with Cranberries and Oranges, 59
  Winter White Pasta Salad, 69
  Za'atar-Spiced Chicken Salad with Tahini Dressing, 153
Salisbury Steak, Vegan, 114–15
salmon
  Corn and Zucchini Omelet with Smoked Salmon, 28
  Poached Salmon with Basil Vinaigrette, 144
  Salmon and Spinach Patties, 142–43
salsas. *See* sauces and salsas
sandwiches
  Avocado Egg Salad Sandwiches, 103
  Chipotle Turkey Sloppy Joes, 171
sauces and salsas
  Alabama Sauce, 110
  Buffalo Sauce, 150
  Fresh Mango Salsa, 140
  Ground Pork Bolognese, 180
  Honey Dijon Sauce, 183
  Marinara Sauce, 126
  Meat Sauce, 200–201
  Mushroom Sauce, 114–15
  Mustard Sauce, 149
  Pesto, 156
  Pink Applesauce, 245
  Salsa Picante, 262
  Sesame Peanut Sauce, 158
  Tzatziki, 264
  Yogurt Sauce, 27
sausage
  Pasta, Bean, and Sausage Soup, 82
  Seitan Chickpea Chorizo Sausages, 104
  Tamale Casserole, 113
seafood
  Cioppino Pasta, 134
  Seafood Risotto, 136
  See also individual seafoods
seitan. *See* vital wheat gluten
Sesame Peanut Noodles with Seared Tofu, 121
Sesame Peanut Sauce, 158
shirataki, 13
shortcuts, 14–15
shrimp
  Cod and Shrimp Stew with Tomatoes and Saffron, 139
  Shrimp and Avocado Toast, 132
  Shrimp Ceviche with Sweet Potatoes and Corn, 133
Slaw, 149
Sloppy Joes, Chipotle Turkey, 171
Smoothie, Chocolate and PB Yogurt, 37
soups
  Beet Borscht, 75
  Cabbage and Potato Soup, 90
  Chicken Drumstick Soup, 94
  Chicken Pho, 95
  Cream of Zucchini Soup, 77
  Greek Lentil Soup, 84
  Green Minestrone, 81
  Hearty Multibean Soup, 87

Korean Hot Pot with Tofu and Mushrooms, 123
New England Fish Chowder, 137
Pasta, Bean, and Sausage Soup, 82
Red Lentil and Spinach Soup, 83
Roasted Garlic and Potato Soup, 89
Sweet Potato Soup, 88
Tomato–Red Pepper Bisque with Basil Oil, 78
Vegan Red Pozole, 91
Vegetable Beef Soup, 92
Winter Squash Miso Soup, 76
Southern Smothered Chicken, 162
Soy Curls, 13
"Chick'n" and Brown Rice Pilaf, 119
Vegan Soy Curls Chili, 97
Spanish-Style Pork and White Beans, 184
spelt, 266
spice blends, 13
spice pastes, 12
spinach, 267
Beef and Spinach Lasagna, 200–201
Chicken Cutlets in Tuscan Cream Sauce, 165
Dairy-Free Pesto Chicken Penne, 156
Florentine Beef Meat Loaf, 193
Josephine's Special, 112
Pasta, Bean, and Sausage Soup, 82
Red Lentil and Spinach Soup, 83
Salmon and Spinach Patties, 142–43
Spinach and Pea Risotto, 54
Vegan Creamed Spinach, 225
spreads, vegan, 14
squash, 267
Butternut Squash Steel-Cut Oatmeal, 19
Spaghetti Squash Marinara with Vegan Parmesan Cheese, 126
Steamed Butternut or Spaghetti Squash, 125
Vegan Mac 'n' Greens, 66–67
Winter Squash Miso Soup, 76
See also zucchini
strawberries
Strawberry-Chia Jam, 20
Yogurt Bowl with Ginger-Almond Granola, 36
Sunshine Salad with Bulgur, Kale, and Mango, 62
sweeteners, natural, 13
sweet potatoes, 267
Mashed Sweet Potatoes, 234
Shrimp Ceviche with Sweet Potatoes and Corn, 133
Steamed Sweet Potatoes, 229
Sweet Potato and Arugula Frittata, 31
Sweet Potato Cottage Pie, 195
Sweet Potato Soup, 88
Swiss chard, 267
Vegan Mac 'n' Greens, 66–67

T

Tabbouleh, Chickpea and Brown Rice, 58
Tahini Dressing, 262
Tamale Casserole, 113
tamari, 13
Tandoori-Spiced Chicken Thighs, 168
tea
Virgin Toddy Tonic, 241
Tilapia, Thai Green Curry, 145
Toddy Tonic, Virgin, 241
tofu
Josephine's Special, 112
Korean Hot Pot with Tofu and Mushrooms, 123
Sesame Peanut Noodles with Seared Tofu, 121
Tomatillo Chicken Chili, 98
tomatoes, 267
Beef and Spinach Lasagna, 200–201
Cincinnati Chili Mac, 198–99
Cioppino Pasta, 134
Cod and Shrimp Stew with Tomatoes and Saffron, 139
Ground Pork Bolognese, 180
Italian Braised Green Beans and Tomatoes, 219
Marinara Sauce, 126
Mixed-Vegetable Korma, 108–9
Mussels with Tomatoes and White Wine Broth, 131
paste, 13
Salsa Picante, 262
Spaghetti Squash Marinara with Vegan Parmesan Cheese, 126
Tomato–Red Pepper Bisque with Basil Oil, 78
Tri-Tip and Bean Chili, 99
Vegan Red Pozole, 91
Vegan Soy Curls Chili, 97
Whole-Wheat Penne Arrabbiata, 70
tools and accessories, 9–11
Torte, Flourless Chocolate, 256–57
tortillas
Fish Taco Salads with Fresh Mango Salsa, 140–41
Tostada Salads, Ground Beef, 190
turkey, 266
Chipotle Turkey Sloppy Joes, 171
Paella Turkey Meatballs, 170
turnips, 267
Tzatziki, 264

V

vegetables
canned, 14–15
colorful, 15
cooking times for, 267
Crunchy Vegetable Dip, 222
dried, 12
frozen, 14
Giardiniera Salad, 226
Low-Sodium Vegetable Broth, 261
Mixed-Vegetable Korma, 108–9
Vegetable Beef Soup, 92
See also individual vegetables
vinaigrettes
Basil Vinaigrette, 144
Champagne Vinaigrette, 218
Italian Vinaigrette, 152
vital wheat gluten
Seitan Chickpea Chorizo Sausages, 104
Tamale Casserole, 113
Vegan Salisbury Steak, 114–15

W

Waffles, Yeasted Buckwheat, 40
Walnuts, Quinoa with Pears and, 64
wheat berries, 266
wild rice, 266
Wild Rice Salad with Cranberries and Oranges, 59
Wine-Poached Pears, 244
Worcestershire sauce, 14

Y

yams, 267. *See also* sweet potatoes
yeast, nutritional, 13
yogurt
Chocolate and PB Yogurt Smoothie, 37
Crunchy Vegetable Dip, 222
Curry Dip, 206
Frozen Yogurt Fudge Ice Pops, 242
Greek Yogurt Cheesecake, 254–55
making, 34–35
Tzatziki, 264
Yogurt Bowl with Ginger-Almond Granola, 36
Yogurt Crema, 161
Yogurt Sauce, 27

Z

Za'atar-Spiced Chicken Salad with Tahini Dressing, 153
zucchini, 267
Beet Borscht, 75
Corn and Zucchini Omelet with Smoked Salmon, 28
Cream of Zucchini Soup, 77
Green Minestrone, 81
Mixed-Vegetable Korma, 108–9
Tamale Casserole, 113
Zucchini with Olive Oil and Parsley, 228

Published in the United States by Ten Speed Press,
an imprint of Random House, a division of
Penguin Random House LLC, New York.

www.tenspeed.com

Library of Congress Cataloging-in-Publication Data
is on file with the publisher.

Hardcover ISBN: 978-1-9848-5754-5

eBook ISBN: 978-1-9848-5755-2

Printed in the United States of America

Design by Isabelle Gioffredi

Food styling by Nathan Carrabba

Prop styling by Claire Mack

10 9 8 7 6 5 4 3 2 1

First Edition